THE BEGINNINGS OF
UNITARIANISM IN AMERICA

THE BEGINNINGS OF
Unitarianism in America

CONRAD WRIGHT

published by
STARR KING PRESS

distributed by
THE BEACON PRESS · BOSTON

TO
MY FATHER AND MOTHER

Acknowledgments

This book was begun as a doctoral dissertation at Harvard, under the direction of Professor Perry Miller; to him my indebtedness over many years is great. Publication in this much-revised form has been made possible by a grant from the Carnegie Fund of the American Historical Association. I am grateful both to the Association, and to Professor Raymond P. Stearns and his committee, who made the recommendation for the award.

The research was facilitated by the hospitality and kindness of the librarians and staffs of the Harvard College Library, the Andover-Harvard Library, the Houghton Library, the Massachusetts Historical Society, the Boston Public Library, the Congregational Library, and the American Antiquarian Society. I am especially indebted to Miss Carolyn Jakeman at the Houghton Library.

Professor Samuel E. Morison placed at my disposal the manuscript commonplace book of Ephraim Eliot. Professor Robert E. Moody of the Boston University Library, Mr. Stephen T. Riley of the Massachusetts Historical Society, and Dr. Clifford K. Shipton of the Harvard University Archives have permitted me to quote from manuscripts in their custody. Quotations from the Harvard College Records have been made with the permission of the President and Fellows of Harvard College.

Dr. Erwin Raisz generously consented to prepare the maps. I have profited from discussions with colleagues, and some of them have taken the time to give the manuscript a critical reading. The following deserve particular acknowledgment: the late Robert K. Lamb, Professor Lynwood S. Bryant, Professor Thomas F. O'Dea, Professor Lawrence W. Towner, and Professor Karl W. Deutsch. Assistance in the preparation of the typescript was given by Miss Bernice Bianchi and Mrs. Nancy Chivers. An earlier version of Chapter 4 has previously appeared in the *Harvard Theological Review*, October, 1942.

Finally, for specific criticism as well as general encouragement, my wife deserves very special mention.

Contents

THE BEGINNINGS OF
UNITARIANISM IN AMERICA

Introduction

This book is concerned with the liberal movement which developed within the congregational churches of New England in the eighteenth century, emerging as Unitarianism in the nineteenth. Its terminal dates are 1735, the year of the outbreak of the Great Awakening, and 1805, the year in which the Unitarian controversy was precipitated by the election of Henry Ware as Hollis Professor of Divinity at Harvard. Between these dates, two generations of religious liberals, commonly called Arminians, rejected traditional Calvinistic patterns of thought and developed a new set of basic assumptions about human nature and human destiny.

The doctrinal position of the liberals combined three tendencies which may be logically distinguished: Arminianism, supernatural rationalism, and anti-Trinitarianism. Arminianism asserted that men are born with the capacity both for sin and for righteousness; that they can respond to the impulse toward holiness as well as the temptation to do evil; and that life is a process of trial and discipline by which, with the assistance God gives to all, the bondage to sin may be gradually overcome. This assertion of human ability contrasts with the Calvinist belief that the innate bent of all men is toward sin, that God has decreed everlasting happiness to some and eternal torment to others, and that salvation comes as the unmerited gift of God's Holy Spirit.

Supernatural rationalism, accepted by many Calvinists as well as by the liberals, was virtually the orthodox theology of the Age of Reason. It asserted that the unassisted reason can establish the essentials of natural religion: the existence

of God, the obligations of morality, and a divine order of rewards and punishments. But unlike Deism, it insisted that
natural religion must be supplemented with a special revelation of God's will. The Bible is such a revelation, which re-
inforces natural religion by stating its obligations more
clearly and impressively; and it proclaims the gospel of redemption through the perfect obedience of Christ, which unassisted reason could never have discovered. The authority
of the Bible rests on internal and external evidences, particularly the miracles of Christ, which attest that he was a divinely inspired messenger. Human reason must examine and
assess such evidences, and determine the true meaning of obscure or disputed passages of Scripture. But while reason is
essential, it must not substitute its own speculations for gospel
truths. The Arminians condemned equally the orthodox insistence on creeds and confessions of faith of human origin,
and the deistic confidence in natural reason unassisted by divine revelation.

Finally, the liberals tended to be anti-Trinitarian, largely
because they were not convinced that the doctrine of the
Trinity is scriptural. Most of them were Arians, believing
that Christ, while not a part of the Godhead, is a being of a
far higher rank in Creation than mere man. They were not
" Unitarian " as that term was then understood, since only
a small minority believed in the simple humanity of Jesus.

Important as the Arminian movement was in bridging the
gap between seventeenth-century Puritanism and nineteenth-
century Unitarianism, its history has never been told in detail. It has been treated only tangentially, by scholars whose
chief interest has been something else. Historians of Unitarianism in America have been aware of it; but in their eagerness to get to the period of controversy, they have usually
spoken briefly of only a few eighteenth-century figures, like

Charles Chauncy, Jonathan Mayhew, and Ebenezer Gay. Such treatment leaves the impression that the Arminians were isolated forerunners of a movement which did not achieve coherence until the nineteenth century. Biographers of Jonathan Edwards know that he regarded Arminianism as a constant and living threat, but they have ordinarily viewed it through his eyes. No movement can be understood, however, if seen only through the perspectives provided by its enemies. Historians of Deism, finally, have tended to look upon the supernatural rationalism of the liberals as a compromise between orthodoxy and Deism, adopted by social conservatives who sought to avoid the odium attached to an unambiguous acceptance of natural religion. The implication here seems to be that these men were really deists who lacked the courage of their convictions.

Several things emerge clearly as soon as the Arminian movement is put in the center of the field of vision. In the first place, Arminianism was not a disembodied set of ideas, adopted for various capricious reasons by scattered individuals. It was part of the culture of a group, of which Chauncy and Mayhew were leading figures. The group was united by personal relationships of various kinds, and it developed a sense of coherence long before the close of the eighteenth century. The Arminians may be defined in terms of their position within the social structure of New England as well as in terms of their theology. To understand Arminianism, it is necessary to investigate that social structure, as well as to analyze the logical structure of the theology.

The inception of the Arminian movement must therefore be sought in the social and intellectual situation of New England in the early eighteenth century. There was a tendency at one time to begin the story of Unitarianism in Transylvania and Poland, and to assume a widening influence and a continuous tradition which eventually reached the Low Countries, England, and America. Dr. Earl Morse Wilbur has reminded us, however, that Unitarianism in America was of indigenous origin, largely independent in its earliest stages of similar tendencies in English thought. English latitudinarianism and dissent helped to shape the growth of a movement whose roots were already deep in New England Puritanism. The New England liberals were called Arminians, not because they were influenced directly by Jacobus Arminius (1560–1609), the Dutch Remonstrant, but because their reaction against Calvinism was similar to his. They were descended spiritually as well as biologically from the settlers of the Bay Colony, and to a very significant extent, their Arminianism was a development out of Puritanism under the pressure of social as well as intellectual forces.

The dissemination of Arminianism within New England was uneven. Throughout the eighteenth century, it was largely restricted to eastern Massachusetts, and within that area it appealed especially to men of prestige and influence. This pattern has been variously explained. Unitarian publicists of a later generation have sometimes implied that liberalism so obviously appeals to the more intelligent and better educated members of the community that no other explanation need be sought. This hypothesis of course leaves it a mystery why equally intelligent and well-educated people in other parts of New England remained Calvinists. The clue to an understanding of the pattern of Arminian success and failure must be sought elsewhere. By the end of the eighteenth century, a decision-making élite had developed in Boston, which was in communication with similar groups in such towns as Salem and Worcester, and with the clergy, at least, in many smaller communities. Over a period of two generations, Arminianism had become the theology of this élite. It did not expand beyond the area which this élite controlled, nor within that area did it penetrate to groups significantly lower in the class structure. Liberal Christianity was roughly coterminous with a particular social class.

Why, then, did this set of religious attitudes and principles become part of the culture of this group? The Reverend George Batchelor argued that it was the contact of Salem shipowners with foreign nations and oriental religions, rather than a monopoly of brains and education, that liberalized their theology. Shipmasters and supercargoes, he suggested, learned that the heathen were often more honest than " civilized " peoples, " and it was hard for them to accept off-hand the dogmas of the Church which in those days consigned to wholesale perdition the majority of the human race." [1] There may well have been a Salem shipmaster, now and again, who was influenced in this way, but this is not satisfactory as a general explanation. Salem merchants were a part of the élite group in eastern Massachusetts, but they were hardly in a position to do the theological thinking for the whole group, or to have more than a local influence on religious ideas.

There was admittedly a certain congruity between upper class attitudes in general and the antirevivalism of the opposers of the Great Awakening. There was also a certain congruity between the Boston or Salem merchant's sense of worldly achievement and his rejection of the doctrine of total depravity. But important as these factors may have been in setting limits or in establishing a predisposition towards liberalism, they did not make Arminianism inevitable. They were quite consistent with a mild and tolerant Calvinism.

What finally happened must be explained in terms of a unique sequence of events, as well as on the basis of certain

[1] George Batchelor, *Social Equilibrium* (Boston, 1887), p. 283.

general tendencies. The shaping of the culture of the Boston élite in the direction of Arminianism seems to have depended very much on the leadership of Charles Chauncy at the First Church and Jonathan Mayhew at the West Church. Within the social structure of New England, these were key positions for influencing the religious attitudes of a whole group; and both Mayhew and Chauncy accepted the responsibilities of community leadership which their ministry to these churches implied. They were Harvard graduates, concerned with affairs of the college, and not without influence on younger Harvard men. Their sermons and polemical writings achieved a wide circulation. They served long enough — sixty years in Chauncy's case — to fix the bent of their parishes permanently. Yet at the time of the Great Awakening, it was by no means foreordained that these two positions of influence should be occupied by Arminians. Chauncy was orthodox when he was installed as colleague to Thomas Foxcroft in 1727; Mayhew might have ended in a country parish. And the theology of the upper classes of eastern Massachusetts might easily have developed as a moderate and undogmatic Calvinism, like that which prevailed at Harvard College.

Be that as it may, the actual sequence of events promoted the rise of Arminianism in Massachusetts. That development is worth examining, both for a clearer understanding of the Unitarian movement which emerged from it, and for a sharper focus on Jonathan Edwards, who was its chief opponent. It may also be regarded as a case study of the dissemination of ideas within a well-structured social system. And the ideas themselves, specifically the Arminian concept of man, may appear somewhat less trivial and superficial when examined directly than when observed through the unsympathetic eyes and uncomprehending mind of Edwards.

CHAPTER ONE

Arminianism Before the Great Awakening

I

In the year 1726, when Cotton Mather undertook to explain the peculiarities of the polity and discipline of the New England churches, he found it unnecessary to discuss their doctrine. It is well known, he wrote, that " they perfectly adhere to the Confession of Faith, published by the Assembly of Divines at Westminster, and afterwards renewed by the Synod at the Savoy: . . . I cannot learn, That among all the Pastors of Two Hundred Churches, there is one Arminian: much less an Arian, or a Gentilist." [1]

A decade later, he would have had to speak less confidently. Referring to the year 1734, Jonathan Edwards declared: " About this time began the great noise that was in this part of the country, about Arminianism, which seemed to appear with a very threatening aspect upon the interest of religion here." [2] New England was approaching the period of bitter religious controversy known as the Great Awakening. By 1745, the uniformity which had delighted Mather had vanished, and the heresies he had condemned were advocated by some of the most respected of the clergy. Arminianism was openly preached before mid-century; coupled

[1] Quoted in Williston Walker, *A History of the Congregational Churches in the United States* (New York, 1894), p. 216.
[2] Jonathan Edwards, *The Works of President Edwards*, 4 vols. (New York, 1843), III, p. 233.

with anti-Trinitarianism, it became dominant in eastern Massachusetts in the years following the Revolution. Deism itself was a menace before the century closed.

The Arminianism that Cotton Mather dismissed and Jonathan Edwards feared was the first phase of the liberal movement in theology which in the nineteenth century was named Unitarianism. It rejected the awful and inscrutable Deity of the Calvinists, and replaced him with a God of benevolence and law. It rejected the concept of human nature as totally corrupt and depraved, and supplanted it with one in which the ability of every man to strive for righteousness was admitted. It was, in a sense, the New England version of the theology of the Age of Reason, occupying a middle ground between orthodoxy on the one hand and infidelity on the other.

II

Arminianism in Massachusetts resembled the prevailing English theology of the Age of Reason; and indeed, colonial thinkers owed much to men like Archbishop Tillotson, Daniel Whitby, Samuel Clarke, and John Taylor of Norwich. But Arminianism was not simply an imitation of fashionable English intellectual currents. Its roots were deep in New England Puritanism; and the drift toward liberalism that it represented was greatly stimulated by native social and intellectual pressures. Had the colonies been entirely cut off from outside intellectual influences, the New England doctrine would still have been transformed under the pressure of insistent social forces. To understand the rapid spread of Arminianism after the Great Awakening, it is necessary first of all to recognize that New England for a century had been moving in that direction.

Seventeenth-century New England congregationalism had

been a bold attempt to build a church order on the basis of regenerate membership. According to the Reformed theology, some men are predestined to everlasting life and others foreordained to eternal death, by God's decree and according to his secret counsel and good pleasure. Although it is not possible in this life to tell with absolute certainty who will be numbered among the saints on the final day, ordinarily those who truly love God and believe in Christ will feel the spirit of God working in their hearts, and a conviction of their lost and sinful estate will be followed by exceeding joy in the grace of God manifest unto the worst of sinners. Assurance that one is of the elect is a doctrine of probabilities only; but the New England Puritan claimed that assurance is probable enough to be the basis for church membership. A particular church, they said, should be made up of visible saints, those men and women who are presumably God's elect. They are united by a covenant or agreement to walk in harmony and mutual helpfulness one with another; and they share the exclusive privileges of admission to the Lord's Table for themselves and of baptism for their children.

The visible saints had political as well as religious privileges, since in order to be a freeman of the Bay Colony, one had to be a member of a particular church. It is clear that the founders of the colony had rested their civil society as well as their church order on the assumption that it is possible to distinguish in this life between the saints and the sinners. The perpetuation of the Puritan institutions in New England depended on the appearance in successive generations of men and women who could give testimony that they had had the experience of conversion.

The founders of the colony had grown up in England amid the excitement of religious turmoil and debate. They had had deep religious experiences of their own, and they assumed that conversion was part of the normal course of events. But the New England in which the children of the settlers were reared was a far less exciting place than England had been. Here were no agents of the king trying to silence Puritan lecturers and impose uniformity by harassing dissent. Now men's concerns were more mundane: clearing the land and tilling it, or fishing in the waters of Massachusetts Bay. The Puritan experiment, which had thrived on adversity, was threatened by political and economic success. Insensibly, by slow degrees, the temperature of religious fervor dropped, and the rate of conversions fell off. Even the children of the saints, who had been baptized in infancy on the assumption that they, like their parents, were in convenant with the Lord, failed to experience the new birth when they reached maturity. New England was then confronted by an extremely uncomfortable fact, for which theory gave no adequate explanation. It was a group of men and women who were in full sympathy with the purposes of the church order, who lived God-fearing and upright lives, who did not lie or swear or cheat their neighbors, who had a full intellectual knowledge of the Gospel, but who could not say that they had personally felt the regenerating spirit of God in their hearts. The experience of regeneration was the only sensible evidence men could have of God's act of justification. But if the only criterion for separating the saints from the sinners was disappearing, how could one build a church order on regenerate membership?

The resulting social pressures soon produced changes in the practices of congregationalism. The first of these was the Half-Way Covenant, recommended to the churches by a synod convened in Boston in 1662. This modification of the original scheme provided that the parents of a child might present him for baptism, even though they were not them-

selves regenerate, provided they would "own the covenant " — that is, avow their general sympathy with the purposes of the church order. By this device the leaders sought
to keep the children within the influence of church watch and
discipline. But adoption of the Half-Way Covenant did not
stay the decline of piety in New England; if anything it encouraged it. Many "half-way" members became satisfied
if they did no more than own the covenant, and made no effort to achieve the true blessing that would admit them to
full communion. The low state of religion and the decay of
godliness continued to be a matter of concern to the clergy.
A "Reforming Synod" which met in 1679 had no percepti-
ble effect on the downward trend, and the complaints and
lamentations of the ministers continued until the outbreak of
the Great Awakening.[3]

One of the few ministers who did have some success in
producing conversions among his flock was Solomon Stoddard
of Northampton.[4] It is significant that he succeeded only at
the expense of further modifications in the original practices
of New England congregationalism. Stoddard still insisted
that the distinction between regenerate and unregenerate was
important, so important that every possible means should be
used to produce conversions. His innovation was to treat the
Lord's Supper as a converting ordinance, and to urge everyone to participate. Full communion had always been restricted to the regenerate; by urging the unregenerate to
attend, Stoddard broke down the institutional distinction between saints and sinners. When that happened, the distinction itself was threatened.

At first, orthodox doctrine was not affected; by no stretch

---

[3] A choice collection of such complaints was made in Thomas Prince, Jr.,
ed., *The Christian History* (Boston, 1744–45), I, pp. 93–106.
[4] Perry Miller, "Solomon Stoddard, 1643–1729," *Harvard Theological
Review*, XXXIV (1941), pp. 277–320.

of the imagination could Solomon Stoddard be regarded as a theological liberal. But the congregational polity could not be modified without at least encouraging a corruption of doctrine. New England stood at a parting of the ways. If the familiar doctrine was to be maintained, the distinction between saints and sinners would have to be revived in actual fact, and find expression in church polity. That road led to revivalism and evangelical orthodoxy. The connection between doctrine and polity could not be discarded in New England, as the ensuing development showed. When Jonathan Edwards, Stoddard's grandson, used revival methods to produce men and women who were conscious that they were of the elect, he rejected Stoddardeanism and returned to the theory of regenerate membership. Once again it was possible to tell a saint from a sinner, to include the one and exclude the other.

But there was an alternative. Edwards revived Calvinism and restored the polity that had traditionally gone with it. Others accepted the modifications of polity produced by the decline in religious fervor, and began, often without realizing what they were doing, to adjust their doctrine to fit. Conversion as a tumultuous religious experience had become unreal to them; how then could they retain a conviction of election, of which conversion was the sensible evidence? Or, to put it another way, if the distinction between saints and sinners was disappearing, how could they retain a vivid sense of total depravity? But when these doctrines faded away, the whole system of theology had to be reconstructed. The result was Arminianism.

III

The transition from Calvinism to Arminianism was in many cases a gradual one, because New England Puritanism held within it a latent ambiguity. Even the doctrine of the first settlers was not strict Calvinism. The Massachusetts Bay Puritans belonged to the " Covenant " or " Federal " school of the Reformed theology, which had considerably modified the teachings of Calvin before they were transplanted to the new world.[5] As this theology developed in the early seventeenth century, it seems to have been an attempt to restate Calvinism in terms that would prevent it from falling into the pitfall of Antinomianism on the one hand or Arminianism on the other. If the Calvinist stressed too much the doctrine that God elects men according to his own pleasure, regardless of their actual moral state, one might ask: Why bother with morality at all? No one can do anything which will entitle him to salvation, because no man can perfectly obey the law of righteousness. And after he is converted, and feels God's spirit working in him, he need give no thought to his behavior. He is above the law because he has the rule of righteousness in his heart, and can surrender to the glorious certainty of salvation. But if this Antinomian argument stressed election and God's grace at the expense of codes of morality, Arminianism emphasized human initiative at the expense of God's sovereignty. The Arminians said that the efficacy of God's grace depends on whether man receives or rejects it. If men will only improve their natural abilities, and endeavor to love God and do his will, his grace will not be denied them. In other words, whether any man is saved is no longer a question of God's election apart from moral worth, but rests on the individual and his behavior as a free moral agent. Finite man would then have a power that the infinite God has not.

[5] Perry Miller, *The New England Mind* (New York, 1939), pp. 365–397; Perry Miller, " The Marrow of Puritan Divinity," *Publications of the Colonial Society of Massachusetts*, XXXII (1937), pp. 247–300.

Thus the problem that the Puritans tried to solve by the Covenant theology was how to maintain God's sovereignty without sacrificing the obligations of morality. They did it by an ingenious device, which gave them all the advantages of the Arminian concept of a God who insists on morality, without sacrificing their basic recognition that in the final analysis, God is inscrutable, and his ways beyond our finite understandings. The infinite God, they said, entered into a covenant with his chosen people, whereby he agreed to act in the matter of their salvation according to rules that they could understand. God voluntarily restricted himself to act in a predictable fashion. If any man lived within hearing of the preaching of the word, this covenant was offered to him; if he declined it, he had only himself to blame. If he accepted it, as of course he would do if he were of the elect, he bound himself in return for salvation not only to have faith in God, but also to strive for holiness. Morality was not the condition on which justification was granted; but anyone who entered into a covenant with God by which he would be justified because of his faith, would discover that he was also bound to the struggle for righteousness.

The seventeenth-century Puritan would have said that only those whom God elected could accept the covenant, and even they did so by God's grace. But a covenant involves a voluntary act on both sides, and by adopting such a device, the Puritans began a development which, by magnifying the part played by man in his own salvation, inevitably carried them farther and farther from strict Calvinism. When the fever of New England piety declined after the first generation, the ministers began to " preach up " the means of grace, insisting that their charges should attend worship, should read the Scriptures and pray to God, and even approach the Lord's table in the hope of being converted. All these were matters of human choice. The ministers went a step further. If you will believe, if you will have faith, they argued, God has covenanted to save you. Do this, and you will be entitled to call upon him to make good his promises. Such preaching was sound enough doctrinally as long as the people remembered that only the elect would be able to respond. But the trouble was that the doctrine of election was becoming only a formal concept, divorced from experience. In such circumstances, the result was to spread the notion that every man could be saved if he chose, and that the power of choice was his.

After one hundred years, then, the accepted theology in New England was still essentially orthodox, but changed conditions had made a great change in emphasis. The doctrine of election was not denied, but the average listener was left with the impression that his salvation was within his own control. The Westminster Confession had balanced God's decrees with human liberty; now human liberty was stretched to such a point that it almost had possession of the field. Sooner or later, someone was bound to recognize that the doctrine of election was disappearing, would consciously reject it, and would start to revise the whole structure of his theology to fit. Then the Covenant theology would develop into something that may properly be called Arminianism.

IV

The orthodox ministers had a cause for concern in addition to the Arminian tendencies which threatened their churches from within. Ever since the days of Archbishop Laud, Arminianism had been common in the Church of England; by the turn of the century, it was wholly dominant there. The growth of the Anglican church in New England was therefore a doctrinal as well as a political threat to the churches of the Standing Order. That growth was particularly rapid in the 1720's, the decade in which King's Chapel in Boston twice produced new churches by a process of fission — Christ Church in 1723 and Trinity five years later. In Connecticut, the conversion of several Congregationalists to the Church of England seemed ominous. In 1722, a group of tutors of Yale College, including Samuel Johnson and Rector Timothy Cutler, conformed. A few years later, the Reverend John Beach, who had been the Congregational minister at Newtown, Connecticut, was converted and took charge of the Episcopal church there. In 1734, the Reverend Ebenezer Punderson of Groton, Connecticut, became a convert, carrying with him part of his parish; and that same year, the Reverend Jonathan Arnold of West Haven followed suit.[6] The reaction of the orthodox to this turn of events was immediate. The trustees of Yale deposed Rector Cutler for his apostasy, and tightened the bonds of orthodoxy by voting to impose a loyalty test:

. . . all such Persons as shall hereafter be elected to the Office of *Rector* or *Tutor* in this College shall, before they are accepted therein, before the Trustees, declare their Assent to the *Confession of Faith*, . . . and shall particularly give Satisfaction to them of the soundness of their Faith, in opposition to *Arminian* and Prelatical Corruptions. . . .[7]

It may be argued that, in Boston, one of the factors in the growth of the Church of England was social prestige, reinforced by the support of the royal governors. In the case of the Connecticut converts, intellectual influences were chiefly responsible. Samuel Johnson declared in his auto-

[6] Francis A. Christie, " The Beginnings of Arminianism in New England," *Papers of the American Society of Church History,* Ser. 2, III (1912), pp. 170, 171; also W. W. Manross, *A History of the American Episcopal Church* (New York, 1935), pp. 104, 105.

[7] Henry Wilder Foote, *Annals of King's Chapel,* 2 vols. (Boston, 1882, 1896), I, pp. 314, 315.

biography that he had always been " much embarrassed with the rigid Calvinistical notions in which he had been bred." A large collection of English theological and philosophical books given to Yale in 1714 by Jeremiah Dummer was the means by which Johnson and his associates found release:

When therefore the library came, and he and his friends above-mentioned came to read and consider those excellent divines of the Church, especially Scot and Whitby, and conversed together on these subjects, it was with vast satisfaction that they saw infinite reason to make their minds easy about them.[8]

The source of contagion was well known to the orthodox. " I hear some in Connecticut complain that Arminian books are cried up in Yale College for eloquence and learning, and Calvinists despised for the contrary," the Rev. Joseph Morgan reported to Cotton Mather, " and none have the courage to see it redressed." [9]

Although the converts were well tainted with Arminianism, they showed some hesitation in avowing it openly, in the face of the strong Calvinist tradition of New England. In the pamphlet warfare occasioned by the spread of Anglicanism, men like Samuel Johnson stoutly denied that they were Arminians; but the course of the controversy made it clear that they rejected the name while accepting the doctrine. Johnson declared that he held no doctrines except those of the Church of England, which long antedated Arminius. But, he went on to say, " if *Arminius* happened to agree with them in some of his notions, I know no reason however, why we should be called after his name." [10] When

---

[8] Herbert and Carol Schneider, ed., *Samuel Johnson, President of King's College* (New York, 1929), I, p. 11.
[9] Franklin B. Dexter, *Biographical Sketches of the Graduates of Yale College* (New York, 1885), I, p. 260.
[10] Samuel Johnson, " A Letter from a Minister of the Church of England to his Dissenting Parishioners," in Schneider, *Samuel Johnson*, III, p. 26.

an opponent in the controversy persisted, Johnson went so far as to say, " I hate the name of that Dutch Presbyterian." But he explicitly denied that the Church of England was Calvinistic: ". . . if we take the articles, prayers and homilies altogether, and candidly interpret one passage by another, and by the general tenor of the whole, we shall find nothing in them that can be justly interpreted to express the Calvinistic doctrine of absolute predestination and reprobation." [11]

The same fear of incurring the open hostility of the Calvinists may well have been the motive behind the anonymous publication about 1719 of *Choice Dialogues Between a Godly Minister and an Honest Country Man, Concerning Election & Predestination.* The authorship was never openly admitted, but it was generally understood that the pamphlet was the work of John Checkley, a layman of King's Chapel, noted for his high church zeal.[12] The *Dialogues* represent a sturdy attack on strict Calvinism, charging that its doctrines take away the free will of man, and make God the author of sin. They admit that redemption comes from God's grace; but by analogy with the cultivation of the soil, man's labor is necessary to remove obstacles which would prevent the sun from producing the harvest. The rigid Calvinistic notions of predestination, the author declared, " are not only most *absurd,* but likewise *blasphemous* against *God,*" [13] and they have the unfortunate result of tormenting the souls of those who believe them. A reply to Checkley was made by a friend of his, one Thomas Walter, who charged him with inconsistency

---

[11] Samuel Johnson, "A Second Letter from a Minister of the Church of England to his Dissenting Parishioners," in Schneider, *Samuel Johnson,* III, pp. 50, 51.

[12] Edmund F. Slafter, *John Checkley; or the Evolution of Religious Tolerance in Massachusetts Bay,* 2 vols. (Boston, 1897); also Foote, *Annals,* I, pp. 286 ff.

[13] Slafter, *John Checkley,* I, p. 160.

as well as unsound doctrine, and implied that most of the *Choice Dialogues* was derived from the English divine, Charles Leslie.[14]

V

But neither the spread of Arminianism resulting from the growth of the Church of England, nor a similar tendency in the Baptist churches,[15] is enough to explain the alarm shown by orthodox Congregationalists in the 1730's. They had good reason to believe that lax doctrine was beginning to corrupt their own churches.[16] In 1734, John White published a lamentation over the sad state of New England, in which one of the complaints was:

That some of Our *Young Men*, and such as are devoted to and educated for, the *Ministry* of the *Gospel*, are under *Prejudices* against, and fall off from, important Articles of the *Faith* of these *Churches*, and cast a favourable Eye upon, embrace, and as far as they dare, *argue* for, *propagate*, and *preach* the *Arminian Scheme*. There are many dark Clouds hang over *New-England*, and the *Churches* of *Christ* therein; but I apprehend this to be as dark and dismal as any.[17]

In the pages that followed, he outlined at length the Arminian scheme; and if the Young Men for whom he lamented were as familiar with it as he, the orthodox had good reason to be alarmed.

[14] [Thomas Walter], *A Choice Dialogue Between John Faustus a Conjurer, and Jack Tory His Friend. . . . By a Young Strippling* (Boston, 1720).

[15] A. H. Newman, *A History of the Baptist Churches in the United States* (New York, 1894), pp. 38–56, 84–95, 239–271.

[16] Professor Francis A. Christie believed that Arminianism in the Congregational churches and clergy before the Awakening was a myth. "What Edwards saw and feared," he maintained, "was not a spread of Arminianism among the Congregationalists, a desertion of the old orthodoxy, but the rise of Episcopalianism." See Christie, "Beginnings of Arminianism," *loc. cit.* III, p. 169. But a careful survey of the evidence makes it hard to avoid the conclusion that the fear was not only great but well founded that Arminianism was beginning to infect the churches of the Standing Order.

[17] John White, *New England's Lamentations* (Boston, 1734), pp. 16, 17.

The orthodox observed with dismay that the contagion from Arminian books was not confined to Yale, but was beginning to spread around Boston as well. John White believed that the chief source of infection was " corrupt Books " which young men found " agreeable as to the Matter, suiting their Proud and self conceited Hearts, by exalting and extolling *free Will*, and *self Sufficiency*." [18] The anonymous author of *A Faithful Narrative of God's Gracious Dealings with a Person Lately Recovered from the Dangerous Errors of Arminius* attributed his downfall to reading " *Arminian Books*, and some of the Writings of such as are called Free-Thinkers." He gave testimony as to the circulation of such books: " About this Time, I went into a Stationer's Shop, as I used frequently to do; and there I espy'd some of the *Arminian Books*; such as I had read but too much in; and the Bookseller told me, of what esteem they were in *England*." [19]

Other complaints of the infiltration of undesirable books were occasionally made. One of the causes for dismay at the opinions of Robert Breck of Springfield, about whom controversy raged in 1735, was that he had apparently been reading Chubb.[20] And Benjamin Colman wrote to William Hooper on February 15, 1739/40, about the books read at Harvard: " I truly wish many of our *modern & new Books* had never *arrived* or been read there; & particularly such as *Mr. Chubb*. . . . These corrupt our young Men's Judgment & Style too." [21]

Three important disputes in the 1730's involved the question of unsound doctrine. They were the cases of Benjamin

---

[18] *Ibid.*, p. 26.
[19] [Samuel Moody], *A Faithful Narrative of God's Gracious Dealings* (Boston, 1737), pp. 1, 7.
[20] *A Narrative of the Proceedings of those Ministers of the County of Hampshire, &c.* (Boston, 1736), p. 5.
[21] Benjamin Colman to William Hooper, February 15, 1739/40. Ms, Massachusetts Historical Society.

Kent, Robert Breck, and Samuel Osborn. Kent graduated from Harvard in 1727, and was ordained at Marlborough on October 23, 1733. Some suspicion was voiced at that time as to the soundness of his faith, and the Marlborough Association of Ministers examined him, especially on the articles " chiefly relating to the controversy with the Remonstrants." He was able to satisfy them enough to gain their assent to the ordination; but some doubt apparently lingered in their minds, for they added a proviso: ". . . as long as they should see that what he had exhibited were his *real* sentiments." [22] But this did not end the matter, for scarcely had he been settled when one of the prominent members of the church charged that he was a " profest Arminian." A council, called on February 4, 1735, found the charges fully sustained. It declared that Kent believed " that there were several answers in the Assembly's Catechism which had not a word of Scripture to support them, particularly that respecting the Decrees "; " that he denied an absolute Election, and asserted a conditional one on the foresight of good works "; " that he said in his preaching, that if God dealt with Adam as a moral agent he could not have hindered his fall or his sinning against him "; and " that infants came into the world free and clear of original guilt." [23] The council advised that Kent be suspended from his pulpit. There is no record that he ever retracted. He moved to Boston where he became a lawyer, celebrated for his eccentricity and wit.[24]

Robert Breck graduated from Harvard in 1730, his college record having been clouded for a time by accusations that he had filched property from some fellow-students. After a

[22] Joseph Allen, *The Worcester Association and its Antecedents* (Boston, 1868), pp. 15, 16.
[23] Levi A. Field, *An Historical Sketch of the First Congregational Church in Marlborough, Mass.* (Worcester, 1859), p. 26.
[24] The best summary of the Kent episode is in Clifford K. Shipton, *Sibley's Harvard Graduates*, VIII (Boston, 1951), pp. 220–230.

short period of further study, he began to preach in Windham, Connecticut, where his Harvard theology attracted the
attention of the Reverend Thomas Clap, later President of
Yale. In 1734, when not yet twenty-one, Breck was asked
to preach to the First Parish in Springfield with a view to a
settlement. The Church and Parish gave him a call, but
Clap tried to mobilize the ministers of the Hampshire Association against him to refuse him ordination. Breck, in turn,
appealed for support to a group of Boston ministers. The
climax to the whole affair was an ecclesiastical council, which
included ministers from outside the county, and which was
broken up by the local civil authorities acting on the instiga-
tion of the anti-Breck faction. There seems to be some evidence that the Boston ministers were to be arrested; but actually it was Breck who was clapped into jail, escorted to
Connecticut, and turned over to the authorities there for
prosecution, only to be quietly released.

Throughout the dispute, Breck's conduct seems to have
been a bit disingenuous, both with respect to his troubles in
college and with respect to his theological views. The alle-
gations against him suggest that he was toying not only with
Arminianism, but with rationalism and Arianism as well. In
the course of the dispute, he presented to the Boston ministers
a Confession of Faith which was thoroughly orthodox, containing none of the errors charged against him. But in 1748,
he published a sermon in which he declared: " That GOD will
judge and reward or punish Men according to their Works,
is as plain as any Thing can be." [25] Ultimately he lived down
the notoriety surrounding his ordination. He became one of
the most respected ministers of the Connecticut valley, even
though his theology was more liberal than that of most of his

[25] Robert Breck, *The Duty of Ministers, not only to Establish Their Hearers in a Well-Grounded Belief of the Christian Religion, but to Exhort Them
that Believe Carefully to Maintain Good Works* (Boston, 1748).

colleagues, and he was a leading figure in the council which dismissed Jonathan Edwards from the Northampton parish in 1750.[26]

Unlike Breck, Samuel Osborn, who was dismissed from the Second Parish in Eastham on November 20, 1738, did not hedge or retract his views under pressure. Ever since his settlement in 1718, Osborn had been repeatedly attacked by the Reverend Nathaniel Stone, the contentious minister of the neighboring church in Brewster. Stone seems to have thought that the way to lend plausibility to the charge that Osborn was " venting erroneous doctrines " was to allow no one to forget that he was " upon court record as the reputed father of a bastard child." [27] In 1743, Osborn readily admitted having preached that " what Christ did and suffer'd, did nothing abate or diminish Men's Obligation to the holy Law of God "; that " Men can do that upon the doing of which they shall certainly be saved "; and that " Men's Obedience is a Cause of their Justification." He told his people frankly that they were accountable creatures, capable of being either virtuous or vicious.[28] After his dismissal, Osborn was unable to get another settlement, although he did retain the friendship and support of a number of his fellow-ministers who were opposers of the Awakening.

Such incidents are fragmentary evidence, to be sure, but they are indicative of laxity of doctrine in the churches of the Standing Order. One result was that the orthodox began to

[26] The best summary is in Shipton, *Sibley's Harvard Graduates*, VIII, pp. 661–680; see also Ezra Hoyt Byington, *The Puritan in England and New England* (Boston, 1897), pp. 335–368. Original documents were printed in the *Narrative of the Proceedings*.

[27] Gustavus Swift Paine, " Ungodly Carriages on Cape Cod," *New England Quarterly*, XXV (1952), pp. 190, 191.

[28] Samuel Osborn, *The Case and Complaint of Mr. Samuel Osborn, Late of Eastham* (Boston, 1743), pp. 5–11; also Enoch Pratt, *A Comprehensive History, Ecclesiastical and Civil, of Eastham, Wellfleet and Orleans* (Yarmouth, 1844), pp. 56, 57.

be more careful on such occasions as the ordination and installation of ministers. The New North Church in Boston, for example, was considering various candidates in 1739 to succeed Peter Thacher, and as a precaution passed the following vote:

Inasmuch as sevral of the great & important Doctrines of Christianity are vigorously opposed at this Day by *Deists, Socinians, Arians* & *Arminians,* and the Faith of many professors in great danger of being suburted by this means:

Voted, That it is the Desire and Expectation of the Church, That the Committee abovementioned take more especial care to enquire of the Reverend Mr. *Thomas Prentice* concerning *his soundness in these present Truths;* and to desire of him the most explicit confession of his Faith concerning them.[29]

After the outbreak of the Awakening, when many ministers had become more doctrinally-minded, there was a tendency for them to look back on the previous decade as one in which Arminianism was notorious and widespread, rather than concealed and sporadic. Such testimony must be treated with caution, coming as it does after the outbreak of the revival, which inflamed men's feelings and made them exaggerate the evils they saw. Some of their complaints may be found in the accounts of revivals published by Thomas Prince in the *Christian History.* The Reverend Josiah Crocker described the situation in Taunton as follows: " As to *Doctrines,* I would only observe; that as far as I have learned, *Arminianism* or Doctrines verging that Way awfully prevailed among them." [30] The most alarming report of the spread of heresies was made by William Shurtleff of Portsmouth, New Hampshire: " How did not only *Pelagianism,* but *Arianism, Socinianism,* and even *Deism* itself, and what is falsely call'd

[29] Henry H. Edes, " Rev. Andrew Eliot, 1719–1788," *Publications of the Colonial Society of Massachusetts,* XIII (1912), pp. 237, 238.
[30] Prince, *Christian History,* II, p. 324.

by the Name of *Free-thinking*, here and there prevail? " [31]
But this comment probably tells more about Mr. Shurtleff
than it does about the actual state of affairs in Portsmouth in
the days before the Awakening.

[31] William Shurtleff, *A Letter to those of his Brethren in the Ministry who
Refuse to Admit the Rev. Mr. Whitefield into their Pulpits* (Boston, 1745),
p. 4.

CHAPTER TWO

The Great Awakening

1735–1745

I

Toward the end of December, 1734, Jonathan Edwards observed signs of an awakened interest in religion in Northampton. In the months that followed, a concern for things of the eternal world became general among people of the town, old and young alike, of both high and low estate. Even the " vainest, & Loosest Persons in Town " were " siezed with strong convictions." [1] Participation in all kinds of religious exercises increased; the people showed great concern over their wicked and unconverted state; many of them for the first time developed a Christian spirit of love and affection, so that Edwards felt that party and factional strife in the town were disappearing. Some of the people had impressions on their imaginations of Christ shedding his blood for sinners, but on the whole this revival was not marked by extremes of what the eighteenth century called " enthusiasm." From Northampton the revival spread to other Connecticut valley towns — to Hadley first, and then to communities as far upstream as Northfield and as far south as New Haven.[2]

Edwards knew that such intense interest in the things of

---

[1] Jonathan Edwards, " Narrative of Surprising Conversions," original version in Clarence H. Faust and Thomas H. Johnson, *Jonathan Edwards* (New York, c. 1935), p. 75.

[2] Jonathan Edwards, *The Works of President Edwards* (New York, 1843), III, pp. 231–272.

religion would not last. He had a sense of the revival as following a well-defined course. Beginning with scattered instances of conversions, it would gradually widen its influence until the whole community was drawn into it; then the excitement would die down, to be followed by a period, perhaps years, of deadness and dullness. It behooved every man, therefore, to hope that the sudden outpouring of the spirit of God would not pass him by. Once the revival had died away, the chances of eternal salvation for anyone who had not been savingly wrought upon were obviously slim. In the case of the 1735 revival, excitement mounted in intensity, as Edwards expected; but its peak was marred by an awful and irregular event, the suicide of Edwards' own uncle under the influence of religious melancholy. After that, the tumult began to subside, so that by the end of the year the town had returned to normal.

Five years later, stimulated by the itinerant preaching of George Whitefield, the revival broke out anew. This time it was no longer a local Northampton and Connecticut valley affair, but was part of an intercolonial Great Awakening. Whitefield made his first visit to New England in the fall of 1740. Between September 14 and October 29, he preached many times in Boston, traveled as far north as York, Maine, spent several days with Edwards at Northampton, and finally proceeded down the Connecticut River through Hartford to New Haven, Stamford, and New York. Everywhere his preaching attracted large crowds, and many people were moved to tears by his words.[3]

No sooner had Whitefield departed, leaving New England in an uproar, than Gilbert Tennent took his place. Tennent, a leader of the evangelical wing of the Presbyterians in New Jersey, had had success in promoting revivals in his own par-

[3] Joseph Tracy, *The Great Awakening* (Boston, 1842), Ch. 7.

ish comparable to that of Edwards in Northampton. His sermon on the *Danger of an Unconverted Ministry* had produced a dispute over revivalism in the middle colonies much like the one that was developing in New England. Tennent spent three months in and around Boston, from December 13, 1740, to March 2, 1741. He was followed in turn by a swarm of exhorters and itinerants, of whom the most notorious was James Davenport (Yale, 1732) of Southold, Long Island. Davenport's accusations that settled ministers were unconverted got him in trouble with the civil authorities in Connecticut; while in Massachusetts he was presented by the Grand Jury of Suffolk County for slander, was tried, and released on the ground that he was insane.[4]

Whitefield returned in the fall of 1744. His admirers welcomed him as warmly as ever, but the excesses of Davenport had turned many earlier supporters of the revival against it and had stiffened the opposition of those who had distrusted evangelical preaching from the beginning. Many ministers now excluded Whitefield from their pulpits, and Testimonies against him were signed by the members of several ministerial associations, especially in eastern Massachusetts. The repercussions of the Awakening were slow in dying away, but by 1745 its initial force was largely spent.[5]

II

The Great Awakening was a reaction against the formalism of an accepted orthodoxy, and was the American counterpart of that religious unrest which produced Pietism in Germany and Methodism in England. But it was much more than a theological controversy. It was a complex episode, involving not only religion, but politics as well, and the whole social structure of the colonies. A society was in upheaval; and in

----

[4] *Ibid.*, Chs. 9, 14.   [5] *Ibid.*, Chs. 16, 18.

an age when religion was a dominant concern, and the churches were among the most important social institutions, the language of theology was naturally used as the language of controversy. Tension and social conflict whose origin was social or economic were easily translated into theological debate. Some knowledge of the social structure of New England, then, is essential for an understanding of the Awakening itself, and of the Arminian movement which emerged from it.

Even before 1740, cleavages existed in New England which awaited only a controversial issue to cause deep rents in the fabric of society. Social classes had existed in the Bay Colony from the very earliest times; as the colony matured, its class structure became more complex and class divisions were accentuated. There was a primary difference between those who were involved in the commercial life of such ports as Boston and Salem, and the farmers of the interior. In addition, in the seaports, there was a growing gulf between the merchant class and the small shopkeepers and artisans. Capital accumulation meant the beginning of colonial fortunes: Thomas Amory died in 1728 leaving an estate in Boston valued at £20,000, not including his property in Carolina and the Azores.[6] Travelers who visited Boston around 1740 often commented on the similarity between the life of the merchants there and of the corresponding classes in London. One of them reported:

The Conversation in this Town is as polite as in most of the Cities and Towns of *England;* many of their Merchants having traded into *Europe,* and those that staid at home having the Advantage of Society with Travellers; so that a Gentleman from *London* would almost think himself at home at *Boston,* when he observes the Number of People, their Houses, their Furniture, their Tables, their Dress

[6] J. T. Adams, *Revolutionary New England, 1691–1776* (Boston, 1923), p. 115.

and Conversation, which perhaps is as splendid and showy, as that of the most considerable Tradesman in *London*.[7]

A conflict of interest between economic groups was a serious matter in the 1730's.[8] The debtor classes were advocating inflation of the currency by the emission of paper money to be secured by land. It was Thomas Hutchinson's testimony that the promoters of this " land-bank " scheme were persons " some few of rank and good estate, but generally of low condition among the plebeians and of small estate, and many of them perhaps insolvent." [9] The merchants and wealthy classes opposed the plan, proposing a substitute bank with notes based on silver. The Governor, acting on advice of the Council, issued proclamations warning the people against accepting land-bank notes, and made use of various sanctions to discourage their circulation.

The conflict might well have ended in armed rebellion, had it not been for two events: Parliament came to the rescue of the sound-money party by declaring that the Bubble Act of 1720 applied in this case, and the Great Awakening diverted popular attention to religious matters. But the transfer of public excitement from the currency problem to religious revivals did not mean that social cleavages were erased. The tension between classes now took a religious instead of an economic form. The same sort of people who had been agitating for the land-bank and cheap money turned their attention to undermining the established church order. Itinerant preaching, the rise of exhorters, rejection of the ideal of an educated clergy, aspersions cast on settled ministers — all these were

[7] John Oldmixon, *The British Empire in America* (2nd ed., London, 1741), I, p. 197.
[8] Adams, *Revolutionary New England*, pp. 154–159; also John C. Miller, " Religion, Finance, and Democracy in Massachusetts," *New England Quarterly*, VI (1933), pp. 29–58.
[9] Thomas Hutchinson, *The History of the Colony and Province of Massachusetts-Bay*, L. S. Mayo, ed., (Cambridge, 1936), II, p. 299.

symptoms of social unrest, directed now against upper-class ministers instead of upper-class merchants.

Social cleavages could readily be translated into theological terms because, in a very broad way, certain attitudes and doctrinal positions correspond to particular social classes. Churches of the disinherited are commonly marked by an attitude of severe condemnation of luxury, gay apparel, and worldly pleasures. Furthermore, there has often been a connection between the doctrine of the new birth and lower-class religious movements. The Anabaptists, the Quakers, the Methodists were all lower class in origin, and only as the decades rolled by did they become prosperous and respectable. They had in common a sense of a direct communication between God and the individual soul, particularly at the moment of regeneration, which was available to every man regardless of rank or education. Perhaps education has a sobering effect on the tendency to have mystical visions; perhaps emotionalism does not comport with prosperity and social position. In any event, evangelical revivalism tends to disappear as one rises in the social scale.

III

In addition to cleavages between classes in New England, there were important variations between the culture and religious traditions of the Connecticut valley towns, and of Boston and the eastern seacoast.[10] At the turn of the century, the Mathers were the dominating figures in and around Boston, although their leadership was not undisputed; in the valley, Solomon Stoddard was virtual dictator. The Mathers led the group which supported the Half-Way Covenant; Stoddard stood for the use of the Lord's Supper as a convert-

---

[10] See Perry Miller, *Jonathan Edwards* (New York, c. 1949), pp. 3–34; also Perry Miller, " Solomon Stoddard, 1643–1729," *Harvard Theological Review*, XXXIV (1941), pp. 277–320.

ing ordinance that all the townspeople were exhorted to attend, and gradually most of the churches of the valley adopted his position.   In Boston, the tradition of unemotional religion became well established, and there was developing a " free and catholic " spirit which emphasized practical morality at the same time that it maintained a gentlemanly tolerance of theological differences. Stoddard, on the other hand, was evangelical in his preaching, and at five different times during his ministry he had seen revivals in Northampton.

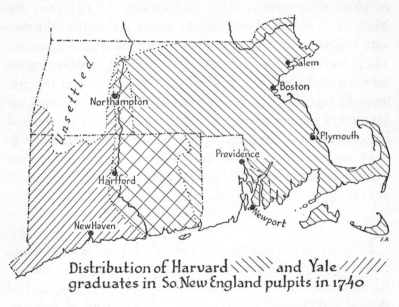

Distribution of Harvard \\\\\\ and Yale ////// graduates in So. New England pulpits in 1740

The intellectual focus of the seacoast area was Harvard College, where the free and catholic tradition was exemplified in men like Tutor William Brattle, Presidents Leverett and Holyoke, and Professor Edward Wigglesworth.   The valley had come to distrust the liberalizing tendencies of Harvard, even though no clear departure from orthodoxy had taken place, and was shifting its allegiance to Yale, which was founded in 1701 in order to maintain unimpaired the faith once delivered to the saints. Year by year, men trained at Yale were replacing Harvard graduates in the pulpits of Connecticut and western Massachusetts. By 1740, southern New England was clearly divided into three culture areas, one dominated by Harvard, another by Yale, and the third by Baptists who for the most part had no college training.[11] The Harvard area included Massachusetts and Connecticut, as far west as the Connecticut River. Rhode Island was Baptist territory, except for such towns on the eastern shore as Bristol, Little Compton, and Newport, where there were Congregational churches served by Harvard men. The Yale area included all of Connecticut except for the northeast corner, and Yale had driven two salients into Massachusetts along the Connecticut and Housatonic Rivers. This distribution meant that Harvard and Yale competed for control of about one-third of Connecticut and the river towns in Massachusetts.

Admittedly, the line between Boston and the valley — or

[11] This "religious ecology" of southern New England is based on a detailed analysis of the biographies of ministers as given in the following: Frederick Lewis Weis, *The Colonial Clergy and the Colonial Churches of New England* (Lancaster, 1936); William B. Sprague, *Annals of the American Pulpit* (New York, 1856–1865), Vols. 1, 2, 5, 6, 8; "Complete List of the Congregational and Presbyterian Ministers in Massachusetts," County of Suffolk by B. B. Edwards, Berkshire County by David D. Field, *American Quarterly Register,* VII (1834–35), pp. 28–38; Joseph B. Felt, "A List of the Congregational and Presbyterian Ministers, who have been Settled in the County of Essex, Mass.," *American Quarterly Register,* VII (1834–35), pp. 246–261; Thomas Noyes, "Complete List of the Congregational Ministers, in the County of Norfolk, Mass.," *American Quarterly Register,* VIII (1835–36), pp. 42–58; Thomas Noyes, "Complete List of the Congregational Ministers, in the County of Plymouth, Mass.," *American Quarterly Register,* VIII (1835–36), pp. 144–159; Thomas Noyes, "Complete List of the Congregational Ministers, in the County of Worcester, Mass.," *American Quarterly Register,* X (1837–38), pp. 47–62, 126–145; B. B. Edwards, "Complete List of the Congregational Ministers in the Old County of Hampshire, Ms.," *American Quarterly Register,* X (1837–38), pp. 260–276, 379–407; Samuel Sewall, "A Brief Survey of the Congregational Churches and Ministers in the County of Middlesex, and in Chelsea in the County of Suffolk, Ms.," *American Quarterly Register,* XI (1838–39), pp. 45–55, 174–197, 248–279, 376–402; XIII (1840), pp. 37–57.

between Harvard and Yale — did not correspond exactly with the line between the opposers and the friends of the revival. Boston ministers like William Cooper (Harvard, 1712), Thomas Prince (Harvard, 1707), and Thomas Foxcroft (Harvard, 1714) were closer in sympathies to Jonathan Edwards (Yale, 1720) of Northampton than they were to Charles Chauncy (Harvard, 1721), the junior minister at the First Church in Boston. On the other hand, there were opposers of the revival among the Tutors at Yale, like Chauncy Whittelsey (Yale, 1738), who was Charles Chauncy's cousin. David Brainerd accused him of having no more grace than a chair, and promptly found himself in trouble with the college authorities. Yet the distinction between the areas dominated by graduates of the two colleges was of major consequence. There were opposers of the revival in Yale territory; but it was in the Harvard area that opposers developed into Arminians. There were evangelicals among Harvard men, but it was only among Yale graduates that one found, as the decades went by, increasing numbers of Edwardeans, or " New Divinity " men.

In Boston, Charles Chauncy occupied a strategic position which made it possible for him to rally the forces of opposition to the revival as few of his colleagues could have done.[12] Born there on January 1, 1704/5, he was the great-grandson and namesake of the second president of Harvard. Following graduation he read theology, and was chosen in 1727 to be the colleague of Foxcroft at the First Church. This post was one of prestige and influence, especially after Foxcroft was stricken with paralysis in 1736. Chauncy's virtues were the prosaic ones — diligence, sobriety, common sense, and devotion to scholarship — and he might well have been over-

---

[12] The best brief sketch of Chauncy is in Clifford K. Shipton, *Sibley's Harvard Graduates*, VI (Boston, 1942), pp. 439–467.

shadowed by his more brilliant colleague had the latter retained his health. As it was, Foxcroft's influence in favor of
moderate Calvinism and revivalism was sharply diminished,
and Chauncy's position correspondingly enhanced. He assumed the chief burden of pastoral and community responsibilities. He was frequently called on to participate in ordaining councils and installation services; he was an obvious choice
to preach before the governor on the occasion of the annual
election. Funeral sermons for prominent members of his
congregation promptly found their way into print. He interested himself in the college, for he was automatically a member of its Board of Overseers.

Nor did he hesitate, during the Awakening, to make use of
the opportunity for leadership that his position afforded him.
He began to collect information about the excesses of the revival, partly from the newspapers, partly through correspondence with friends, and partly by means of a grand tour
of New England. It is said that he traveled three hundred
miles on this mission, and he must have established personal
contact with dozens of ministers and leaders of opinion in
many communities throughout southern New England. One
of the results was the long list of sponsors, filling eighteen
pages, who made possible the publication in 1743 of a fat volume entitled *Seasonable Thoughts on the State of Religion
in New-England*.

Chauncy's mind was less incisive than that of Edwards,
and his literary style much more lumbering. He never swept
a congregation off its feet, either by oratorical eloquence or
by persuading it of the very presence of the Spirit of God in
its midst. But he was able and energetic; he knew the prejudices of the people to whom he appealed, and he understood
how to work through existing social and institutional structures to achieve his ends. Edwards was repudiated by his

own congregation in 1750; his vindication did not come until after his death. Chauncy was never repudiated, even though in the beginning he was almost alone among the Boston ministers in denouncing the revival. Instead, he lived to see his views, which became increasingly liberal after the Awakening, substantially accepted by the leaders of opinion in Boston and the area for which it was the cultural metropolis.

IV

George Whitefield did not preach doctrines of economic levelism or attempt to array class against class. Certain of the men who followed him did much more than he to exploit class differences. But even Whitefield's preaching tended to undermine the social order, by weakening the traditional New England parish system and by diminishing the prestige of established ministers. The New England parish system was strictly territorial except in Boston. There was but one congregational church in each town or precinct. All the inhabitants were expected to attend and required by law to support public worship in the meetinghouse. The minister was customarily settled for life, and an inhabitant of the town had no option as to the preaching he would hear. In the seventeenth century, the people were tied into a coherent and united church order, which was central in the whole structure of community and colony. By the 1730's, to be sure, breaches had been made in this system, and exceptions granted under certain circumstances to Quakers, Baptists, and members of the Church of England. But the system itself was still the normal and accepted thing.

To appreciate how the Awakening tended to undermine the New England church order, one need only examine some of the practices of the revivalists. First, there was itinerant preaching. Heretofore a minister would preach in a pulpit not his own only in the course of regular exchanges with nearby ministers. It was unheard of for him to travel from town to town, speaking wherever he could find a congregation, whether the settled minister welcomed him or not. The itinerants justified their course by declaring, with John Wesley, that all the world was their parish; that they were called of God to do his work wherever it needed to be done. Their actions, however, seemed insulting to many of the settled ministers, for the implication was that the duly appointed religious teachers were not fit for their positions. Hence the opposition to itineracy arose partly from resentment at this implied judgment passed on the ministry, and partly from fear of the consequences to church order.

In the sermons of the men who became liberal or Arminian, there was unbroken opposition to the practice, and a tenacious defence of the traditional New England way. William Balch argued in 1744 against ministers who " go from Place to Place," having no parish of their own, or neglecting it if they have, " and rambling about in those of other Men's, exciting Parties and Factions." [13] Charles Chauncy put itinerant preaching first on his list of things of a bad and dangerous tendency in his *Seasonable Thoughts*. What is the meaning of such actions? he inquired. " Is it not obviously this? The *settled Pastors* are Men, not qualified for their Office, or not *faithful* in the Execution of it; They are either *unfit* to take the Care of Souls, or *grossly negligent* in doing their Duty to them. . . ." [14] The outcome could only be confusion and disorder:

If one Pastor may neglect his *own* People to take Care of *others*, who are already taken Care of; and, it may be much better than he can take care of them: I say, if one Pastor may do thus, why not another,

[13] William Balch, *The Duty of Ministers* (Boston, 1744), pp. 17, 18.
[14] Charles Chauncy, *Seasonable Thoughts on the State of Religion in New-England* (Boston, 1743), p. 50.

and another still, and so on, 'till there is no such Thing as *Church Order* in the Land? . . . And if this should become the general Practice, what might be expected, as the Effect, but an intire Dissolution of our *Church State?* [15]

The second tendency that concerned Chauncy and the other opposers was the rise of exhorters, that is, " *Men of all Occupations,* who are vain enough to think themselves fit to be *Teachers* of others; Men who, though they have *no Learning,* and but *small Capacities,* yet imagine they are able, and without Study too, to speak to the *spiritual Profit* of such as are willing to hear them. . . ." [16] For the most part, these were young men or boys, but women and girls were sometimes guilty. One notorious example was a certain Richard Woodbury of Rowley, who professed to come as a special messenger from God. He pretended to cast out devils, and drank healths to " King Jesus." His blasphemous excesses alarmed even the friends of the revival, who sent a delegation to Ipswich to look into the matter.[17] Chauncy's condemnation of such men was based on medieval and Puritan social theory, which taught that each man was called by God to fill a certain place, whose boundaries should be respected:

And as to *others,* who *abide not in their own Calling,* but take upon them the *Business* that is *assign'd to others,* they throw the *Body of* CHRIST into great Disorder. For as in the *Body natural* there are various Members, adapted to *various* Uses; so 'tis in the *mystical Body of* CHRIST.[18]

A third tendency of the revival with obvious social implications was the attempt to discredit the ideal of an educated ministry. George Whitefield was a chief offender, by virtue of slights he cast on the colleges. He preached at Cambridge on September 24, 1740, and his impressions of Harvard were

[15] *Ibid.,* p. 51.   [17] Tracy, *Great Awakening,* pp. 335, 336.
[16] *Ibid.,* p. 226.   [18] Chauncy, *Seasonable Thoughts,* p. 227.

published in his Journals for all the world to read: " Tutors neglect to pray with and examine the Hearts of their Pupils. Discipline is at too low an Ebb. Bad Books are become fashionable amongst them." He therefore preached on the text, " We are not as many who corrupt the Word of God," and in the Conclusion he " made a close Application to Tutors and Students." [19] On leaving New England, he passed judgment in general terms: " As for the Universities, I believe it may be said, their Light is become Darkness, Darkness that may be felt, and is complained of by the most godly Ministers." [20]

Not all the extreme revivalists and itinerants were uneducated, but some of them were, and their argument was that they spoke by inspiration of the Spirit, while human learning was a snare for the unwary. Chauncy declared that this was a revival of Antinomian errors.[21] " You ought not to expect *immediate inspiration*," he insisted; " nor may you depend upon the assistance of heaven, but in the way of previous diligent study." [22] The minister should be above the common level in capacities, and his talents should be cultivated by a good education. " He ought to have Skill in the learned Arts and Languages, so as to be ready to make use of them in the Service of the Sanctuary, as Occasion may call for it. . . ." [23] William Balch pointed out that many of the adversaries of Christianity were men of learning, " and what a miserable, pitiful Figure will an *illiterate* Minister make, should he chance to fall into such Hands! " [24]

[19] George Whitefield, *A Continuation of the Reverend Mr. Whitefield's Journal . . . The Seventh Journal* (London, 1741), pp. 28, 29.
[20] *Ibid.*, p. 55.
[21] Chauncy, *Seasonable Thoughts*, pp. 256–263.
[22] Charles Chauncy, *The Gifts of the Spirit to Ministers* (Boston, 1742), p. 28.
[23] Charles Chauncy, *Ministers Cautioned Against the Occasions of Contempt* (Boston, 1744), p. 14.
[24] Balch, *Duty of Ministers*, p. 15.

A final form which the revolt against the Standing Order took was rash, censorious, and uncharitable judging of the settled ministers. The excuse was the same as for itinerant preaching, that is, fear that many of the settled ministers were unconverted. Here, too, Whitefield set the example. Recording the events of October 9, 1740, he said: " the Lord gave me to open my Mouth boldly, against unconverted Ministers. . . . *For I am verily persuaded, the Generality of Preachers talk of an unknown, unfelt Christ.*" [25] The constant theme of Tennent's preaching was the dangers of an unconverted ministry. He was often heard to declare that the greatest part of the ministers of New England were carnal, unconverted men. [26] One of the first things James Davenport did when he arrived in Boston was to attempt to interview all the ministers, and inquire as to the state of their souls. The rebuffs he received only confirmed him in his previous opinion, and he proceeded to engage in familiar conversation with the Almighty on a subject of great concern to them both : " *Good* LORD, . . . *I will not mince the Matter any longer with thee, for thou knowest that I know, that the most of the Ministers of the Town of* BOSTON *and the* COUNTRY *are unconverted, and are leading their People blindfold to Hell.*" [27]

Chauncy spoke for all the opposers when he pointed out that the tendency of such preaching was " to set People against their Ministers as not fit to preach to them, and in this Way, to sow among them the Seeds of Contention and Separation." [28]   And a writer in the Boston *Evening-Post* declared: " the *Engine* which they artfully manage is that of *Detraction.* . . . From which Practice it is very just to infer,

[25] Whitefield, *Seventh Journal,* p. 38.
[26] Chauncy, *Seasonable Thoughts,* pp. 147–149.
[27] *Ibid.,* p. 166.
[28] *Ibid.,* p. 141.

that there is a Design carrying on to *subvert* and *eject* the *standing settled Ministers*." [29]

In 1747, Jonathan Mayhew described the supporters of Whitefield in a letter to his father: " When he was lately in Boston, many persons attended him, but chiefly of the more illiterate sort, except some who went out of curiosity." [30] But it would be oversimplification to say that the economic and religious groupings were identical, that all revivalists were of the lower and all opposers of the upper classes. During the course of the revival, actually, there developed three rather than two points of view. Some men condemned the Awakening from the outset, declared that it was more likely to prove the work of the Devil than of God, that it was destructive of order in Church and State, and that all its excesses were so much a part of it, that to condemn them was to condemn the whole. This group was led by men of position and respectability, like Charles Chauncy. At the opposite extreme were the supporters of the revival and all that went with it: itinerant preaching, exhorting, visions, tumults and disorders in public worship, and physical manifestations of the presence of the Holy Spirit. In increasing degrees of violence, they were typified by Whitefield, Tennent, and Davenport. They spoke for the " rabble," " those of the lowest Rank," and " idle and ignorant Persons," [31] who found in the Awakening an outlet for their attack on the upper classes. Many of these people abandoned the churches of the Standing Order and swelled the ranks of Baptist or " Separate " Congregational churches.

[29] *Ibid.*, p. 150.

[30] Alden Bradford, *Memoir of the Life and Writings of Rev. Jonathan Mayhew, D.D.* (Boston, 1838), p. 102. (This source gives the date incorrectly as 1749.)

[31] These contemporary epithets from the Boston *Evening-Post* were quoted by John C. Miller, " Religion, Finance, and Democracy in Massachusetts," *New England Quarterly*, VI, p. 46.

But between these two extremes was a large group, certainly much larger than the outright opposers of the revival, who saw in it much to be grateful for, and who argued that its excesses were not an essential or inevitable part of a glorious Work of God.   Jonathan Edwards was their chief spokesman; in Boston, Benjamin Colman and Thomas Foxcroft would be reckoned among them.   While these men differed from the opposers on certain questions of doctrine, they were of the same social class, and stood firmly with them when church order was threatened.   As the social implications of the Awakening became more apparent, the members of this middle group became more discriminating, or even lukewarm, towards it.   By 1743, many supporters of the revival were ready to testify against its excesses.   When some opposers gained control of the Massachusetts Convention of Ministers in May of that year, there resulted, as one might have expected, a wholesale condemnation of errors in doctrine and disorders in practice.[32]   But when the friends of the revival called a meeting the following July to counteract this testimony, they too demanded:

That laymen do not invade the ministerial office, and, under a pretence of exhorting, set up preaching; which is very contrary to gospel order, and tends to introduce errors and confusion into the church. That ministers do not invade the province of others, and in ordinary cases preach in another's parish without his knowledge, and against his consent. . . .[33]

And Jonathan Edwards was as zealous as Charles Chauncy in defending an educated and settled clergy.   " Order is one of the most necessary of all external means of the spiritual good of God's church," he wrote; and it is requisite even in Heaven itself: " order is maintained among the glorious angels there." [34]

---

[32] Tracy, *Great Awakening*, pp. 287–288.
[33] *Ibid.*, p. 298.
[34] Edwards, *Works*, III, p. 379.

v

In matters of church order, Chauncy and the opposers regarded themselves as defenders of the traditional New England way. In matters of doctrine also, they insisted that the revivalists were the innovators, and they called to their support the shades of John Winthrop and Thomas Shepard, of Increase and Cotton Mather. The doctrinal debate was concerned with the nature of conversion. Is it possible for a man to be saved, even though he has never experienced the intense emotional experiences to which the revivalists pointed as evidence of their gracious estate? How can one distinguish between true religious experiences and the delusions of an overheated imagination which may be Satan's work? Is assurance of one's saved condition an essential part of the process of conversion? To questions such as these, the opposers gave answers which they believed to be wholly orthodox and scriptural.

The process of conversion begins, according to Chauncy, with an awakened conviction of sin. The guilty creature realizes how hateful to the Divine Majesty he is, and how precarious is his situation. The awful disharmony between the perfections of God and the corruptions of the sinful soul are impressed on him with increasing force, so that he must admit that he deserves nothing better than eternal torment. Conviction of sin is accompanied by another gift of the Holy Spirit, true gospel faith. This means much more than an intellectual knowledge of the gospel. It means that the awakened sinner for the first time feels as an immediate and living thing the presence of Christ as mediator, and the necessity of " trusting in him, and in him alone for *righteousness* and *eternal life*." [35]

[35] Charles Chauncy, *The Out-Pouring of the Holy Ghost* (Boston, 1742), p. 15.

Chauncy insisted, as did the seventeenth-century Puritan, that " the degrees of distress, from a consciousness of sin and fear of wrath, are vastly various in different persons." [36] The conviction of sin might come about in a variety of ways: suddenly by the immediate impact of God's power, or by the example of another's conversion, or gradually, through the reading of the gospel and preaching of the word. It might come more or less suddenly; the terrors might be of varying intensity. Indeed, the process could very well take place, even though the subject could not afterwards remember the precise moment when the awakening began. The possibility could not be excluded that some were sanctified from childhood, and would inherit the kingdom without any agonies of soul. " This, I doubt not, is sometimes the Case; and might oftener be so, if parents were more generally faithful in the religious education of their children." [37]

But the conviction of sin is not the same thing as conversion, regardless of the amount of emotional turmoil accompanying it. " 'Tis only the *first step* towards it, a preparation of mind making way for it: Nor unless it end in this blessed change, will it signify any thing, if persons are under ever so deep distress." [38] The important thing is whether one is a partaker of the new nature. The difference between the unregenerate and the regenerate man is two-fold: in the inward frame of the mind, and in the outward course and manner of life.[39] The unconverted have only an intellectual, or " notional," idea of the being and perfections of God, and the truths of Christian doctrine. They are perhaps aware of sin, but dismiss it lightly, as of no great concern. If they make

---

[36] *Ibid.*, p. 13.
[37] Charles Chauncy, *The New Creature Describ'd and Consider'd* (Boston, 1741), p. 23.
[38] Chauncy, *Out-Pouring*, p. 13.
[39] Chauncy, *New Creature*, pp. 7–17.

any feeble attempts to obey God's will, they readily forget their purpose when confronted by difficulties and obstacles. Their greatest concerns are worldly: the enjoyment of earthly pleasures and carnal desires. The motives that move them are grief at worldly disappointments and losses, fear of the threats or displeasure of men rather than God, and anger at those who oppose them in their search for earthly gain. But the regenerate man centers his love, his hope, and his fears on God instead of man. The beauty of holiness appeals to him above all else, and sin now appears an awfully evil and bitter thing. Not the things of the world, but " the things of GOD and CHRIST, are now the chief object of their delight." [40] Love of God and fear of his righteous anger are now the springs of action, and they sustain his purpose through all doubts and disappointments.

There is an equally great change in men's outward conduct. They earnestly try to abandon their sins, and do their duty to God and their neighbors. Once they were accustomed to curse and swear, and were guilty of fornication and all uncleanness. Now their manners are reformed and all these sins are put away. And this change is positive as well as negative: " 'tis a Change not only from Sin, but to Holiness." The new creature spontaneously indulges in piety and devotion toward God, in private prayer and public worship. Towards his neighbors he is courteous and kind, full of love and good will:

. . . if you have indeed been *renewed in the spirit of your minds,* it will shew it self in your *lives.* The change that has been wrought in you will have an influence upon your whole outward conduct and behaviour. You will leave off former sins, and put in practice neglected duties. As the grace of GOD teaches, you will deny ungodliness, and worldly lusts, and live soberly, and righteously, and godlily in the world.[41]

[40] Chauncy, *New Creature,* p. 10.
[41] Chauncy, *Out-Pouring,* pp. 36, 37.

Hence the process of conversion is not just an intellectual affair, " not *meerly* an *assent* of the mind to *gospel truths*," [42] although rational argument may help to bring it about. Nor is it an emotional experience that has no fruit in conduct. " It hereby means that glorious change, whereby men are *turned from darkness to light;* whereby, of *slaves to diverse lusts and pleasures,* they are made the *servants of* GOD *and righteousness.*" [43]

As for assurance, Chauncy declared that it is attainable, " yet however it comes about, or wherever the fault lies, 'tis the attainment of but few; and the experience of the greatest part of true christians is a sad proof of this." So Chauncy admonished his listeners to do what they could to obtain it, but not to give up hope if their search was vain: " You may notwithstanding be real christians, *new creatures.*" [44] He reiterated this position in numerous sermons throughout the Awakening,[45] and it was adopted by the Massachusetts Convention of Ministers in May, 1743.[46] In short, for the opposers, the test of conversion is the fruit of the process. The thing to be satisfied about is whether one has forsaken worldly delights and motives for heavenly ones. " But in what is previous, or preparatory to this, there is a latitude, and so great a one, that there are but few christians, whose experiences are just alike." One should, therefore, be " rather concern'd about the thing, than the way in order to it. Get satisfied you have been thus wro't upon, and you need be at no further pains." [47]

---

[42] *Ibid.,* p. 15.
[43] Chauncy, *New Creature,* p. 18.
[44] *Ibid.,* pp. 31, 32.
[45] Charles Chauncy, *Ministers Exhorted and Encouraged to Take Heed to Themselves, and to their Doctrine* (Boston, 1744), p. 19; Chauncy, *Out-Pouring,* p. 39; Chauncy, *Seasonable Thoughts,* pp. 271–274.
[46] Chauncy, *Seasonable Thoughts,* p. 298.
[47] Chauncy, *New Creature,* pp. 25, 26.

When judging of his own spiritual state, a man's conduct is one of the chief evidences; in judging another, it is the only one. To be sure, it is not infallible — if it were, it would anticipate and render needless the Last Judgment. Conversion is an internal process, and only God can see into the hearts of men. They may relate their experiences to us, but they may be deceived or they may be hypocrites.[48] Because of the danger of deception, one should be careful not to indulge in rash and censorious judging of others, especially of ministers. Such uncharitable defamation of character is usually a surer sign that the accuser is unconverted than that the accused is. Chauncy readily agreed that the visibly wicked minister " is the greatest *Scandal* to *Religion*, and *Plague* to the *Church* of GOD," and that such should be exposed. But the case is different when a minister's character and profession agree. Then it is " an *Abuse* of *them*, and an Injury to the *Church* of GOD, to insinuate *Suspicions* against them." [49] Besides, it is false to suppose that unconverted ministers are of no use to the Church of God. They ought to seek assurance, for their own peace of mind if for no other reason. But to compare " the *Instrumentality* of *unconverted* Ministers, in the Business of *Regeneration* " to that of " a *naturally dead Man in begetting Children*," reveals " gross Ignorance of the unavoidable State of the *visible Kingdom of* GOD." [50] In this position, Chauncy was supported by the Convention of May, 1743.[51]

---

[48] Chauncy, *Seasonable Thoughts*, pp. 6–8.
[49] *Ibid.*, pp. 141, 142.
[50] Chauncy, *Ministers Exhorted*, p. 7.
[51] Chauncy, *Seasonable Thoughts*, pp. 299, 300. Chauncy repeated these warnings about judging others as unconverted on numerous occasions. See Charles Chauncy, *Enthusiasm Described and Caution'd Against* (Boston, 1742), p. iii; *Seasonable Thoughts*, p. 244; *Ministers Cautioned*, p. 19. Solomon Stoddard had defended unconverted ministers, the report being that he himself had not been converted until after his ordination and settlement.

VI

If opposers like Chauncy stressed the possible variety of
Christian experience, revivalists like Davenport tended to
narrow its range. The course which the individual soul must
take on its way to salvation was confined to a standardized
pattern; and the elements in the process that were stressed
were those setting it apart conspicuously from the ordinary
experience of men, which emphasized the immediate presence
and extraordinary working of God. His presence seemed to
call for remarkable and unusual manifestations, and for sudden and conspicuous effects. Invariably conversion seemed
to the convert to be produced from without, not by his own
efforts; and its effects were so out of the ordinary that they
were clearly beyond the normal power of men.

The various extravagances and excesses of the revival were
defended because they seemed to reveal the hand of God directly at work. Thus the revivalist felt that no conviction of
sin was real without physical manifestations of the presence
of the Holy Spirit, such as " *swooning away* and *falling to the
Ground,* where Persons have lain, for a Time, speechless and
motionless; bitter *Shriekings* and *Screamings; Convulsion-
like Tremblings* and *Agitations, Strugglings* and *Tum-
blings.*" [52] Once the awakened sinner knew the spirit of God
was within him, he was confident that every impulse was divine and every utterance inspired. Chauncy declared that
" The Rev. Messieurs BARBER and DAVENPORT claim Pre-
cedence of all others " in their regard for impulses and impressions, especially when these were accompanied by texts
of scripture.[53] The inspiration of the Lord extended to the
sermons that Davenport preached. Often he had no idea in
advance as to what he would say; but when the time came,

[52] Chauncy, *Seasonable Thoughts,* p. 77.   [53] *Ibid.,* p. 183.

the Lord placed the words in his mouth, and he spoke freely, finding more to say than he could possibly utter. Such inspiration made education unnecessary for a revivalist; indeed, human learning was regarded as a clog on the free workings of the spirit.

One fruit of conversion, according to the revivalist pattern, was a sudden light and joy, and very much raised affections. This religious joy was sometimes expressed in hearty laughter, a shocking practice which Chauncy said stemmed from the fact that Whitefield " was sometimes observed to speak of the Affairs of Salvation, with a *Smile in his Countenance* "; and Gilbert Tennent " could scarce hear of a Person's being under the slightest Conviction, but he would *laugh*." [54] Under the influence of the Holy Spirit, converts were known to have had trances and visions. Some saw Christ on the cross, with the blood running from his wounds, or on his throne in heaven, among shining ranks of saints and angels. Such experiences naturally led their subjects to an absolute and unshakable assurance that they were saved: " there is no true Believer, but hath *Assurance* for some Space of Time, longer or shorter; so that he could once say, *He knew in whom he had believed, and that he had passed from Death to Life*." [55] Anyone whose religious life did not fit the established pattern, but was less intense or stressed mere morality, was regarded as unconverted.

Those who were able to testify that they were saints were often filled with spiritual pride, which was expressed in rash and censorious judging of others. It seemed a simple matter to inquire into the experience of settled ministers, and pass judgment on their spiritual state. Surely, the revivalists insisted, anyone who has experienced conversion himself can

[54] *Ibid.*, p. 127.
[55] Andrew Croswell, quoted in Chauncy, *Seasonable Thoughts*, p. 271.

tell from another's description of his conversion whether it was genuine or not. On one occasion the minister in a town where Davenport was itinerating was approached for permission to use the meetinghouse. The minister's reply was to ask Davenport what were his reasons for leaving his own people, traveling through the country, and censuring ministers. Davenport then began to inquire into the spiritual health of the minister, but " an Account thereof was refus'd him, until he shewed his right to demand it: And thereupon he expressed his Fears that I was a *Stranger to* CHRIST; and said, that my refusing to give *him an Account* was a *dark sign* thereof." After his rebuff, Davenport mounted his horse, and rode back to his lodgings, singing lustily all the way. That evening he preached at his lodgings, denounced the minister as unconverted, and urged the people to withdraw from his ministry, " declaring, that to attend it would be as dangerous to their *Souls,* as *Bowls of Poison to their Bodies.*" [56]

Chauncy did not deny that religion should arouse the emotions. " These will be excited, in a less or greater degree, in the business of religion: And 'tis proper they shou'd." [57] What he protested was the assumption that emotionalism of the most extreme sort was the norm by which religious experience should be judged. Raised affections taken by themselves do not prove anything as to their origin. They might be a gift of the Holy Spirit; but they might also be the disordered passions of the natural man. When he saw a whole society disrupted by revivalism, Chauncy argued that the evidence of its divine origin was not persuasive. To the excesses of the Awakening he boldly applied the term " enthusiasm," in the eighteenth-century sense of fanaticism or religious hysteria. In those days it was a term of reproach, which was resented by the supporters of the revival, just as the opposers

[56] *Ibid.,* p. 157.   [57] Chauncy, *Enthusiasm,* p. 20.

resented being called Arminians. Chauncy shrewdly played on the dislike of anything identified as enthusiasm. A sermon preached in 1742 he called *Enthusiasm Described and Caution'd Against;* and the Preface to *Seasonable Thoughts* was devoted to proving that the errors in practice and doctrine prevalent in the days of Anne Hutchinson, which all good New Englanders regarded with abhorrence, had been exactly duplicated in 1740.

The error of the enthusiast, said Chauncy, is to regard certain wholly natural phenomena as of supernatural origin. The enthusiast believes he is favored with the extraordinary presence of God, " when all the while, he is under no other influence than that of an overheated imagination." He is the victim of a " bad temperament of the blood and spirits; 'tis properly a disease, a sort of madness." [58] To be convinced of this, one need only test the private revelations of the enthusiast against the truths of the Bible. That God's will is revealed in the sacred Scriptures none will deny; and God " cannot be suppos'd to be the author of any *private* revelations that are contradictory to the *public standing* ones, which he has preserved in the world to this day." [59] The Scriptures condemn an undue preference for one minister over another; they command charity, condemn self-conceit over spiritual gifts, and require a just decorum in speaking in the house of God. How then can the characteristic behavior of the revivalists be regarded as divinely inspired?

" Next to the Scripture," Chauncy wrote, " there is no greater enemy to *enthusiasm,* than *reason.*" [60] This is not to say that reason should be set up in opposition to revelation. But the Holy Spirit deals with men as reasonable creatures, who can perceive and be persuaded of the truth of Christian

[58] *Ibid.,* p. 3.
[59] *Ibid.,* p. 7.

[60] *Ibid.,* p. 18.

doctrine by a due use of reason. The only way to prevent the emotions from running headlong into enthusiasm is to keep them under rational control:

> . . . the *human passions* are capable of serving many valuable purposes in religion, and may to good advantage be excited and warmed: always provided, that they are kept under the restraints of *reason;* for otherwise they will soon run wild, and may make those in whom they reign to do so too. *Light* and *heat* should always go together; and if there be not some good proportion of the former, it will turn to little account, if there be ever so much of the latter.[61]

Despite the fact that Chauncy was the foremost of the opposers, while Edwards was the ablest defender of the revival, there was a considerable area of agreement between them. Edwards was careful to distinguish between his own defence of the religious affections, and enthusiasm.[62] He agreed that " Holy affections are not heat without light," [63] and that in the course of conversion the subject receives no new doctrinal knowledge as a private revelation. He insisted strongly that all the characteristic marks of conversion emphasized by the Davenports and Whitefields prove nothing one way or the other. It is no sign either way that the emotions are very much stirred; or that they cause those who have them to be fluent, fervent, and abundant in talking of things of religion; or that they have great effects on the body; or that the subject is convinced that he did not produce such effects himself. It is inconclusive when impulses are accompanied by texts of Scripture, for there is nothing in that beyond the power of Satan to produce. It is no sign that people spend much time in religion, or that they are exceedingly confident that they have been saved. And no one can tell infallibly from another's relation of his experience whether he is saved or not. The difference between the unregenerate and the regener-

---

[61] Chauncy, *Gifts of the Spirit*, p. 8. [63] *Ibid.,* III, p. 108.
[62] Edwards, *Works*, III, pp. 121, 122.

ate man, said Edwards, is that the Spirit of God dwells within the latter, producing through him the effects of holiness. This will manifest itself by a love for divine things as they are in themselves, apart from any bearing they may have on the selfish interest of the person. It is attended by genuine humility, in contrast with the spiritual pride of the revivalists. It turns men away from sin to holy things. And finally, " Gracious and holy affections have their exercise and fruit in Christian practice." [64]

Between Chauncy and Edwards, therefore, the dividing line was at least as much one of temperament and diverse traditions as anything. Born to the evangelical tradition of the Connecticut valley, Edwards was temperamentally inclined to accept revivalism, and regarded the Awakening as a glorious and extraordinary work of the Spirit of God, though unfortunately marred by excesses and extravagances which were no essential part of it. Edward's mature concern was to distinguish between the work of God in the revival, which he defended, and the excesses which he deplored.[65] Chauncy, on the other hand, was heir to the sober traditions in religion that had long prevailed in Boston. He was temperamentally predisposed against revivalistic methods, and was not inclined to try to justify the Awakening despite its excesses. If these were eliminated, he argued, there would be nothing left differing in any way from the work of God's Spirit in converting men that had been familiar for a century.

Let us only consider this Work *strip't* of these *remarkable Appearances*, — such as crying out, — falling down, — Twitchings and convulsive Motions, — Foamings and Frothings, — Trances and Visions and Revelations — Exhorters, — Censoriousness, — Pharisaism, &c. and I *demand* where its *Extraordinariness* is — If these Things were *deducted* from the Religion of the present Day, what

[64] *Ibid.*, III, p. 182.
[65] In the *Treatise Concerning Religious Affections*, published in 1746.

would there be in our Religion that would make it appear *different* from what it used to be.[66]

VII

In taking a stand against the Great Awakening, Chauncy and the opposers had no idea that they were starting down the path to Arminianism. They thought they were defending the truths for which the first settlers had stood. In the attack on revivalism from 1740 to 1745, the opposers were no more explicitly Arminian than Bostonians had been for at least two generations, ever since the adoption of the Half-Way Covenant. In all that Chauncy wrote, there may have been Arminian tendencies, yet he never overstepped the boundaries of orthodoxy. He insisted that " the *principal Opposers* are among those of an establish'd Reputation for their Orthodoxy." He declared it to be a " base Slander " to spread abroad the report that any ministers in the country were Pelagians; and added, " Nor can I suppose, there are so many, as some suggest, who think with ARMINIUS." [67]

One test of Chauncy's sincerity in his protestations of orthodoxy is the list of books he was reading, as revealed in references in his published sermons. Most men read books which corroborate their opinions, rather than ones which might change them. By and large, the authors to whom Chauncy and the opposers turned for inspiration and corroboration were of unimpeachable orthodoxy. Chauncy quoted most frequently from seventeenth-century Puritans, both English and native, such as Thomas Shepard, Richard Mather, William Perkins, John Owen, and Richard Baxter. He referred to " the excellent CALVIN, whose Words are as well worthy of Regard in *this*, as in other Articles." [68] Of

---

[66] [Charles Chauncy?], *The Late Religious Commotions in New-England Considered* (Boston, 1743), pp. 35, 36.

[67] Chauncy, *Seasonable Thoughts*, pp. 398, 399.

[68] *Ibid.*, p. 338.

these men, only Baxter was in the least suspect; he was a mediating theologian, accused of being a Calvinist by the Arminians and an Arminian by the Calvinists. He was sound enough, however, to assent to the decisions of the Synod of Dort, and described the Shorter Catechism as " the best catechism I ever saw yet." [69] On one occasion, Chauncy did defend Archbishop Tillotson against the strictures of Whitefield, and Tillotson was both Arminian and rationalist. But the question at issue was the Archbishop's personal character rather than his doctrine. After all, both Increase Mather and Benjamin Colman had done as much. [70] When Whitefield charged in 1740 that evangelical writers were neglected at Harvard, an investigation showed that the authors commonly taken from the library were Owen, Baxter, Flavel, Bates, Howe, Doolittle, Willard, Watts, and Guyse [71] — all of them of accepted orthodoxy.

There is no indication that either Chauncy or the Harvard students were reading Daniel Whitby's Arminian *Discourse on the Five Points*, even though it had appeared as early as 1710; nor Samuel Clarke's rationalistic Boyle Lectures of 1704 and 1705; nor Thomas Emlyn's anti-Trinitarian *Humble Inquiry*, dated 1702; nor John Taylor's *Scripture Doctrine of Original Sin*, published in 1740. These were the truly unorthodox books of that generation, and represented the staple diet of the liberals after 1745. But New England did not discover them until after the Awakening, and the suddenness with which they then began to be cited in sermons and other polemical literature makes their absence before 1745 all the more striking.

The effect of the revival was not so much to spread Ar-

---

[69] James Hastings, ed., *Encyclopaedia of Religion and Ethics*, II, p. 440.

[70] Chauncy, *Seasonable Thoughts*, pp. 143–147.

[71] Edward Wigglesworth, *A Letter to the Reverend Mr. George Whitefield* (Boston, 1745), p. 31.

minianism as to prepare the way for its rapid growth. Down to the Awakening, a sense of community in New England still existed. For all Stoddard's differences with the Mathers, he still came to Boston every year at Harvard Commencement time. He could argue with the Mathers, because all felt they had a stake in a common enterprise. But after 1745, New England was so divided that there was a sense of community among the liberals and a sense of community among the evangelicals, but any wider sense of common purpose was wearing very thin. Communication between the two groups increasingly took the form of debate, rather than the search for agreement; and the gap between the two widened rapidly. The opposers of 1745 were Arminians by 1755.

But if their Arminianism was not a product of the years of the Great Awakening, their permanent and unyielding bias against revival methods was. From that day to this, no Arminian or Unitarian has ever hit the sawdust trail.

CHAPTER THREE

Original Sin

1743–1760

I

Edwards declared in his Farewell Sermon in 1750 that the progress made by Arminian doctrines " within this seven years " was greater than in any similar period of time previously. He expressed concern lest these doctrines prevail in Northampton " as they very lately have done in another large town I could name." He had been alarmed by " the danger of the prevailing of these corrupt principles, near sixteen years ago "; but he identified the rapid spread of the infection with the years after the Awakening.[1]

Edwards' concern in 1750 presumably resulted from a series of episodes in which the line between Calvinist and Arminian was clearly drawn. That line had seldom been clear before the Awakening, when many ministers had failed to emphasize the doctrines of election and original sin, yet none could tell whether they were unorthodox or simply concerned with other things. It had not been clearly drawn during the Awakening, when debate centered on the nature of conversion and the doctrine of assurance, and opposers accused of unsound doctrine replied by quoting Thomas Shepard and the Shorter Catechism. But after 1743, the doctrines of grace

---

[1] Jonathan Edwards, *The Works of President Edwards* (New York, 1843), I, pp. 79, 80.

came to the fore, and the basic issue could no longer be evaded.

The point at which the structure of Calvinist theology first came under sustained attack was the doctrine of original sin. Samuel Niles referred to this doctrine as the one " most eagerly struck at, and virulently oppos'd by many, in the present Age." [2] There were two phases to this dispute. The first was a series of controversies in such local communities as Bradford and Braintree, Massachusetts, and Ashford, Connecticut. Later, from 1757 to 1760, there developed a general pamphlet debate which was sharply focused on the doctrine of original sin. Samuel Niles published *The True Scripture-Doctrine of Original Sin* in 1757, and Jonathan Edwards' *Great Christian Doctrine of Original Sin Defended* appeared the following year. At the same time, Samuel Webster of Salisbury, Peter Clark of Danvers, and Charles Chauncy were engaged in pamphlet warfare on the same subject. Some, at least, of the orthodox, seemed to realize that the battle with Arminianism would be won or lost on this issue; for if the concept of total depravity should disappear, the rest of the orthodox scheme would become irrelevant.

II

A dispute in the Second Church in Bradford was the opening round of the conflict. Although William Balch (Harvard, 1724), the minister of the church, had sometimes been suspected before the Awakening, his real difficulties began in 1743, when he preached and published a sermon reconciling Paul and James on the doctrine of justification by faith. This sermon did not assert justification by the merit of good works, but it did attack the notion that a wicked man who

---

[2] Samuel Niles, *The True Scripture-Doctrine of Original Sin Stated and Defended* (Boston, 1757), p. 40.

makes no attempt to do God's will can be regarded with favor by him, or receive the benefits of Christ's suffering and obedience.

Some members of Balch's church took exception to his opinions, expressed in this and other sermons, believing that they were of unsound tendency. One member, Ichabod Cheney, went so far as to indulge in disorderly speaking in the house of God on February 27, 1743/44, saying that the doctrine preached that day was false and tended to lead souls to destruction. Cheney and some of his associates compiled articles against the minister under ten headings, which included such charges as that he had said that " Man by Nature is more inclined to Vertue than Vice," and that " Morality is the Height of Christianity." [3] The church held several meetings in March and April, 1744, and voted to suspend Cheney for disorderly speaking. It declared that it was offended with Cheney's supporters for giving their evidence to him, instead of taking the matter up with the minister directly. The aggrieved members requested a council, but were denied, whereupon they called on neighboring churches, and finally persuaded the First Church in Gloucester to proceed " in the Third Way of Communion " as defined in the Cambridge Platform — that is, by admonition. This was done on July 2, 1744, in a letter which introduced a long and acrimonious exchange of views between the two churches. The rights of churches under the Cambridge Platform, and the manner of handling the dispute, soon obscured the doctrinal issue. The argument was still in progress when, on August 1, 1744, at the call of the Bradford church, a council met which vindicated the church's actions against the aggrieved members, and accepted Balch's explanations of doc-

---

[3] *Letters from the First Church in Glocester to the Second in Bradford, with their Answers* (Boston, 1744), pp. 29, 30.

trine. The Bradford church declined to listen further to the Gloucester church, and two years later the aggrieved brethren were still unsatisfied.

This dispute called attention to Balch's doctrinal irregularity. In 1746, the ministers of the churches in Beverly, Samuel Wigglesworth and John Chipman, examined and condemned Balch's sermon on Paul and James, and his explanations of doctrine given to the council in 1744. Balch's evident design, they declared, was " to attribute to *Works*, or christian Obedience, such a Part in Man's *Justification*, as is contrary to Scripture." [4] To this, Balch replied in *A Vindication of Some Points of Doctrine*. The whole controversy was much embittered, and confused by issues of polity and personality, but it clearly revealed the doctrinal stresses that were present in the churches of New England, even if expression of them did not often reach such a bitter height. Balch remained minister of the church until his death in 1792, after sixty-five years of service. [5]

At the same time, similar troubles were disrupting the church in Abington, of which Samuel Brown (Harvard, 1709) was minister. Brown was an opposer. On June 11, 1744, charges against him " respecting doctrines delivered by him in public and private " were discussed at a church meeting. Among the false doctrines of which he was accused was this: " That the seed of grace is implanted in the soul before

[4] Samuel Wigglesworth and John Chipman, *Remarks on Some Points of Doctrine, Apprehended by Many as Unsound, Propagated . . . by the Reverend Mr. William Balch* (Boston, 1746), p. 5.

[5] For a sketch of Balch's life, see Clifford K. Shipton, *Sibley's Harvard Graduates*, VII (Boston, 1945), pp. 296–304. In addition to the tracts already cited, the documents in the case include: William Balch, *The Apostles St. Paul and St. James Reconciled with Respect to Faith and Works* (Boston, 1743); William Balch, *False Confidences Exposed, or Men Warned of Self-Righteousness* (Boston, 1743); [John Bayly and others], *A Brief Narrative of Some of the Brethren of the Second Church in Bradford* (Boston, 1746); *The Vindication of the Second Church in Bradford* (Boston, 1746); William Balch, *A Vindication of Some Points of Doctrine* (Boston, 1746).

conversion, and there grows till it is ripe for the new birth." Brown was able at the time to explain to the satisfaction of the majority, but four years later the issues were revived. In February, 1748, the town tried to coerce him by reducing his salary. On August 31, 1748, after another set of charges had been preferred against him, a mutual council was called. He was accused of errors in doctrine, of admitting to his pulpit ministers " not friendly to the great and soul-humbling doctrines of the Gospel," of arbitrariness in church government, and of lying. The council cleared him, but a minority of the church absented themselves from communion and church meetings. They called a meeting of their own, and " voted the pastor out of his office." Finally, Brown agreed to resign, provided the town would pay him £100 old tenor annually for life, exempt his estate from taxation, and join him in choosing arbitrators to decide how much was due him for back salary; but he died while the matter was still under discussion. On the settlement of his successor, a new covenant was adopted specifically expressing assent to the doctrines of the Westminster Shorter Catechism.[6]

The cleavage between Arminians and Calvinists was widened in June, 1747, when Jonathan Mayhew was ordained over the West Church in Boston. Mayhew and Chauncy must be ranked together as the two great leaders of the first generation of New England Arminians.[7] Jonathan was the

---

[6] Aaron Hobart, *An Historical Sketch of Abington* (Boston, 1839), pp. 40–45; Clifford K. Shipton, *Sibley's Harvard Graduates*, V (Boston, 1937), pp. 479–481.

[7] The chief printed source for the life of Mayhew is Alden Bradford, *Memoir of the Life and Writings of Rev. Jonathan Mayhew, D.D.* (Boston, 1838). A more recent study is an unpublished dissertation by Charles W. Akers, " The Life of Jonathan Mayhew, 1720–1766," Boston University, 1952. This dissertation makes use of the same letters and manuscripts Bradford used, which are now in the Boston University Library; and in addition, the author drew extensively from the newspapers of the time. A recent brief treatment, emphasizing political theory rather than religious ideas, is in Clinton Rossiter, *Seedtime of the Republic* (New York, 1953), Ch. 9.

son of Experience Mayhew, missionary to the Indians at Chilmark, and his ancestors for four generations had been the patriarchal and feudal rulers of Indians and white settlers of Martha's Vineyard.[8] He was born on the island on October 8, 1720, and spent his first twenty years there. He entered Harvard in 1740, just in time to encounter the revivalism of George Whitefield who preached to a large crowd — he himself estimated it at seven thousand — in the College Yard. Many students were deeply impressed; and incongruous as it may seem, in view of his later comments on Whitefield, Mayhew was among the number. Tutor Henry Flynt recorded in his diary that he was one of a group of about thirty students who " prayed together Sung Psalms & discoursed together 2 or 3 at a time and read good books." [9] About a year later, he made a special trip to York, Maine, to observe a revival. He described it in a letter to his brother which was so fervent and evangelical in tone as to suggest that he had within him the makings of a revivalist.[10] But his father was an opposer, and the influence of the President and Tutors of Harvard was soon thrown against the extravagances of the Awakening; so whatever leanings he had in that direction received no support.

Following graduation, Mayhew remained in residence in Cambridge, pursuing theological studies. Tradition has it that he also studied with Ebenezer Gay of Hingham, who was to preach at his ordination.[11] By 1746, he was looking for a settlement, and candidated in Worcester; but Thaddeus Maccarty, an admirer of Whitefield, was chosen instead.

[8] See Akers, " Life of Jonathan Mayhew," Ch. 1; also Lloyd C. M. Hare, *Thomas Mayhew, Patriarch to the Indians* (New York, 1932).

[9] " Diary of Henry Flynt," entry marked Dec. and Jan. 1740. Ms, Harvard College Library.

[10] Jonathan Mayhew to Zachariah Mayhew, March 26, 1742. Mayhew Papers.

[11] Bradford, *Mayhew*, p. 21.

Early in 1747, he received two calls, one right after the other, to Cohasset and to the West Church in Boston. Since the latter was in the metropolis, and supported by a congregation of wealthy merchants, he had little difficulty in making a choice.

Although the West Church was only ten years old, it already had something of a reputation for laxity in the pulpit. Its first minister was William Hooper, who on more than one occasion had caused his clerical brethren some uneasiness. He was a Scotsman, educated at Edinburgh, and a recent arrival in Boston. In 1740, Benjamin Colman found it necessary to take him to task for remarks in a Thursday Lecture which appeared critical of the traditional doctrines of grace. Hooper's letter of reply quieted, if it did not wholly satisfy, Colman and the other orthodox ministers to whom it was shown. But their suspicions were horribly confirmed some years later, for Hooper abandoned his pastorate at the West Church in 1746, sailed to England to secure Episcopal orders, and returned to become the Rector of Trinity.[12]

Furthermore, some hint of doctrinal unsoundness on Mayhew's part seems to have been spread abroad even before his ordination. The church was apparently uncertain as to how its choice would be received, since invitations to participate in the ordination were sent to only two of the Boston churches, Brattle Street and the First Church. These were the only ones before which Mayhew had ever been invited to preach, and their junior pastors, Samuel Cooper and Charles Chauncy, were friends of his. But when Deacon Henry Berry and Harrison Gray brought the invitation to Dr. Colman at Brattle Street, he freely told them of " the great Uneasiness & Displicency it must be to me to be asked without

---

[12] The correspondence between Colman and Hooper is in the Massachusetts Historical Society. One letter is reprinted in William B. Sprague, *Annals of the American Pulpit*, V (New York, 1859), pp. 124–126.

the Presence of the Rev'd Dr Sewal, Prince, Webb &c "; and he dashed off a note immediately to Foxcroft at the First Church to find out what he was going to do. " Our Peace & Edification at home, is I fear threatned whether we send, or not," he explained.[13] Samuel Cooper, Colman's colleague, was out of town at the time; and Colman seems to have had no trouble persuading his church not to send. At the First Church, according to an anonymous biographical sketch in the Mayhew Papers, the members first voted to participate, much to Foxcroft's surprise. But one of them doubted the vote, whereupon " Mr. Foxcroft for reasons best known to himself, left the desk in an abrupt manner, so that nothing was done by that church —." [14]

On May 20, 1747, the day originally set for the ordination, Mayhew's father was delayed en route from the Vineyard; so of the five clergymen originally invited, only Gay of Hingham and Appleton of Cambridge were present. They advised that the ordination should be postponed until a more representative body could be summoned. A new date was set — June 17, 1747 — and this time the West Church studiously avoided sending invitations to the other Boston churches. Instead, fifteen of the country churches were appealed to, and eleven accepted. Among the ministers in attendance were Ebenezer Gay and Lemuel Briant, both of them Arminians or virtually such. Others, like Mayhew's father, Nathaniel Appleton, and John Hancock of Lexington, while not heretical, were not disposed to insist on rigid tests of orthodoxy in matters of fellowship among the churches.[15]

Mayhew's relationships with his fellow ministers in Bos-

[13] Benjamin Colman to Thomas Foxcroft, *Publications of the Colonial Society of Massachusetts*, VIII (1906), pp. 352–353.
[14] " Biographical Sketch," p. 6. Mayhew Papers, Ms, Boston University Library.
[15] Bradford, *Mayhew*, pp. 25–27; Akers, " Mayhew," Ch. 3.

ton continued to be cool, at any rate until the 1760's, when he led the common fight against encroachments of the Church of England. He never became a member of the Boston Association of Ministers, because of the opposition of a few of the orthodox. Chauncy tried to have him admitted, but did not press the point because Mayhew himself did not care enough to make an issue of it. His preaching burden was somewhat heavier as a result, since he did not exchange regularly with the others. " But thro' God's Goodness to me," he wrote to his father, " I live very happily and contented without them." [16]

With Chauncy, his relations were always close. The two complemented one another well. Chauncy was solid, respectable, and careful not to allow his Arminianism to show too early or too conspicuously. Mayhew was temperamentally bolder and more forthright; with the support of his church behind him, he had no hesitation about saying quite bluntly the sort of thing that Chauncy would write down at length on paper and then set aside until the time was ripe for publication. In a sense, Chauncy influenced from within, while Mayhew goaded from without; under their combined influence, Boston merchants soon became accustomed to a liberal gospel.

Mayhew always had the support of his church; his friend Lemuel Briant (Harvard, 1739) was not so fortunate. Briant was only twenty-seven years of age when a sermon on *The Absurdity and Blasphemy of Depretiating Moral Virtue,* first preached before Mayhew's congregation, embroiled him in controversy both with members of his own church and with neighboring ministers.[17] The purpose of the sermon was

[16] Jonathan Mayhew to Experience Mayhew, October 5, 1747. Mayhew Papers.
[17] Briant was one of the men named by John Adams in 1815 as having preached Unitarianism sixty-five years previously. His sermon was published as delivered at Mayhew's church in Boston, but it had apparently been preached

to declare that: " It is the Righteousness of the Saints that renders them amiable in God's Sight, that is the Condition of all his Favours to them, and the sole Rule he will proceed by in judging of them. . . ." [18]   This statement of doctrine seems to be carefully worded to avoid the question whether the unregenerate man has any righteousness that commends him in any degree, however slight, to God; but Briant's true sentiments were revealed obliquely in one paragraph, the implication of which was a denial of particular election, original sin, the accepted doctrine of salvation by grace, and the perseverance of the saints:

Hence it has come to pass that when Men read of God's choosing whole Nations to certain Privileges (and these in this Life only) they have rashly concluded that *particular Persons* are *unconditionally* chosen to eternal Life hereafter.   — That when they have laid before them the Character of a very loose and abandoned People, who by their *own* long practised Wickedness, have rendered themselves the Children of Wrath, and fitted themselves for Destruction, they are induced to vilify humane Nature itself with the same vicious Character.   — That when they hear of our being *saved by Grace,* they conceive of it so as to destroy all moral Agency, and set themselves down with this vain Thought, that nothing on their Part is necessary to Salvation, but if they are designed for it, they shall *irresistably* be driven into Heaven, whether they will or not.   — And if they are not, no Prayers, nor Endeavours will avail.   — And finally; when they meditate on the constant unchangeable Affection God bears to *good Men,* they make this groundless Inference from his Unchangeableness, that they are unchangeable also.[19]

---

elsewhere on exchange.   It is reported that when he delivered it in Scituate, the Rev. Nathanael Eells said to him: " Alas! Sir, you have undone to-day, all that I have been doing for forty years."   Eells was himself liberal in tendency, and the story continues that he preached a series of sermons with a view to correcting Briant's errors.   His efforts had little effect, however, because his congregation found it hard to detect any difference between his doctrine and Briant's. See Samuel Deane, *History of Scituate, Massachusetts* (Boston, 1831), p. 199.

[18] Lemuel Briant, *The Absurdity and Blasphemy of Depretiating Moral Virtue* (Boston, 1749), p. 20.

[19] *Ibid.,* p. 7.

This paragraph was surely not the work of a man who had much sympathy with the orthodox scheme. At any rate such was the conclusion of Briant's contemporaries. One of them, John Porter, of the church in Brockton, replied in *The Absurdity and Blasphemy of Substituting the Personal Righteousness of Men in the Room of the Surety-Righteousness of Christ*. An attestation at the end of the pamphlet, signed by five of Porter's brethren, declared that " we cannot but lament the dreadful Increase of *Arminiasm* and *other Errors* in the Land, among Ministers and People." [20] In a rejoinder called *Some Friendly Remarks,* Briant challenged Porter to point out a single passage in his sermon " where the Doctrine of Justification by the *merit* of Man's *personal* Righteousness is asserted, or from whence it can by good and necessary Consequence be inferred." [21]

Almost a year passed before Porter appeared in print again, with a vindication of his sermon, to which were appended some comments by John Cotton of Halifax, one of his previous attestors. Porter printed parallel columns of his views and those of Briant on election, original sin, perseverance, and personal righteousness. In the Appendix, Cotton mildly declared his purpose was " rather to *unmask* Errors, than to *refute* them." [22] While Briant might complain that he was not an Arminian because he did not hold with Arminius on every point, and pretended to get his doctrine from the Bible, still he was as much an Arminian as his opponents were Calvinists. In short, Cotton declared that he had never read " a more *bare-faced* Piece of *Arminianism,* or

[20] John Porter, *The Absurdity and Blasphemy of Substituting the Personal Righteousness of Men in the Room of the Surety-Righteousness of Christ* (Boston, 1750), p. 31.

[21] Lemuel Briant, *Some Friendly Remarks on a Sermon Lately Preach'd at Braintree* (Boston, 1750), p. 10.

[22] John Porter, *A Vindication of a Sermon Preached at Braintree, Third Parish, December 25th 1749* (Boston, 1751), p. 33.

worse, than Mr. *Briant's* Sermon is." Thomas Foxcroft, who was seeing the pamphlet through the press in Boston, added a note at this point, calling Briant a Socinian rather than an Arminian.[23]

Briant could not bear to let Porter have the last word. He immediately came out with *Some More Friendly Remarks*, which proved him to be a shifty controversialist.[24] He declared that Porter had originally attacked his method of opening a text from Isaiah, and therefore he had been quite justified in assuming that that was the question at issue between them. If there proved to be other grounds of dispute, he should not be charged with prevarication for not dealing with them before being called upon to do so. Even if there were a real opposition between them, Briant defied them to prove it from his sermon. Because he said the doctrine of grace had been weakly supported and impertinent texts urged in proof of it, did that make him a denier of it? Because he did not wish human nature represented worse than it is, should he be taxed with denying that it is as bad as it is? All this was a bit disingenuous, and Samuel Niles was more than half justified in declaring that when Briant " can't fairly grapple with an Argument, he knows how to shuffle and *evade*." [25]

Niles' *Vindication of Divers Important Gospel-Doctrines* closed the pamphlet exchange, but the case was not by any means settled. Some members of Briant's church had become alarmed by his irregularities, and in 1752 they sought redress by means of a council of seven churches. When this council met on December 5, 1752, it sought to have Briant

[23] *Ibid.*, pp. 43, 44.
[24] Lemuel Briant, *Some More Friendly Remarks on Mr. Porter & Company* (Boston, 1751).
[25] Samuel Niles, *A Vindication of Divers Important Gospel-Doctrines, and of the Teachers and Professors of Them* (Boston, 1752), " Preface," p. 11.

meet with it but was rebuffed. It sought to have him join in forming a mutual council, and was again refused. It proposed adjournment until January 9, 1753, in the hope that Briant would then cooperate, and directed that in the meantime, the charges be reduced to writing. Six of the seven churches met according to adjournment; and since Briant remained obdurate, the council " tho't it proper to go into the Hearing of the Matters of Difference." [26] The troubles in the church were in part personal, as was so often the case in such episodes. There was the question of the suspension of Ebenezer Adams, a member of the church; and there was also the charge made by Briant's wife that he had been guilty of " several scandalous sins." As Jonathan Mayhew explained it in a letter to his father, " Some say she is distracted; and others that he did not use her well." [27] But the council found that the doctrines expressed in the notorious sermon were " sufficient Reasons of Offence "; condemned him for substituting Mr. Peirce's catechism for the Assembly's; and found his recommendation of " Mr. *John Taylor's* Book (which we esteem very erroneous) to the prayerful perusal of some of his Brethren " to be justly obnoxious to them. [28]

A majority of the church, however, seem to have gone along with their minister. They had already reached a very broad position on the right of private judgment, declaring " we cannot but commend our Pastor for the pains he takes to promote a free and impartial examination into all articles of our holy religion, so that *all may judge, even of them-*

---

[26] *The Result of the Council of a Number of Churches Held at Braintree, Massachusetts, December 5, 1752* (Boston, 1753), p. 2.

[27] Jonathan Mayhew to Experience Mayhew, Aug. 21, 1752. Mayhew Papers.

[28] *The Result*, pp. 2, 3. John Taylor of Norwich, to whom reference was made, was an English dissenting clergyman, whose Arminian *Scripture-Doctrine of Original Sin* was beginning to circulate in New England.

selves, what is right." A church committee soon met, but was unable to find any doctrinal differences " so great as to justify *any Breach or Schism* in the Church, or to cause any uncharitable Censures from Men of a Christian Disposition." [29] Furthermore, in the unhappy separation between Briant and his wife, they found he was not to blame. But he did not long survive his vindication. The following October he requested dismissal because of ill-health, and the Parish voted on October 22, 1753, to accept his resignation. He died a year later. [30]

Meanwhile, John Bass had been forced out of the church in Ashford, Connecticut. He had been born in Braintree in 1717, and graduated from Harvard in 1737. Ashford, where he was settled in 1743, is in the northeast part of Connecticut, in precisely that part of the colony where Yale influence was increasing at the expense of Harvard. Although Bass regarded himself as a " Calvinian " at the time of his settlement, his Calvinism must have had a Harvard flavor, for he was persistently charged with Arminianism. But Calvinistic principles, he concluded, were evidently " a Clergyman's main Defence; the best he can hit upon to provide him Food and Raiment, and to fix him in the good Graces of the

[29] *The Report of a Committee of the First Church in Braintree, Appointed in March, 1753* (Boston, 1753), p. 6.

[30] William P. Lunt, *Two Discourses, Delivered September 29, 1839* (Boston, 1840), pp. 132, 133. It has been asserted that Briant's dismissal was because he was " too liberal for the period in which he lived." (George Whitney, *Some Account of the Early History and Present State of the Town of Quincy*, Boston, 1827, p. 37.) But there seems to be no reason to doubt that ill health was the cause for his leaving the pulpit. For some time he had been unable to give instruction to the children of the church in the catechism, for that reason; and the warrant for the precinct meeting included the following clause: " or if otherwise the Parish shall think best to wait patiently some time longer, to see if it may not please God in his good Providence to restore our Rev. Pastor to his former state of health." (Lunt, *Two Discourses*, p. 133.) The point is a minor one, except as it shows the extent to which the liberal views of the minister had won support in his congregation.

Populace." [31] He was imprudent enough to re-examine his position, in order to satisfy his own conscience, and was driven to change some of his opinions. Certain members of his congregation became suspicious of his failure to preach on doctrines peculiar to Calvinism, withdrew from the communion table, and requested a church meeting which was called on January 23, 1750/51. The opponents charged Bass specifically with failure to " preach up " original sin, the new birth, and election. He was asked, *" Sir, Don't you think that a Child brings Sin enough into the World with it to damn it forever? "* — to which he bluntly replied, " No." After fruitless meetings of the church and the local association of ministers, the matter was taken over his protests to the consociation of Windham County, which dismissed him on June 4, 1751. His statement of doctrine made to the consociation was Arminian, and drew heavily on the writings of John Taylor of Norwich. Bass's last entry in the church records at Ashford read as follows:

June 5th, 1751. I was dismissed from my pastoral relation to the church and people of Ashford, by the Rev. Consociation of the county of Windham, for dissenting from the Calvinistic sense of the Quinquarticular Points, which I ignorantly subscribed to before my ordination; for which, and all my other mistakes, I beg the pardon of Almighty God.[32]

Bass published the chief documents in the case in his *True Narrative of an Unhappy Contention in the Church at Ashford*, which was one of the frankest records of a change in

[31] John Bass, *A True Narrative of an Unhappy Contention in the Church at Ashford* (Boston, 1751), p. 3.
[32] Ellen D. Larned, *History of Windham County, Connecticut*, 2 vols. (Worcester, 1874), I, p. 548; see also Carlton A. Staples, *An Historical Discourse Delivered on the One Hundred and Fiftieth Anniversary of the Organization of the First Congregational Church in Providence, R. I.* (Providence, 1879), pp. 22, 23.

doctrinal position written by any New England Arminian. This pamphlet was evidently read with interest in Massachusetts, appearing as it did at the very time that Briant's sermon was under discussion. In his reply to Briant, Samuel Niles took time to comment on the Ashford case and commend the actions of the consociation.[33] Bass then published a rejoinder to Niles, to deny that he had acted from a designing and mercenary spirit.[34] From Ashford he went to Providence, Rhode Island, where he served the congregational church from 1752 to 1758. Then, because of ill health and discouraging response from the people, he left the ministry to practice medicine.[35]

In 1757, a controversy in the church in Leominster also resulted in the dismissal of the minister. The town had been set off from Lancaster in 1740, and three years later, it voted to settle John Rogers (Harvard, 1732), " a learned orthodox minister, as they have been advised by the neighboring ministers." [36] Three of his sermons published in 1756 and another in 1757 revealed how grievously mistaken those

---

[33] Niles, *Vindication*, p. 95n–p. 98n.

[34] John Bass, *A Letter to the Rev. Mr. Niles of Braintree, Containing Some Remarks on his Dying Testimony* (Boston, 1753).

[35] Edward B. Hall, *Discourses Comprising a History of the First Congregational Church in Providence* (Providence, 1836), pp. 23–24. Bass's experiences as a Harvard man in Connecticut were matched by those of James Dana (Harvard, 1753) who was called by the church and society in Wallingford, Connecticut, in 1758. Before he had been ordained, controversy arose, and the opponents called a meeting of the consociation of the county, charging irregularity in the proceedings of the church, and heterodoxy in the preaching of the candidate. The church and society denied the authority of the consociation, and proceeded with the ordination. Dana's theological position soon became a very minor matter, attention being directed chiefly to the questions of polity involved, and it is impossible to say how much of an Arminian he was at the time of his ordination. See William B. Sprague, *Annals of the American Pulpit*, I (New York, 1857), pp. 565–571; also Benjamin Trumbull, *A Complete History of Connecticut, Civil and Ecclesiastical*, 2 vols. (New Haven, 1818), II, pp. 480–526.

[36] Rufus P. Stebbins, *A Centennial Discourse Delivered to the First Congregational Church and Society in Leominster, September 24, 1843* (Boston, 1843), p. 12.

neighboring ministers had been. The church called an *ex parte* council to meet on July 26, 1757. From Rogers' printed sermons, his approval of Samuel Webster's *Winter Evening's Conversation* on original sin, and " from many coincident testimonies," the council concluded that " he denies the doctrine of original sin, both the imputation of the guilt and the corruption of our nature." It even found that " the aggrieved brethren had just ground of suspicion, that the Rev. Mr. Rogers did not hold or believe the essential Divinity of Christ as it is revealed in the Divine Word." [37] The council advised a delay of three months, to give Rogers a chance to change his mind. On January 28, 1758, however, both church and town voted to dismiss him. His supporters withdrew from the parish, and in 1762 were incorporated into a poll parish under his ministrations.[38]

III

A shift in the reading of the liberals away from evangelical writers appears very clearly in the record of these controversies. One document tells almost the whole story. It is an advertisement appended to John Bass's *True Narrative* of the dispute at Ashford, and it shows New England

[37] *Ibid.*, p. 84.

[38] Liberal historians in the nineteenth century have declared that some of the neighboring ministers, including at least one on the council, were of the same views as Rogers, but studiously concealed their opinions. Timothy Harrington of Lancaster and John Mellen of Sterling were most frequently mentioned. An examination of John Mellen's *Fifteen Discourses* (1765) reveals that they present the Covenant theology with some of the Calvinistic doctrines which particularly offended the Arminians, *e.g.*, election and the fall, played down. Perhaps the fairest judgment in his case and that of Harrington is that they regarded themselves as orthodox at the time of the Rogers case, and, as the historian of Leominster suggested in discussing Harrington, they did not become liberal until some years later. See Isaac Goodwin, " History of the Congregational Church in Sterling," *Worcester Magazine and Historical Journal*, II (1826), pp. 217–219; Joseph Willard, " History of Lancaster," *Worcester Magazine and Historical Journal*, II (1826), p. 324; Aaron Bancroft, *A Sermon Delivered in Worcester, January 31, 1836* (Worcester, 1836), p. 37; David Wilder, *The History of Leominster* (Fitchburg, 1853), p. 183.

suddenly confronted with the Age of Reason in an advanced stage of development:

TO BE SOLD,

By Daniel Gookin,

Opposite to the Reverend Dr. SEWALL'*s Meeting-House,*

THE Scripture Doctrine of *Original Sin,* proposed to a free and candid Examination.   ALSO,
A Paraphrase with Notes on the Epistle to the *Romans,*
To which is prefixed a Key to the Apostolic Writings.
These by Mr. *JOHN TAYLOR.*

CHRISTIANITY as old as the Creation.

Dr. *Whitby* on the Five Points, and Original Sin.

Stackhouse's Body of Divinity.

Bp. *Hoadley's* Terms of Acceptance.

Emlyn's Sermons, and Tracts.

Bp. *Butler's* Analogy, and Sermons.

Dr. *Foster's* Sermons.

WITH

Diverse other Authors of the highest Character.[39]

Two books by John Taylor of Norwich appropriately head this list. Of all the English dissenters, Taylor was the most influential and widely read in New England. Perhaps the reason was that his own intellectual development closely paralleled that of the colonial Arminians, so that his reaction

---

[39] Bass, *True Narrative,* p. 29. One wonders what the feelings of Dr. Sewall were when he saw his name in such company. Both Dr. Sewall (Harvard, 1707) and Dr. Thomas Prince (Harvard, 1707), his colleague at the Old South Meeting House, were supporters of the revival, and Sewall was so evangelical in his preaching that he was sometimes called the " weeping prophet."

against Westminster standards was phrased in precisely the terms that could be most useful to them. He was of orthodox or Calvinist dissenting background, and did not abandon this position until after 1733, when he became minister at Norwich. Then he examined some of the works of Samuel Clarke with his congregation, and found his views radically altered. His *Scripture-Doctrine of Original Sin* was consciously modeled on Clarke's *Scripture Doctrine of the Trinity*.

The New England Arminians derived two things from Taylor. One was a carefully worked out argument against the traditional doctrine of original sin; the other was a technique of studying the Bible which was of continuing importance, since it could be applied to other doctrines as well. This technique involved a careful comparison of all texts relevant to a particular doctrine, a determination of the meaning of obscure words by a linguistic analysis which called for thorough knowledge of the original tongues, and the elucidation of obscure passages by paraphrases. Taylor had not invented these techniques, to be sure. Sir Isaac Newton and Thomas Emlyn had attempted to establish an uncorrupted text by examining the evidence for the disputed passage I John 5:7; Samuel Clarke had attempted to determine the nature of the Trinity by a comparison of texts; and the device of paraphrasing had been used by Locke, Daniel Whitby, James Peirce, George Benson, and others. But for many New England ministers, Taylor's use of these methods was enormously stimulating. The resulting concern for the true meaning of scripture and interest in biblical scholarship became widely diffused among New England Arminians, until it became a characteristic part of the theological training of the early Unitarians.

Taylor's works were mentioned frequently in the controversies of the 1750's. Lemuel Briant recommended them to one of his parishioners, though he afterwards hedged and explained that he merely wanted the man to judge for himself.[40] John Bass openly cited Taylor's " Key to the Apostolic Writings " and quoted from it a definition of faith with the challenge: " This is, with an immaterial Alteration, Mr. TAYLOR's Definition of FAITH; and I believe no *Calvinist* will say but that it is Evangelical, and consequently Saving."[41] Charles Chauncy spent seven years, after the Awakening, engaged in the kind of biblical study that Taylor advocated;[42] many years later, when he published his *Salvation of All Men,* he acknowledged his indebtedness:

I should not be just to what I account *distinguished merit,* if I did not take this opportunity publicly to acknowledge my obligations to the writings of the late reverend Dr. *John Taylor* of *Norwich.* Had it not been for his *Scripture Doctrine of Original Sin,* and his *Paraphrase and Notes upon the Epistle to the Romans,* with the previous *Key to the Apostolic Writings* in general, I should never, I believe, have been able to have composed this work. I do not mean, by what I now say, to insinuate to the world, as though this excellent writer was of the opinion, that *all men shall finally be saved;* for I know he had quite other sentiments of the matter: But what I would suggest is, that it was his *example* and *recommendation* that put me upon studying the *scriptures* in that *free, impartial,* and *diligent* manner, which led me into these sentiments.[43]

[40] *The Result of the Council,* p. 3; *The Report of a Committee,* p. 6.

[41] Bass, *True Narrative,* p. 21n; see also p. 16n.

[42] Chauncy's health suffered during the Awakening, but he took up systematic study of the Bible as soon as he was sufficiently recovered. He read everything he could lay hands on in Boston and Cambridge " that had an aspect upon illustrating the scriptures." He even sent to England " for a considerable number of writers recommended by Doct. Doddridge," of which he believed he had the only copies in the colonies. See Charles Chauncy, " A Sketch of Eminent Men in New-England. In a Letter from the Rev. Dr. Chauncy to Dr. Stiles," *Collections of the Massachusetts Historical Society,* X (1809), p. 162.

[43] Charles Chauncy, *The Mystery Hid from Ages and Generations . . . or, the Salvation of All Men the Grand Thing Aimed at in the Scheme of God* (London, 1784), pp. xi, xii.

Closely associated with Taylor was a group of dissenters, including George Benson (1699–1762),[44] Nathaniel Lardner (1694–1768),[45] and James Foster (1697–1753).[46] Their influence in New England was very direct in at least one case, that of Jonathan Mayhew. On reading Mayhew's *Seven Sermons* (1749), these three men were surprised and pleased to find a kindred spirit in New England. Together with Governor Shirley and Benjamin Avery of London, they were instrumental in obtaining for him the degree of Doctor of Divinity from Aberdeen. The resulting correspondence between them and Mayhew continued as long as they lived, giving him a personal contact with English dissenting opinion which was of great importance in shaping his views. Dr. Benson wrote to Mayhew in July, 1750, sending a volume of

[44] Like Taylor, Benson began his career as a Calvinist; afterwards becoming an Arminian, he was forced to leave the church in Abingdon over which he had been settled. In later life, he was the colleague of Dr. Lardner, at the Presbyterian meetinghouse in Poor Jewry Lane, Crutched Friars. He prepared paraphrases of the Epistles, wrote a *History of the First Planting of the Christian Religion* (1738), and *The Reasonableness of the Christian Religion as Delivered in the Scriptures* (1743). His *History of the Life of Christ* appeared posthumously. He combined Arminianism, rationalism, and anti-Trinitarianism. See John Hunt, *Religious Thought in England from the Reformation to the End of Last Century*, 3 vols. (London, 1870–73), III, pp. 180–183; Thomas Amory, "Memoirs" prefixed to George Benson, *The History of the Life of Jesus Christ* (London, 1764); *Dictionary of National Biography*.

[45] Nathaniel Lardner's most famous work was an apology for Christianity, *The Credibility of the Gospel History*, which appeared in many volumes over a period of thirty years. It was an attempt to verify the facts stated in the gospels from references in other contemporary writers. Lardner began as a Trinitarian, but progressed steadily downward, first becoming an Arian of the school of Samuel Clarke, and finally, in the letter on the Logos (1759), a Socinian. See Hunt, *Religious Thought in England*, III, p. 239; *Dictionary of National Biography*.

[46] James Foster was one of the most eloquent preachers among the dissenters. In his early years at Exeter, he was closely associated with James Peirce and Joseph Hallett, Jr., whose Arianism occasioned a famous dispute and their own expulsion. Foster, like them, was forced to leave his pulpit. In 1720, he published an *Essay on Fundamentals*, which argued that the Trinity was not one of them. He attacked Tindal in *The Usefulness, Truth, and Excellency of the Christian Revelation Defended* (1731), and published several volumes of sermons. See Hunt, *Religious Thought in England*, III, pp. 226–237, 251–254; *Dictionary of National Biography*.

his sermons. Mayhew replied at once, thanking him for the sermons and the recommendation to the University of Aberdeen, and acknowledging his intellectual indebtedness:

It is several years since I have been your debtor, with many others unknown to you, for your first quarto volume on the Epistles. The second, I have lately procured; from which I expect to reap equal pleasure and profit, when I have read it with equal attention.[47]

At about the same time he thanked Dr. Foster: " I have been indebted to you, almost ever since I was able to read, for those excellent sermons, and other writings, which you have published." [48]   The *Seven Sermons* had indeed mentioned Foster's sermon on Providence.[49]   Mayhew wrote to Lardner also: " I have long been greatly obliged, in common with the rest of the world, for your ' Credibility of the Gospel History '; which I have read, more than once, with great satisfaction, and, I hope, not without advantage." [50]

The exchange of letters and published works across the Atlantic continued through the years; and after Mayhew's death, Lardner corresponded with the moderate Calvinist, Ezra Stiles.[51]   Despite Mayhew's clear indebtedness, he mentioned these four men only twice in his published writings — a fact which may serve as a warning that citations in

[47] Bradford, *Mayhew*, p. 92.
[48] *Ibid.*, p. 93.
[49] Jonathan Mayhew, *Seven Sermons* (Boston, 1749; reprinted London, 1750), p. 111.
[50] Bradford, *Mayhew*, p. 98.
[51] In June, 1767, Lardner wrote to Stiles that he had finished the concluding part of the *Credibility* in four volumes. " And I have determined to send *six* sets of that Collection to our Friends in America: *vid.* one set for the Harvard College at Cambridge in N.E.: a second to the Yale College in Connecticut: a third set for your Ecclesiastical Library at Newport: the fourth set for the College in New Jersey: a fifth for the Revd. Mr. Sam. Mather at Boston in N.E. who at times has favour me with several letters, & divers publications of his own: the sixth for the Revd. Dr. Chauncy at Boston, who preachd the funeral sermon for Dr. Mayhew." F. B. Dexter, ed., *Extracts from the Itineraries and Other Miscellanies of Ezra Stiles, D.D., LL.D.* (New Haven, 1916), pp. 528, 529.

sermons are an inadequate measure of intellectual influence. Mayhew did acknowledge a debt to Foster's friend, James Peirce, in a volume of sermons published in 1755: " How much, or how little, I have been beholden to this learned Commentator, in other parts of this discourse, where I have not expressly mentioned him, may be easily seen by those who think it worth while." [52]   Other New England ministers, who did not have the direct contact with the English dissenters which was so profitable to Mayhew, were nevertheless influenced by them.   As early as 1743, Thomas Barnard made reference to Peirce,[53] and Lemuel Briant substituted a catechism by him for the Assembly's.   Briant likewise quoted from " a late elegant Writer and Instructor how to *preach* CHRIST "; and John Porter, hot on the trail of heresy, discovered that the passage came from the writings of James Foster.[54]

While the personal contacts of the New England liberals were, appropriately enough, with English dissenters, their intellectual indebtedness also included members of the Church of England.   The Church of England divines whose Arminianism was most influential seem to have been Daniel Whitby (1638–1726),[55] and Thomas Stackhouse (1677–1752).[56]   Whitby's *Discourse* on the Five Points (1710) and

---

[52] Jonathan Mayhew, *Sermons* (Boston, 1755), p. 144n.

[53] Thomas Barnard, *Tyranny and Slavery in Matters of Religion, Caution'd Against* (Boston, 1743), p. 29.

[54] Porter, *Vindication*, p. 26.

[55] Whitby began as a Calvinist: " I was bred up seven Years in the University under Men of the Calvinistical Persuasion, and so could hear no other Doctrine, or receive no other Instructions from the Men of those Times, and therefore had once firmly entertained all their Doctrines."   But he became stoutly anti-Calvinistic, and thoroughly conscious of the extent to which he had rejected his earlier position.   See Daniel Whitby, *A Discourse Concerning [the Five Points]*, 2nd ed. (London, 1735), p. i.

[56] Stackhouse's *Complete Body of Divinity* appeared in 1729, with a second edition in 1734.   The great distinction of this massive folio was the manner in which it presented an historical view of different doctrines, and placed the opinions of Calvinists and Arminians side by side for comparison.   The author's

his *Treatise Concerning Original Sin* (1711, translated 1739) were both advertised by Daniel Gookin in 1751. Samuel Webster used Whitby in his controversy with Peter Clark in 1757;[57] while Clark protested that Whitby was Pelagian rather than Arminian, " for even *Arminius* himself taught more soundly, and more agreably to Scripture, than the said Writer, touching the Derivation of *Adam*'s Sin to his Posterity." [58] Stackhouse's *Complete Body of Divinity* was not quoted so frequently as Whitby's writings, but in addition to the mention in Gookin's advertisement, there was one in Webster's *Winter Evening Conversation Vindicated,* in terms that implied that it was something of a standard book of reference.[59]

The influence of these English Arminians probably confirmed and deepened convictions which the colonists would have reached independently in any event. But the self-confidence of the New England liberals must have been enhanced by the realization, which now meant something to them, that there was a well-marked tradition which avoided Calvinism on the one hand and freethinking on the other. Taylor, Whitby, and the others made that tradition available to them. Through these men, the New Englanders were drawn into the main stream of liberal theology, which may be traced back at least as far as the Dutch Remonstrants and which produced such men as Locke and Tillotson. The rejection of the alternative Calvinist tradition then became

---

own sympathies were not concealed, however. He reached the conclusion: " In such abstruse Points, each Man, I suppose, is left to his own Persuasion. . . ." Thomas Stackhouse, *A Complete Body of Speculative and Practical Divinity,* (2nd ed., London, 1734), p. 163.

[57] [Samuel Webster], *A Winter Evening's Conversation upon the Doctrine of Original Sin* (Boston, 1757), p. 23.

[58] Peter Clark, *The Scripture-Doctrine of Original Sin, Stated and Defended. In a Summer-Morning's Conversation* (Boston, 1758), p. 101.

[59] [Samuel Webster], *The Winter Evening Conversation Vindicated* (Boston, 1758), p. 103.

easier. In 1743, Charles Chauncy spoke of " the excellent Calvin." In 1755, John Adams referred to " the frigid John Calvin." [60] The New England mind had at last discovered the eighteenth century.

IV

In the debate over original sin in the 1750's, the Arminians did not deny that Adam had sinned or that men are sinners. Samuel Webster spoke of " the *actual Degeneracy* and *Apostacy* of *Mankind*, whatever be the Cause " as a melancholy fact which was " too plain to be doubted." [61] Samuel West of Needham, later of Boston, spoke in 1775 of the fallen and ruined state of human nature as " a subject that should be much insisted on by the ministers of Christ." [62] Arminians were well aware of the actual sinfulness of men; it was the doctrines of the imputed guilt of Adam's sin and total depravity which they rejected.

According to the Calvinists, Adam was both the natural and the moral head of all mankind, so that by the constitution of things, his posterity stood and fell in him. Two explanations of the relationship between Adam and his posterity, by which his guilt was imputed to them, had long been familiar in New England; and to them, Edwards added a third. The first two, which commonly appeared together, were natural generation and legal representation. Adam's posterity were in him " in a natural Sense, as Branches are naturally in their Root or Stock, before they grow out of it "; and they were in him " in a relative and moral Sense, as he was their appointed Head and Representative." [63] The third

---

[60] John Adams, *The Works of John Adams*, Charles Francis Adams, ed., (Boston, 1850), I, p. 27n.

[61] Webster, *Winter Evening Conversation Vindicated*, p. 14.

[62] Samuel West, *A Sermon Preached at the Ordination of the Rev'd Jonathan Newell* (Boston, 1775), p. 15.

[63] Experience Mayhew, *Grace Defended* (Boston, 1744), p. 13.

explanation, which was Edwards' innovation, was based on the concept of personal identity which he derived from Locke: " there is no such thing as any identity or oneness in created objects, existing at different times, but what depends on *God's sovereign constitution.*" [64]   It is only by the fiat of God that any man is the same individual from one moment to the next. Similarly, Adam and his posterity are one because God has chosen to regard them as such " for the derivation, either of righteousness, and communion in rewards, or of the loss of righteousness, and consequent corruption and guilt." [65]

The Arminian objections, when they were not biblical ones, revolved around the point that guilt is a personal matter, and that no one can rightly be blamed for the fault of another or for circumstances over which he has no control. This was perhaps the chief argument in John Taylor's *Scripture-Doctrine of Original Sin*, and Samuel Webster might almost have been quoting from Taylor when he said: " *Sin* and *guilt* (so far as I can see) are *personal* things, as much as *knowledge*. And I can as easily conceive of one man's *knowledge* being imputed to another, as of his sins being so. . . ." [66]   John Tucker agreed that sin and guilt " can no more be transfer'd from one to another, than one Man's *Reason* and *Conscience*, can become another man's *Reason* and *Conscience.*" [67]

If the imputation of Adam's sin is explained on the basis of natural generation, Webster argued, then we are guilty of all the sins of Adam as well as the first, and all the sins of all our ancestors in addition. If the doctrine is made to rest on

---

[64] Edwards, *Works*, II, p. 490.
[65] *Ibid.*, II, p. 491.
[66] Webster, *Winter Evening's Conversation*, p. 9.
[67] [John Tucker], *Observations on the Doctrines, and Uncharitableness, &c. of the Rev. Mr. Jonathan Parsons, of Newbury* (Boston, 1757), p. 28.

the concept of legal representation, it is contrary to the relationship actually existing between free men and their representatives, even those of their own choosing. Men may suffer because of the folly of their representatives; they are not guilty of their sins.[68] As for Edwards' doctrine of identity, on many grounds this argument seemed sophistical to Chauncy. Nowhere in Scripture are Adam and his posterity spoken of as one complex person. Such a notion is contrary to the experience of men, who are conscious that they exist personally distinct from Adam, and whose consciences trouble them for their own sins but not for his. The essential fact of personal identity, as Locke said and Edwards himself admitted, was continuity of consciousness. "How then could Adam and his posterity be the *same complex one,* to the purposes of sin and wrath, without the *same* principle of consciousness?" Such a doctrine was "not only an absurdity in speculation, but an impossibility in nature"; it was "as wild a conceit of a vain imagination as was ever published to the world. It cannot be paralleled with any thing, unless the doctrine of *transubstantiation.*"[69] The Arminians, in short, believed that there are some respects in which mankind is one, and some respects in which mankind are individuals, and the two should not be confused.

The opponents of imputed guilt were able to place the Calvinist doctrine in such an unfavorable light that even some of the orthodox were forced into damaging concessions. Is it fair, the Arminians asked, that children who die in infancy should go to Hell, when they had never reached an age of moral responsibility? Can it be reconciled with the goodness

---

[68] Webster, *Winter Evening's Conversation,* p. 8.

[69] Charles Chauncy, *Five Dissertations on the Scripture Account of the Fall; and its Consequences* (London, 1785), pp. 269–272. Although not published until 1785, this book was one of those Chauncy prepared in the midst of his most active period of study, presumably in the 1750's or early 1760's.

of God? " What! make them first to open their eyes in torments; and all this for a sin which certainly they had no
hand in, (being committed before one of them had a being). . . ." [70] Can it be supposed that a just God " should
send millions that die before they come to a capacity of moral
agency, as is the case of all infants, the moment they leave
this world, to the place of ' weeping, and wailing, and gnashing of teeth for ever,' " merely because their first father ate
of a tree thousands of years before they were born? " Were
the posterity of Adam, thousands of years before they had a
being, moral agents? " [71]

The correct answer from the orthodox point of view would
have been to show how all mankind, even infants, possess a
sinful nature, and so damnation is no worse than they deserve. For God to make any exceptions at all is sufficient to
display his goodness. God's justice in the punishment of sinners is more important than the happiness of any particular
sinful creature. But wrenched from its context in the Calvinist system, a doctrine which implied the damnation of infants seemed monstrous, even to Calvinists. Their damnation, Peter Clark declared, is a thing " which few or none
maintain; even tho' some may suppose them liable to eternal
Death, that is, an eternal Privation of Life; as they may be,
and yet suffer the Torments of Hell." He himself regarded
their fate as something which we cannot definitely ascertain
from Scripture, but " we have great Reason to hope the best
of their State." [72] This admission laid Clark open to rebuke
from Chauncy, who declared in an anonymous tract that
Clark, while pretending to be a Calvinist, had gone over to
the enemy. He did not blame Clark for hoping for the best

---

[70] Webster, *Winter Evening's Conversation,* p. 6.
[71] Chauncy, *Five Dissertations,* pp. 141, 151.
[72] Clark, *Summer Morning's Conversation,* p. 8.

with respect to the fate of infants, but it did surprise him that such a man should claim to be a defender of orthodoxy.[73]

Although they rejected imputation, the Arminians admitted that there is a connection between the sin of Adam and the moral situation of his posterity. But this connection involves only their physical inheritance. Samuel Webster named the consequences of Adam's sin in one sentence: " *Pain, sickness, labour, sorrow* and *death*, i.e. as 'tis explained, *returning to the dust*, are the only evils mentioned, or so much as suggested." [74] Charles Chauncy argued that the curse of God brought about an actual physical change in the surface of the earth, " changing it from its *paradisaick* state, to one that was adapted to be an occasion of *toil*, and *sorrow*, and *death*." [75] On Adam, God passed the sentence of death, by which is meant not damnation, or the second death, but the dissolution of the link between the body and the soul. Adam's posterity are included in this sentence, not because of their guilt, but because they must necessarily inherit his physical characteristics. John Tucker surmised that when the first parents sinned, their bodily appetites and passions became stronger. It seemed to him " not irrational to suppose that such a nature is conveyed down to us, as their descendents." [76]

Men, therefore, inherit " a STATE OF NATURE LESS PER-

---

[73] [Charles Chauncy], *Opinion of One that has Perused the Summer Morning's Conversation* (Boston, 1758), p. 1.

[74] Webster, *Winter Evening's Conversation*, p. 12.

[75] Charles Chauncy, *The Earth Delivered from the Curse to which it is, at Present, Subjected* (Boston, 1756), p. 5. In this argument, Chauncy drew heavily on William Whiston's *New Theory of the Earth* (1696) and Thomas Burnet's *Sacred Theory of the Earth* (1681). Chauncy would not affirm for a certainty that the " mechanical causes " Whiston relied on to explain the changes were the means God actually had used; but he did believe that " the state of things he has represented, as what might be owing to these ' causes,' is both intelligible, and credible, upon the strictest philosophical reasoning." Chauncy, *Five Dissertations*, p. 116.

[76] John Tucker, *Remarks on a Sermon of the Rev. Aaron Hutchinson, of Grafton* (Boston, 1767), p. 16n.

FECT, than it might otherwise have been, rendering it morally impossible that they should, upon the foot of STRICT RIGOROUS LAW, attain to the justification of life." [77]   If the physical state of the world has been altered since the fall, it is wholly congruous that the bodily powers of men should have been altered as well.   Then the soul would have a less efficient instrument by which to act.   The result may be a misfortune to men, but the mere inheritance of a weakened nature does not make them blameworthy until they abuse their powers, and by their own actions condemn themselves.   Nor are the weakened powers any argument against the goodness of God, so long as the probation to which men are subjected is proportioned to their weakened intellect and will.

But while man inherits a state of nature less perfect than could be desired, it does not follow that his nature is wholly depraved.   The orthodox view was that when Adam fell and the gracious spirit of God which had kept him from evil was withdrawn, he and his posterity were left totally corrupt. They possessed freedom, but could exercise it only to do evil, in the same way that God, though perfectly free, was free only to do good.   Even if we set aside the argument from Scripture and rely on experience alone, said Edwards, the record of human history is enough to convince us that all men have a tendency to sin.   From a universal result may be deduced a universal cause, " that the natural state of the mind of man, is attended with a propensity of nature, which is prevalent and effectual, to such an issue; and that therefore their nature is corrupt and depraved with a moral depravity." [78]

The essence of the Arminian position, on the other hand, was that all men are a mixture of good and evil tendencies. When we are born, said John Tucker, we are " neither Right-

---

[77] Chauncy, *Five Dissertations*, p. 160.   [78] Edwards, *Works*, II, p. 313.

eous nor Wicked, but capable of being either." God has implanted in us " certain Appetites and Passions," which are innocent of themselves, but capable of leading us astray unless they are kept under proper restraint. But he has also given us " an intelligent Nature: He has bless'd us with the Power of Reason, and implanted in us that *moral Sense* which we call *Conscience.*" These are given us as a balance to the appetites and passions, to keep them under control.[79] The Arminians were as ready as Edwards to admit a universal tendency towards sin in all men; but they insisted this was not the whole story. They pointed out that the argument from experience is double-edged. On one occasion Jonathan Parsons, John Tucker's orthodox neighbor, asked him to explain " what those Inclinations in little Children are, which dispose them to follow bad Examples? " To this question Tucker replied with another: " Why don't he tell us what those Inclinations are in *such*, which dispose them to follow *good* Examples? For that they are dispos'd to follow Good, as well as Bad, is undeniable: — to speak the Truth, as well as to tell Lies, &c." [80] The most that experience can prove is that every man has a nature which *may* bear the fruits of evil, not one which *must* bear those fruits.

v

By the middle 1750's, Arminians no longer pretended they were orthodox, but instead began to condemn Calvinism by name and attack its dangerous tendencies. John Bass used the moral argument against Calvinism in precisely the same way that Channing did seventy years later:

. . . representing our Nature as exceeding Corrupt and Wicked as soon as formed, odious to GOD's Holiness and under his Wrath and Curse; has, so far as I can see a natural Tendency to fill the Mind

[79] Tucker, *Observations*, pp. 9, 10.   [80] Tucker, *Observations*, p. 25.

with the most gloomy Apprehensions of the Author of our Being, to damp our Spirits, to turn away our Hearts from Him; and, in a Word, to the Destruction of all Religion.[81]

The Arminians asserted that the decrees cut the nerve of men's striving for righteousness. Those who believed in total depravity will regard it as " a *natural fountain* of sin in them, and so a *cloke* for all their wickedness." [82] If a man is brought into the world with a sinful nature, nothing that he can do of himself will produce the fruits of righteousness; if the elect have been chosen before the beginning of time, nothing that any man can do will affect his destiny.

While the Arminian concept of human nature was not so pessimistic as that of the Calvinists, neither was it so optimistic as that of the later Unitarians. If the Arminians did not accept total depravity, neither did they particularly emphasize the dignity of human nature.[83] Life for them was a process of trial and discipline by which, with the assistance of God, the bondage to sin may gradually be overcome. But the transformation of character by which men are made fit candidates for eternal life is no easy or automatic process, and the Arminians realistically refused to minimize the difficulties, even as they argued that eventual triumph over human weakness and limitation is possible.

[81] Bass, *True Narrative,* pp. 26, 27.

[82] Webster, *Winter Evening's Conversation,* p. 25.

[83] To this generalization, an occasional exception may be found at the very end of the eighteenth century. The following excerpt anticipates the optimism of nineteenth-century Unitarianism: " Having pointed at the great objects which education ought to embrace, the importance of it will more fully appear by opening our eyes upon that dignity and happiness which the Creator designed for the human race. When we analize man, raptures of solemn joy and gratitude must fill our hearts to see what greatness, sublimity, glory and happiness our faithful Creator designed for him. . . . As an intellectual being, how wonderful is man! . . . As an active and moral being, still more wonderful is man! . . . So exalted is the human race in the scale of beings, that while the Creator, of his other works said, They were very good; of man He saith, In the image of God created He him! " Simeon Doggett, *A Discourse on Education* (New Bedford, 1797), pp. 9–11.

CHAPTER FOUR

The Freedom of the Will

1754–1773

I

Jonathan Edwards believed that the crucial point which divided Calvinists and Arminians was the freedom of the will; that by establishing the doctrine of moral necessity, the Calvinists would have a firm basis from which to confute Arminian objections to the doctrines of total depravity, efficacious grace, absolute, eternal, and particular election, and the perseverance of the saints.[1] His treatise on the *Freedom of the Will* was intended to give a final and crushing reply to his opponents, and in preparation for it he read widely and thought deeply. He believed that he had answered all objections, stopped all crevices in the argument, and written an unanswerable work. It appeared in 1754.

Whatever else its publication may have done, it produced a state of incredible intellectual confusion. Edwards' followers part of the time did not understand him; his opponents often found themselves in a maze of contradictions. With some justice, James Dana of Wallingford introduced his discussion of foreknowledge with Milton's lines:

> Others apart sat on a hill retired,
> In thoughts more elevate, and reason'd high
> Of Providence, foreknowledge, will, and fate,

[1] Jonathan Edwards, *The Works of President Edwards* (New York, 1843), II, pp. 176–179.

Fix'd fate, free will, foreknowledge absolute,
And found no end, in wand'ring mazes lost.[2]

Edwards might declare that the logic of the Calvinist position required an assertion of necessity, and a denial of what he believed was the Arminian view of the freedom of the will. In actual fact, most New England Calvinists asserted that man is a free moral agent in about the same terms that the Arminians used. The Savoy version of the Westminster Confession, which was accepted as the standard, asserted free will in these words: " God hath endued the Will of man with that natural liberty and power of acting upon choice, that it is neither forced, nor by any absolute necessity of Nature determined to do good or evil." Man in his innocency was free to do that which is good, " but yet mutably, so that he might fall from it." [3] Since the fall, the will is still free in the sense that men can make voluntary choices; but because of man's bondage to sin, he is free to do only evil, just as God, whose nature is holy, is free to choose only that which is good. Arminians sometimes declared that Calvinism was really determinism, but there were always Calvinists ready to deny the charge. Stephen West and Samuel Hopkins adopted Edwards' position, but even the Edwardeans rapidly worked around to a reassertion of the freedom of the will.[4] Timothy Dwight, for example, declared that " *men are intuitively conscious of their own free agency, being irresistibly sensible, that they act spontaneously, and without any coercion, or constraint.*" [5] No Arminian could have said more.

The fact that Edwards was apparently departing from the

[2] James Dana, *The " Examination of the Late Rev'd President Edwards's Enquiry on Freedom of Will," Continued* (New Haven, 1773), p. 96.

[3] Williston Walker, *The Creeds and Platforms of Congregationalism* (New York, 1893), p. 377.

[4] Joseph Haroutunian, *Piety versus Moralism* (New York, c. 1932), Ch. 9.

[5] Timothy Dwight, *Theology* (Middletown, Conn., 1818), I, pp. 248, 249.

accepted Calvinist doctrine was not lost on the Arminians. James Dana began his *Examination of the Late Reverend President Edwards's " Enquiry on Freedom of Will "* by setting aside as not germane to the discussion Edwards' system of doctrine. "It is only the *foundation principle* we aim to consider: The system built hereupon, whether true or false, is not, by the generality of Calvinistic Divines, made to depend on the *same* basis."[6] The sense of liberty Dana was defending was " so far from being the peculiar notion of ' *Pelagians, Semi-Pelagians, Jesuits, Socinians, Arminians,* and others' of the same stamp, as Mr. Edwards injuriously represents, that it has been maintained by the most eminent divines called *Calvinists,* as we shall be ready to shew should there be occasion."[7]

In New England, necessity was regarded as a doctrine not of the Calvinists, but of freethinkers; and when Edwards produced the *Freedom of the Will*, he was classed, not with the Westminster divines, but with the Stoics, Hobbes, Leibniz, Spinoza, and Collins. Edwards himself took note of the accusation that his position was that of Hobbes, and denied that he had ever read him.[8] Doubtless few of the Arminians had either, and it seems probable that they knew of Leibniz and Spinoza chiefly because these authors had been specifically named and refuted in Samuel Clarke's writings. But Dana made quite specific the identification of Edwards with the freethinkers in a letter to Andrew Eliot:

A report is circulated, that the english impression of Mr. Edwards on the will was promoted by the *deists* in London; and that the *rakes* in Holland had procured a dutch translation of it. If either of these can be authenticated, I should be glad to be inform'd — and par-

---

[6] James Dana, *An Examination of the Late Reverend President Edwards's " Enquiry on Freedom of Will "* (Boston, 1770), p. ix.
[7] Dana, *Examination Continued*, p. 37.
[8] Edwards, *Works*, II, pp. 140–142.

ticularly obliged to you to send me the information. The friends of Mr. Edwards pique themselves much on the supposed reputation of his book in England & Scotland. If deists & rakes are the persons there by whom it is had in estimation, it might serve the cause of truth to let this be published.[9]

The issue, then, was not the basis for the division between New England Arminians and most New England Calvinists. And whatever Edwards may have thought, it was not even the real basis for the division between him and the Arminians. At the bottom of a tangle of verbal misunderstandings, the analyses of the mind made by Edwards and his opponents were not very different. There are certain elementary distinctions in human experience, such as the difference between the action of a man and of a clock, and between the failure to act which means that a man is physically prevented from acting and the failure to act which means that he does not want to act. Though one might never guess it from the accusations made on both sides, these distinctions were recognized by both parties. The controversy did more to confuse than it did to clarify the real issue that divided Calvinist and Arminian. For the historian, it is a blind alley, which must be explored only because so many good people lost their way in it.

II

When Edwards published his treatise, no New England Arminian had written extensively on the freedom of the will. The Arminian position was revealed only in casual and uncritical comments. Thus Chauncy declared: " As Men are *rational, free Agents,* they can't be *religious* but with the *free Consent of their Wills;* and this can be gain'd in no Way, but that of *Reason* and *Persuasion.*" [10]   Samuel Osborn said

[9] James Dana to Andrew Eliot, July 9, 1773. Ms, Massachusetts Historical Society.

[10] Charles Chauncy, *The Only Compulsion Proper to be Made Use of in the Affairs of Conscience and Religion* (Boston, 1739), p. 10.

that God's making men moral agents is a fruit of his goodness, and " it cannot be tho't (without an Absurdity) that *he
should see better afterwards, and deprive Men of their
Agency, and work upon them as Machines.*" [11] But Chauncy
dismissed the whole question in very characteristic fashion:

. . . the *Divine* SPIRIT acts in, and upon them, in a way suited to
their nature *as Men,* in a way that agrees with their character as
moral agents. . . . But to say *precisely* how the HOLY GHOST en-
lightens the *mind,* and then captivates the *will,* . . . these things,
I say, are difficulties in this dispensation of grace: And as they are
such, the less we puzzle our selves or others about them, the better.[12]

For some understanding of the Arminian position, then, it
is necessary to turn to the English books which were regarded
in Massachusetts as having authority. Three authors stand
out: John Locke, Daniel Whitby, and Samuel Clarke.
Locke's comments may be found in the chapter " Of Power "
in the *Essay Concerning Human Understanding.* The first
assertion is that man is an agent — that is, a being which can
begin or end its actions in accordance with the preference of
the mind. The mind has two powers, the understanding
and the will, which may be termed faculties, if we are not
misled thereby into supposing each faculty to be an agent,
with its own province and authority. The will is the power
of choosing between one course of action and another. What
determines the will? Or, more precisely, what causes a man
to choose one action rather than another? Certainly not the
greatest positive good involved, because sometimes a man
will act contrary to his best interests, even when he knows
what they are. But all men choose that which, at the moment, seems to them to be conducive to their happiness. The

[11] Samuel Osborn, *The Case and Complaint of Mr. Samuel Osborn* (Boston, 1743), p. 10.

[12] Charles Chauncy, *The Out-Pouring of the Holy Ghost* (Boston, 1742),
p. 19.

will, then, is determined by what Locke called "the most pressing uneasiness." Since the will is a power of choice and not a chooser or agent, the word "liberty" is unintelligible when applied to it:

For to ask, whether a man be at liberty to will either motion or rest, speaking or silence, which he pleases, is to ask, whether a man can will what he wills, or be pleased with what he is pleased with. A question which, I think, needs no answer: and they who can make a question of it, must suppose one will to determine the acts of another, and another to determine that; and so on *in infinitum.*[13]

The real question is not whether the will is free, but whether the man is free. The only sensible reply is, that a man is free when he is able to do what he pleases — that is, when his voluntary actions are not thwarted by some external obstacle.

In saying that men choose that which they feel will be conducive to their happiness, Locke recognized that the emotions might dominate the reason. But to guard against the notion that men act entirely on impulse, he ended by pointing out that man is a rational creature. He does not always rush to the satisfaction of his immediate desires, but may stop to consider. Locke did not put it in so many words, but his meaning seems to be that the "most pressing uneasiness" of a rational creature, when presented with a course of action, may well be not to pursue it without consideration, but rather to examine and pass judgment on it. A man is free, not because his will acts from an antecedent state of indifference, but because his will is determined by "his own desire, guided by his own judgment."[14]

Locke denied in strict fact the freedom of the will; Daniel Whitby insisted on it. But clearly, the two men were not talking about the same thing. Whitby said quite specifically

[13] John Locke, *Essay Concerning Human Understanding*, Bk. II, Ch. 21, par. 25.
[14] *Ibid.*, Bk. II, Ch. 21, par. 71.

that " what makes the Will chuse, is something approved by the Understanding, and consequently appearing to the Soul as Good."

Wherefore to say that Evidence proposed, apprehended and consider'd, is not sufficient to make the Understanding to approve; or that the greatest Good proposed, the greatest Evil threatned, when equally believed and reflected on, is not sufficient to engage the Will to chuse the Good and refuse the Evil, is in effect to say that which alone doth move the Will to chuse or to refuse, is not sufficient to engage it so to do; . . . which being contradictory to itself, must of necessity be false.[15]

The freedom that concerned Whitby was men's freedom from any original bias of the mind to good or evil: " from Necessity, or a Determination to one, *i.e.* either to Good or Evil only." [16] In other words, his whole argument refers to the question of original sin and total depravity. If men are naturally endowed with a corrupt bias, then their evil acts are beyond their control, and they can no more be blamed for them than a blind man can be blamed for failing to see.

Whitby began by saying that men are in a state of trial or probation. The problem is " whether he hath a Freedom to chuse Life or Death, . . . or whether he be determined to one, having a Freedom from Coaction, but not from Necessity." Such liberty is no perfection of human nature, but an admission that men are not perfect. This liberty is not essential " to Man as Man, but only necessary to Man placed in a State of Trial, and under the power of Temptation." [17] God and the angels do not possess freedom in this sense, but they are not rightly rewardable. This freedom from necessity to do evil because of the sin of Adam is essential to a system of rewards and punishments; and it implies a rational being who

[15] Daniel Whitby, *A Discourse Concerning [the Five Points]*, (2nd ed., London, 1735), p. 212.
[16] *Ibid.*, p. 344.
[17] *Ibid.*, pp. 299, 300.

can consult and deliberate about his course of action. Whitby did deny that men always act in accord with the " highest " motive, but what he meant was the worthiest motive, not the strongest one. Men do not always follow the strongest rational motive, because they sometimes find that impulses contrary to the dictates of reason are stronger still.

Samuel Clarke's argument may be found in the Boyle Lectures on the being and attributes of God. Its essentials are very simple. God is an agent — that is, a being with a power of initiating mechanical motion — and he has created finite agents. Hence man also is a free moral agent, whose actions are voluntary, rather than merely a part of a physical chain of cause and effect such as prevails in the world of mechanical motion. Whether the will is the seat of men's liberty, Clarke said, is not the question; " but whether there be *at all* in Man any such Power as a Liberty of Choice and of Determining his own Actions; or on the contrary his Actions be all as Necessary, as the Motions of a Clock." [18] He did not deny — in fact he specifically asserted — that the will is determined by the last judgment of the understanding. But this acts as a moral motive, not as a physical efficient.

The *Necessity* therefore, by which the *Power of Acting* follows the *Judgment of the Understanding*, is only a *Moral Necessity*, that is, *no Necessity at all*, in the Sense the Opposers of Liberty understand *Necessity*. For *Moral Necessity*, is evidently consistent with the most perfect *Natural Liberty*.[19]

Clarke concluded by pointing out that God's foreknowledge is not inconsistent with liberty of men's actions. A man who has no control over another person's actions can very often foresee what that person is going to do. God has the same power to a perfect degree. Since foreknowledge " implies no

[18] Samuel Clarke, *A Demonstration of the Being and Attributes of God* (5th ed., London, 1719), p. 91.
[19] *Ibid.*, p. 105.

other Certainty, but only That Certainty of Event which the Thing would equally have without being Fore-known, 'tis evident that *It* also implies no necessity." [20]   In all this discussion, Clarke evidently does not differ in essentials from Locke and Whitby.

III

No philosopher influenced Edwards more than did John Locke, especially in his treatment of the will. The analyses of the two men are basically the same, though Edwards used a different terminology and was able to clear up some inconsistencies in Locke's statement.   Instead of saying that the will is determined by the " most pressing uneasiness," Edwards said that it is determined by the " strongest motive." He meant by this, that a man will do that which appears to him at a given moment to be most desirable, whether for rational reasons or not.   The will chooses the greatest apparent good; and since this connection is inseparable, Edwards often phrased his position: " the Will is as the greatest apparent good is."   This is a definition of moral necessity which leads directly to Locke's definition of liberty as the power of a man to do as he pleases.   Freedom rests in the absence of external compulsion, rather than in any supposed power men have to choose what they will choose.

According to Edwards, the Arminian notion of liberty involved three points:

1. That it consists in a self-determining power in the will, or a certain sovereignty the will has over itself, and its own acts, whereby it determines its own volitions; so as not to be dependent in its determinations, on any cause without itself, nor determined by any thing prior to its own acts.   2. Indifference belongs to Liberty in their notion of it, or that the mind, previous to the act of volition, be in equilibrio.   3. Contingence is another thing that belongs and is es-

[20] *Ibid.*, p. 111.

sential to it; not in the common acceptance of the word, as that has been already explained, but as opposed to all necessity, or any fixed and certain connection with some previous ground or reason of its existence. They suppose the essence of Liberty so much to consist in these things, that unless the will of man be free in this sense, he has no real freedom, how much soever he may be at Liberty to act according to his will.[21]

But if Locke, Whitby, and Clarke may be accepted as typical Arminians, it is surely clear that Edwards' analysis of volition was the same as the Arminian analysis, and he was accusing them of holding opinions which in fact they rejected. It was the soundest of Arminian doctrine to say that men choose that which appears to them most agreeable, and to deny that it is the will that is self-determined. The Arminians did insist that God and men are agents; but Edwards' own position involves the same assumption. They did declare, in opposition to materialists, that men's actions are not bound into a system of physical necessity; but they acknowledged that they are determined by moral necessity. Completely misunderstanding what the Arminian position was, when Edwards read Whitby and Clarke and actually found they agreed with him, he accused them of being inconsistent with themselves.[22]

The essential identity of Edwards and the Arminians on this fundamental point cannot be too firmly stressed, since most students know of the Arminians only through Edwards' misdirected attack on them. Readers of the *Freedom of the Will* are so fascinated by the vigorous way in which Edwards demolished the " Arminian " position that they do not stop to inquire whether he was representing his opponents fairly or not.[23]   But if the Arminians did not believe in a self-

---

[21] Edwards, *Works*, II, pp. 18–19.
[22] *Ibid.*, II, pp. 48–52.
[23] Not even Perry Miller has avoided this pitfall. In his recent study of Edwards he declares: " He scored most heavily with a reduction of the Armin-

determining power of the will, or that actions proceed from a state of equilibrium or indifference, where did Edwards get the curious notion that they did? The answer is an ironic one. It was from an anonymous book which was not by an Arminian at all, but by a Calvinist — a moderate Calvinist, to be sure, but still a Calvinist. The book was *An Essay on the Freedom of Will in God and in Creatures*. It was published in London in 1732, and its author was Isaac Watts.

Edwards' use of this book as an example of the " Arminian " doctrine of the freedom of the will did not pass unchallenged at the time. Chauncy Whittelsey wrote to Ezra Stiles on June 30, 1768, expressing dismay at the probable effects of Edwards' book. Its author, he said,

. . . holds up his Subject to view, as of the utmost importance with reference to the Quinquarticular Points. Hence he from time to time speaks of the Arminian Notion of Liberty, which he asserts to be absurd and inconsistent, and of the Liberty, which Calvinists maintain, which he asserts to be the only possible Liberty in the Universe. By which Rate Dr. Watts is the Arminian, and Mr. Lock the Calvinist &c. &c.[24]

Against this volume, Edwards' attack could be quite legitimately directed. Watts believed that it is the will " that is properly the moral principle or agent within us, the proper subject of virtue or vice, and therefore it must be a free and self-determining power, and must chuse of itself, whether it

---

ian proposition of the free, self-determining power of the will into intrinsic nonsense: if the will determines its own acts, there must always be a will before the act; each act must be preceded by an act of will, and that by another, and so on, *ad infinitum*, until we come to the theoretical first act; if this is determined by a still previous decision of will, we take up the march again, but if we call a halt, and say *this* act is first, we have an act that follows from no volition, which is just simply an initial fact, an arbitrarily given, which cannot be the selection of a free will." See Perry Miller, *Jonathan Edwards* (New York, c. 1949), p. 259. Obviously, Edwards was scoring heavily against a straw man, so far as the Arminians were concerned.

[24] Franklin B. Dexter, ed., *Extracts from the Itineraries and Other Miscellanies of Ezra Stiles, D.D., LL.D.* (New Haven, 1916), p. 592.

will follow reason or appetite, judgment or passion." [25]   To be sure, the understanding, which perceives the fitness or unfitness of things, often serves as a " director or guide " to the will.   But the will remains sovereign, not necessarily determined by the greatest apparent good as it is discovered to the mind, or the last dictate of the understanding, or the removal of some uneasiness.   That the greatest apparent good, as Watts understood the phrase, does not determine the will, is shown by the fact that many persons are convinced that piety and virtue will conduce to their happiness, yet their will chooses present sensualities and vicious pleasures.   The will has power over the understanding to the extent that if it has an inclination to an object, it yields to the prejudices on one side, " it fixes the mind upon those arguments, which tend to prove what it wishes, and turns the thoughts away from those evidences, which lie on the other side of the question," and so influences the judgment.[26]   It may also rush the mind to a hasty and ill-advised decision, based on slight and insufficient evidence.   A further mark of the self-determining power of the will is its action when confronted with identical alternatives.   Suppose that a man is shown two cakes, or two eggs exactly alike.   Neither appears more desirable than the other, yet the man can choose one and reject the other.   " The understanding in such instances as these, has no pretence of power to direct or determine the will, because it sees no superior fitness, and the will would be for ever undetermined, if it did not determine itself." [27]   This argument of Watts was not based on any serious misunderstanding of his opponents.   He was able to summarize succinctly the contrary

[25] Isaac Watts, " An Essay on the Freedom of Will in God and in Creatures," in *Discourses, Essays, and Tracts, on Various Subjects* (London, 1753), VI, p. 386.

[26] *Ibid.*, VI, p. 379.

[27] *Ibid.*, VI, p. 388.

view: " that the will of man in every action whatsoever is certainly and necessarily determined by the last dictate or judgment of the understanding, and that the understanding is necessarily determined in it's judgment by present appearances of things as to their fitness or unfitness." [28]   But he rejected this line of thought as leaving no freedom of choice to man, encouraging the principles of fatalists, and taking away the true distinction between virtue and vice.

If Edwards and the Arminians agreed that men's actions are governed by moral necessity — that is, by a necessary connection between acts of the will and the greatest apparent good — what explains all the excitement in New England pulpits?   Why did New England Arminians attack Edwards' treatise?   In the first place, there was a great deal of misunderstanding of Edwards resulting from a different use of terms.   In the second place, Edwards' opponents were by no means his intellectual equals, and were prone to lose their way in the thicket of debate.   Edwards had produced what purported to be a refutation of the Arminian position, so the Arminians felt they were called upon to attack it.   But they sometimes fell into the pitfall of accepting his statement of their position as correct, or else they failed to distinguish between those parts of his treatise with which they agreed and those which they rejected.   They were certain that Edwards' conclusions were false, but they were not quite clear at what point to press the attack.

The real difficulty was that Edwards combined moral necessity with total depravity.   He said that men have inherited a corrupt bias, so that no matter what object or inducement to action is placed before them, their actions will be vicious. This meant, according to the Arminians, that in the last analysis a man's vicious actions are the result of a kind of physical

[28] *Ibid.*, VI, p. 393.

necessity. If a man sins because he has inherited a sinful nature, this is a matter over which he has no control; it is a result of his inheritance just as much as his physical endowment, and so he cannot be blamed, no matter how vicious his acts. The whole controversy would have been vastly simplified if the Arminians had recognized clearly that Edwards' treatise was not wrong, but irrelevant. They should have dismissed the *Freedom of the Will,* and concentrated on the treatise on original sin which complemented it. Moral necessity without total depravity loses all its sting. Arminians like James Dana saw this, but not so clearly as one might wish. Their reply to Edwards was blunted in consequence.

IV

For a decade and a half following the publication of Edwards' book, there was no careful reply to it. Arminians often asserted man's free moral agency, but their comments were loose and ambiguous. Condemnation of the book as fatalistic was more common than analysis of its argument. Henry Cumings of Billerica was heard to say that in his opinion Edwards' treatise was little better than fatalism, and that if he were an atheist he would want no better arguments than he found there to support his position.[29] Ebenezer Gay dodged the issue by ascribing to man " the Power of Self-determination, or Freedom of Choice; his being possessed of which is as self-evident, as the Explanation of the Manner of it's operating, is difficult." [30] In a volume of sermons published in 1755, Jonathan Mayhew did devote a long footnote to the question, but he regarded it as a fruitless undertaking: " if we *exercise ourselves in these things,* I know of

[29] William B. Sprague, *Annals of the American Pulpit,* VIII (New York, 1865), p. 60.
[30] Ebenezer Gay, *Natural Religion, as Distinguish'd from Revealed* (Boston, 1759), p. 12.

no valuable end it can answer — except that of convincing us of our ignorance." [31] The most he would say was that some men choose to conform to the Holy Spirit, while others do not. A careful reading of the footnote, however, reveals plainly the kind of necessity he was opposing:

> . . . if the sinner . . . could not possibly have avoided thus *willing, chusing,* and acting; but was, in every successive moment of his existence, even from the first, laid under a necessity of doing just as he did; whether this were owing to any *external* constraint, or to some *internal, original* byass, or impulse of *nature;* makes not the least alteration in the case, so far as divine justice is concerned in it.[32]

Here the necessity is two-fold: physical necessity of external compulsion; and the necessity that comes from inherited bias, equally beyond the control of the individual. Nothing is said in opposition to that moral necessity which connects acts of the will with the greatest apparent good. Mayhew adopted three arguments for the essential liberty of moral agents: first, men's consciousness of it; second, Clarke's argument that there must somewhere be an agent which is the first cause, and the creator of finite agents; and third, the moral sense of men, who have no difficulty in distinguishing those acts for which they may be blamed from those beyond their control.

Charles Chauncy, like Mayhew, replied to Edwards briefly and incidentally, in *The Benevolence of the Deity.* Chauncy had read Archbishop King's *Essay on the Origin of Evil,* and had borrowed from it extensively in writing his own book. But the significant fact is that Chauncy remained wholly unaffected by King's theory of the freedom of the will. King had argued that an agent is pleased with what he chooses, rather than chooses what pleases him. He denied that the

---

[31] Jonathan Mayhew, *Sermons* (Boston, 1755), p. 291.
[32] *Ibid.,* p. 302n.

will is determined by "any *Uneasiness* arising from the things about which it is conversant." The will is indifferent to external objects. "These Objects then will neither please nor displease till this Indifference be removed, but it is suppos'd to be removed by the Application or Determination of the Power itself; therefor Anxiety does not produce but presuppose its Determination." [33] This position resembles Watts' more than it does Locke's; indeed, Watts acknowledged that King's book had been the inspiration for his own. [34] But Chauncy, despite his indebtedness to King on other points, reverted to the standard interpretation of the freedom of the will as it had been developed by Locke, Whitby, and Clarke. First of all he established that man is an agent. Then, without discussing whether the highest motive determines the will, he set out to prove that man has a power "to direct, suspend, over-rule, or put an intire stop" to his volitions. [35] Men's rational powers may control their impulses; hence men are "self-determined."

Two Arminians, however, made full-dress replies to Edwards: James Dana of Wallingford, Connecticut, [36] and Samuel West of Dartmouth. Dana was the author of *An Examination of the Late President Edwards's "Enquiry on Freedom of Will"* which was published in 1770, and of a continuation which appeared three years later. Samuel

---

[33] William King, *An Essay on the Origin of Evil*. Translated with notes by Edmund Law. (1st English ed., London, 1731), Ch. 5, Sec. 1, Subsec. 3, par. 6.

[34] Watts, *Discourses*, VI, p. 384.

[35] Charles Chauncy, *The Benevolence of the Deity* (Boston, 1784), p. 132.

[36] Dana was minister at Wallingford from 1758 to 1789, and at New Haven from 1789 to 1805. At New Haven, he succeeded the Reverend Chauncy Whittelsey, cousin of the Reverend Charles Chauncy of Boston. Whittelsey and his church were popularly regarded as Arminian in tendency. See Franklin B. Dexter, ed., *The Literary Diary of Ezra Stiles* (New York, 1901), III, p. 8. Dana's writings on the freedom of the will do not reveal a very extreme or outspoken form of Arminianism, but they are clearly not Calvinistic. His later sermons seem to be more orthodox than the earlier ones.

West's first three *Essays on Liberty and Necessity* were not published until 1793; but as he explained in the preliminary Advertisement, they had been composed twenty years earlier. They were reprinted in 1795, with additions. Neither Dana nor West was Edwards' equal in argument, and their work is marred by misunderstanding of Edwards at some points, and by inconsistencies in their statements of their own position. But what they were trying to say is clear; and it is plain that they did not believe, as Edwards supposed the Arminians did, that the will is an autonomous and self-determining faculty of the mind.

The primary assumption of both Dana and West was that man is a moral agent, with a power of initiating motion in the physical world. God is an infinite agent, who has the power of creating finite agents.[37] The actions of a moral agent do not emerge from nothing: " a moral effect cannot exist without a cause any more than a natural effect." [38] But the important thing is that man is not a machine; his actions are determined by moral incentives, rather than by physical causes.

The stimulus to action, according to Dana, is called a " motive." Here, in the use of the word " motive," lay the most persistent source of his misunderstanding of Edwards. " By motives," said Dana, " we mean external reasons or inducements exhibited to the view of a moral agent." [39] Indeed, he sometimes restricted the word even more, to include only rational motives:

[37] Dana, *Examination*, p. 95n.
[38] Dana, *Examination Continued*, p. 33.
[39] *Ibid.*, p. 31. Samuel West's definition was quite similar: " By motive, we understand the occasion, reason, end, or design, which an agent has in view, when he acts; therefore, we say, that the mind acts upon motives; i.e. when the mind acts or chooses, it always has some end, design, or reason, which is the occasion of its acting, or choosing; therefore, motives, in our sense of the term, are the previous circumstances, which are necessary for action." Samuel West, *Essays on Liberty and Necessity* (New Bedford, 1795), Part I, p. 16.

Virtuous or vicious elections must proceed upon motive. And we grant that the greatest good really *ought* to determine moral agents; but that it always *doth,* even where it is perceived, we deny. . . . 'Tis too common, indeed, that the passions bias and pervert the moral judgment. . . . Moral agents many times sin immediately against present light and conviction, while they have *full in their view* the wiser choice. And what is this, but to determine themselves contrary to the greatest apparent good? [40]

The difference between this definition and that of Edwards is that for Edwards the motive is not external to the mind, but is an idea held by the mind. External objects or inducements to action may be the starting point, but action results only insofar as the mind regards them with desire or distaste. The motive is not the object itself, but the object as viewed by the mind. Furthermore, the object is apprehended as desirable or distasteful, not by the reason alone, but by the emotions as well: " the understanding must be taken in a large sense, as including the whole faculty of perception or apprehension, and not merely what is called reason or judgment." [41] The Arminians, then, thought of a motive as something external to the mind — an object, reason, or inducement to action. Edwards conceived of it as internal — an object or inducement as viewed by the mind with favor or disfavor.

Hence, when Edwards declared that " the Will is always determined by the strongest motive," the Arminians were easily misled by his use of words. As applied to an external motive, the adjective " strongest " seemed to suggest the " highest " or " the most compelling to a rational mind." Then Edwards would seem to be saying that there is a necessary and uniform connection between the highest motive and a man's action. But this is not true, as the sins and follies of mankind bear witness. Dana admitted that " motives may,

[40] Dana, *Examination Continued*, pp. 38, 39.
[41] Edwards, *Works*, II, p. 8.

in some cases, be exhibited in so strong a light, that the mind in which they are extant could not but make the choice it doth." But, he continued, " unless this can be shewn to hold true in *every* instance, the doctrine of necessary determination cannot be supported." [42] One clear instance when this did not hold true was Adam's fall. The general trend of Arminian thought was to deny that Adam's capacities were perfectly developed at the time of his creation, and to assert that like his posterity he came upon the earth with mere naked capacities, which had to be trained up to righteousness. Hence Adam's sin " appears to have been a neglect of reason and hasty listning to the sollicitations of appetite." [43] Thus revelation agrees with experience that the most compelling rational motive is frequently ignored.

Furthermore, when the Arminians misunderstood Edwards to mean by " motive " an external object, they inevitably concluded that his scheme was one of mechanistic determinism. If there is a necessary and uniform connection between an external object and a man's actions, then the man is no more than an intricate machine which unites object and action in a mechanical sequence of cause and effect. But since men are not machines, external objects or motives are to be regarded as the occasion of human volitions, rather than their mechanical cause. The actions of men are something more than physical events; they are also moral events which must have moral causes: " And whether any other than an *intelligent mind* can be such a cause, let those who have common understanding judge." [44]

But Dana was not consistent in his use of the word " motive," and sometimes he used it in much the same way that Edwards did. When that happened, the real issue between

[42] Dana, *Examination Continued,* p. 36.
[43] *Ibid.,* p. 24.
[44] Dana, *Examination,* pp. 81–82.

the two men became more sharply focused. On the very first page of the *Examination,* Dana said: " The enquiry in this place is not, Whether the highest motive hath always a causal influence on the will? But, admitting this to be the case, what is it that *causeth* any supposed motive to *be* highest in the mind's view? " [45] He repeated the question in other words: " *How* comes the object to have such a particular *appearance* to the mind . . .? *Whence* is the *state, temper, frame* of the mind what it is? " [46] Obviously, two factors are involved, the external object itself, and the observing mind:

. . . *antecedent* to the mind's view of the object, there must be something in it [the object] to cause it to appear agreable when viewed — something independent on, and prior to the view — or the mind must be in such a particular state, frame, or temper — or view the object under such and such circumstances, in order to it's appearing thus and thus agreable.[47]

That one or the other of these factors is finally responsible for determining the choices a man will make is certain: " Either internal, original bias, or something extrinsic, is the cause, to whose efficiency, determination, command, decision, the will is as much subject, as the motion of the body to the will. . . ." [48]

Dana professed to be in doubt as to which of these two factors Edwards relied on, though Edwards declared plainly that both of them are involved.[49] To be doubly sure, Dana examined both alternatives. If Edwards meant that the will is determined by an extrinsic cause — that is, it is the nature of the object itself that determines how it will appear to the mind — then sinful volitions are not the fault of the individual, but must be charged to God himself. The object is a motive to choice. " But motives to choice are exhibited to

[45] *Ibid.,* p. 1.
[46] *Ibid.,* p. 3.
[47] *Ibid.,* p. 23.

[48] *Ibid.,* pp. 44–45.
[49] Edwards, *Works,* II, pp. 6–8.

their mind by some agent: By whom are they exhibited? " There is no stop in tracing the causal relationship until we reach the first cause. " Will it now be said, that GOD is the cause of those dispositions of heart, and acts of the will, which are so odious in their own nature? On Mr. *Edwards*'s scheme this must be said." [50]

The remaining alternative, that the mind is determined by an " original bias or propensity," raises the question of total depravity. Consider Adam and Eve in their innocency:

Their original bias and inclination, it will be allowed, proceeded immediately from the creator. If then their sin was the effect of a necessity originally in their will, or was their will's original propensity, it was so entirely owing to the *nature of things,* that (by supposition) it could not involve them in guilt — Or if connected with the eternal cause, who alone is necessary in his own nature, it could not upon our author's own scheme; be *their* sin. The whole guilt, if any, must be imputed to the first cause.[51]

But total depravity, involving as it did a man's inheritance, doomed him to sin quite as inescapably as though he were bound by physical necessity.

Since God created men's natures, and gave them their moral capacity or incapacity, Edwards' scheme made God the author of sin. " The examiner begs the reader to keep in mind this single question, *Whether Mr. Edwards's doctrine makes God the efficient cause of all moral wickedness?* . . . To reduce a *Christian* writer to this is sufficient, without going any further." [52] Dana was hardly being unfair to Edwards in charging that such was the outcome of his system. The Edwardeans did object to the bald way in which the Arminians stated their challenge, and much preferred to say that God ordained a system in which sin would infallibly come to pass. But however one phrased it, the effect was the same. The

[50] Dana, *Examination*, p. 49.   [52] Dana, *Examination Continued*, p. vi.
[51] *Ibid.*, pp. 53–54.

Edwardeans were forced to argue that sin was desirable. Samuel Hopkins published *Sin, Through Divine Interposition, an Advantage to the Universe* (1758); and Joseph Bellamy wrote *Four Sermons on the Wisdom of God in the Permission of Sin* (1758), and *The Wisdom of God in the Permission of Sin, Vindicated* (1759). Such an inversion of moral values was incredible to the Arminian. Dana agreed with Bishop Butler that God may bring good out of moral evil, but it still would have been far better if the evil had never existed. To argue that moral evil is an advantage, is to say that the divine law of righteousness is imperfect, and leaves no basis from which to condemn intemperance and all debauchery. Besides, if God ordains sin, " How then is sin such an *infinite evil* as we have been taught to believe it? Does it not turn out an infinite *good?* " [53]

V

The alternatives seemed clear. Either God is responsible for men's sinful volitions, by presenting them with motives to evil or creating in them a sinful nature, or else men themselves are responsible. If men are to be blamed, it is because they are free moral agents. A moral agent is free, not in the sense that he does not choose the greatest apparent good, but in Daniel Whitby's sense, that he is not depraved, or determined by an inherited bias to evil. A free moral agent, when confronted with a course of action or a choice between two courses of action, is not compelled one way or the other by mechanical force, nor is he doomed to choose the sinful path because of an inherited corrupt nature.

A man's volitions, to be sure, are an expression of his nature: a sinful man will make evil choices. But men are seldom wholly good or wholly evil, so that some of their voli-

[53] Dana, *Examination*, p. 12.

tions will be good and others sinful. Character is not something that exists fully developed from birth. Locke taught that the mind of man at birth is a blank sheet of paper on which experience writes. Similarly, moral character is the product of training and experience. The child is endowed with various passions which may tempt him to evil; but he is also endowed with reason, which may control those passions. Hence, in a very real sense, a man's character is what he makes of himself. The bias with which the mature man approaches choices between good and evil has been created in his lifetime, and he can be held very largely responsible for it: " our estimating the moral character from internal dispositions is on a supposition that *these* are within the power of the agent." [54]

The Arminians believed in the determination of character by environmental influences on a plastic original nature. Their position was not always clearly stated, nor was it free from contradictions. It involved problems which they had not faced, let alone solved. For example, they never reached the point of wondering whether environmental conditioning might not also be deterministic, so that no one can ever be held responsible for his moral character. But if their constructive doctrine was ambiguous, their opposition to Edwards was not. They opposed the rigid determinism which attaches a man's moral character to the sin of Adam.

By and large, the problem of the freedom of the will seemed less important to the Arminians than it did to Edwards. Most of the time, they appealed to experience and let it go at that. " Let a man look into his own breast," wrote Dana, " and he cannot but perceive inward freedom — *Inward freedom* — For if freedom be not in the *mind*, it is no where. And liberty in the mind implies *self-determina-*

[54] *Ibid.*, p. 96.

tion." [55] For however one phrased it, the Arminians were convinced that moral agents are free from any initial taint which would prevent them from responding to the monitions of conscience and the dictates of reason.

[55] *Ibid.*, p. v.

CHAPTER FIVE

Justification by Faith

1755–1780

I

The negative side of the Arminian argument was a denial of the doctrine of original sin and the concept of human nature that it implies. Its positive side was a revision of the doctrines of justification and regeneration, to bring them into line with the concept of man as a moral agent free from the taint of Adam's sin. This reconstruction of doctrine proceeded simultaneously with the attack on imputed guilt and total depravity; and by the mid-sixties, the liberals had elaborated and rounded out their version of the doctrines of grace. Charles Chauncy's *Twelve Sermons* (1765) presents the Arminian structure in mature form.

Meanwhile, the pattern of religious parties and factions in the congregational churches was becoming clearer. The main body of the clergy continued to adhere to a moderate Calvinism, but they now found themselves under attack from both sides. As a counterbalance to the growing influence of the Arminians, there was emerging on the opposite wing a small group of evangelicals, who asserted a much higher-toned Calvinism than had ever been accepted in New England. The advocates of this " New Divinity " were the heirs of Edwards. Their chief leader was Samuel Hopkins (Yale,

1741); hence they were frequently known as " Hopkinsians "
or " Hopkintonians."

Hopkins had himself been a student in the parsonage in
Northampton, and was as close a friend as Edwards had. He
served the church in Great Barrington from 1743 to 1769,
and the First Congregational Church in Newport, Rhode Island, from 1770 to his death in 1803. The earmarks of his
system, by which it could be distinguished from ordinary Calvinism, were three. In the first place, Hopkinsians placed
great stress on Edwards' definition of virtue as consisting in
disinterested benevolence. In the popular mind, they were
understood to believe that no one will be saved unless he is
so disinterested in his own fate that he is willing to be damned
for the glory of God. In the second place, Hopkinsians de-
preciated the use of means in man's salvation. If a man is unconverted, all his actions are displeasing to God, no matter
how respectable he may appear to his fellow-men, or how
faithful he may be in attendance at public worship and in the
performance of other religious duties. Nothing that he can
do by himself will entitle him to salvation, and the more
he makes use of the means of grace, if he remains unrepentant,
the more abominable he is in the sight of God. Only when
God has first renewed the heart can a man's prayers and worship be pleasing to his Creator. Finally, the Hopkinsians
were less squeamish than moderate Calvinists in deducing
from the concept of God's omnipotence the conclusion that
sin itself exists because he has ordained it.

In the sixties and seventies, the Hopkinsians were still a
small group. Ezra Stiles estimated that out of five or six hundred ministers in New England in 1773, there were " about
20 or 25 Ministers full in Mr. Hopkins's peculiarities; and
20 more who admire Mr. Edwards writings and have a
hearty Friendship for Mr. Hopkins, tho' rather as they are

friends to all Calvinists than for his Singularities."[1] The group included Joseph Bellamy (Yale, 1735) of Bethlehem, Connecticut; Ephraim Judson (Yale, 1763) of Norwich, Connecticut; David Sanford (Yale, 1755) of Medway, Massachusetts; Levi Hart (Yale, 1760) of Preston, Connecticut; and Nathanael Emmons (Yale, 1767) of Franklin, Massachusetts. These men were all Connecticut-born as well as Yale-bred, and they were united by close ties of friendship.

Although Hopkins' *Inquiry Concerning the Promises of the Gospel* (1765) took the form of a reply to Jonathan Mayhew rather than an attack on the moderate Calvinists, it was the latter who were most active in condemning Hopkinsian innovations. Jedidiah Mills (Yale, 1722) of Huntington, Connecticut, and William Hart (Yale, 1732) of Saybrook, Connecticut, led the attack.[2] But the Arminians were equally disturbed. Charles Chauncy wrote to Ezra Stiles in 1769: " I'm sorry, with my whole soul, that Mr. Hopkins is like to settle at Newport. I have a much worse opinon of his principles than of Sandeman's. He is a troublesome, conceited, obstinate man." Two years later, his dislike had not subsided: " And, in truth, I had much rather be an episcopalian, or that others shd, than that I or they shd be Hopkintonians. The new Divinity so prevalent in Connecticut will undoe the Colony. Tis as bad, if not worse than paganism."[3]

[1] Franklin B. Dexter, ed., *The Literary Diary of Ezra Stiles, D.D., LL.D.* (New York, 1901), I, p. 363.

[2] Joseph Haroutunian, *Piety versus Moralism* (New York, c. 1932), Ch. 3; Frank Hugh Foster, *A Genetic History of the New England Theology* (Chicago, 1907), pp. 131ff.

[3] Franklin B. Dexter, ed., *Extracts from the Itineraries and other Miscellanies of Ezra Stiles, D.D., LL.D.* (New Haven, 1916), pp. 450, 451. Robert Sandeman, to whom Chauncy referred, is an obscure figure in New England religious history, who is remembered, if at all, for a special theory of justification by faith and for an attempt to revive primitive Christian rites of worship. He came to America from Scotland in the fall of 1764, and organized several small congregations in Portsmouth, Boston, Danbury, and elsewhere. Chauncy

II

Although Charles Chauncy was an Arminian, his definition of the word " justification " would have been acceptable to Old Calvinists and Hopkinsians as well. It means " to approve, accept, vindicate or adjudge as just." [4]   All men are sinners; yet if God so decrees, a sinful man may be justified, or receive the status of a just man. Before he is justified, declared the Calvinists, nothing that he does can make him deserving of salvation. He can never fulfill perfectly the divine commandments, and so he cannot be saved by his works. He cannot earn salvation by the merit of his personal righteousness. But God may impute Christ's righteousness to him, and treat him as though he were righteous, before he actually is so. This divine transaction is what is meant by " justification." It is followed by a process of sanctification, in which the newly-justified man attempts, with the aid of the Holy Spirit, to cast aside the evil and indolent habits of his previous sinful state.

In New England, to be sure, this basic Calvinist position had long been phrased in the terms of the Covenant theology. God voluntarily enters into an agreement or bargain. He promises to pardon those who have faith in him, and man in turn agrees to labor for sanctification. It goes without saying that only the elect can respond to this offer. They accept because they have faith, but their faith is itself the gift of God's Holy Spirit. The Covenant theologians agreed with the Hopkinsians, however, in making justifica-

---

took him seriously enough to devote long footnotes in his *Twelve Sermons* on justification to refuting him. He died in 1771, however, and Chauncy's concern proved to have been excessive. See Williston Walker, " The Sandemanians of New England," *Annual Report of the American Historical Association for the Year 1901* (Washington, 1902), I, pp. 131–162.

   [4] Charles Chauncy, *Twelve Sermons* (Boston, 1765), p. 3.

tion a divine operation by which man is saved from guilt, while sanctification redeems him from bondage to sin.

The next step, which takes a man from the Covenant theology into Arminianism, does not seem at first glance to be a very big one. The Arminians accepted the concept of a covenant between God and man. They frequently used the word " covenant," at least in the beginning, with the result that they were able to present their doctrine as less of an innovation than Hopkinsianism. The terms of the contract are very simple: God will pardon those who have faith in him and diligently seek him. The Arminian heresy in this doctrine lies not in what is stated, but in what is omitted. The Calvinists always made it clear that only the elect could accept this bargain, and that they necessarily would do so; the Arminians said that every man has an equal opportunity to accept it or pass it by.

Arminians were often accused of preaching justification by works, or by the merit of personal righteousness. Actually, they took great care to avoid that error. When Chauncy wrote his *Twelve Sermons,* the very first thing he set out to prove was that justification is impossible by works of the law. If the law of righteousness is the standard by which men will be judged, then no man " can be accounted, accepted or vindicated as just, upon the score of any works he has performed in obedience to it." [5] The reason is obvious: all men are sinners. He who would be justified on the basis of his works must not have a single misdeed on his record, " for one bad one only, tho' it should be attended with a great many good ones, would as certainly, if not in so high a degree, expose him to a sentence of condemnation, as if his works were all bad, with the exception of one only that was good." [6] Similarly, Lemuel Briant challenged those who took exception to

[5] *Ibid.,* p. 5.　　　　　[6] *Ibid.,* p. 12.

his sermon on the *Absurdity and Blasphemy* " to point out a single Passage in my Sermon where the Doctrine of Justification by the *merit* of Man's *personal* Righteousness is asserted, or from whence it can by good and necessary Consequence be inferred." [7]   Even in his sermons on striving, which Hopkins regarded as particularly vulnerable, Jonathan Mayhew disclaimed the doctrine of merit: " It is, however, very far from being the design of what is here said, that we should do thus under the notion of meriting salvation thereby; or performing such a righteousness as God is obliged in justice to accept." [8]   If men were to earn salvation by their own merits, no one would be saved — Arminian and Calvinist stood together on this point.

Justification is by faith; in words, at least, the Arminians were loyal to the principles of the Reformation.   Faith means, first of all, a belief in the truth of the Gospel and submission to the will of God.   But faith is something more than a mere intellectual assent to divine truths; it is a persuasion of a very special kind.   It must be a living powerful spring of action, not a dead faith.   It produces repentance and issues in righteousness, and a man's deeds are the chief test by which we can determine whether a man possesses justifying faith.   " The doctrine of the gospel undoubtedly is, that we are *justified by faith;* but it is a great mistake to infer from hence, that we are accepted to the divine favour, and entitled to eternal life, without unfeigned repentance, and new obedience." [9]   Though no man can be justified because of his personal obedience, wrote William Balch, " Yet I believe, at the same Time, that no Man can be justified

---

[7] Lemuel Briant, *Some Friendly Remarks on a Sermon Lately Preach'd at Braintree* (Boston, 1750), p. 10.

[8] Jonathan Mayhew, *Striving to Enter in at the Strait Gate Explain'd and Inculcated* (Boston, 1761), pp. 19–20.

[9] Jonathan Mayhew, *Sermons* (Boston, 1755), pp. 171–172.

without personal Obedience, i.e. without *sincere* Obedience to the Gospel. . . ."[10] There is no contradiction here. The Arminians were simply saying that a man's obedience is not enough to save him, but that the lack of it is enough to condemn him. Or, to put it another way, the reason why a man's obedience is a condition of his salvation is not that it can ever be perfect enough to deserve such a reward, but that God has promised to bestow eternal life on those who make " a sincere tho' imperfect Conformity to the divine Image and Will."[11]

Although the Arminians said they believed in justification by faith, not works, what they did was to put both on the same level, as conditions of salvation: " as both these are manifestly included in the Condition of salvation, it is obvious, that when one of them, only, is mentioned, as such condition, the other must be supposed to attend it, or be included in it."[12] In this way, the Arminians broke down the sharp contrast which Calvinists had long made and which Hopkinsians stressed particularly, between works, which are abominable, and faith, which is gracious. Neither faith nor works has any merit of its own, or places God in debt to man. A man's salvation is by the free grace of God: " It proceeds wholly from his undeserved favour; and is to be acknowledged as *his gift*, not claimed as *our due*."[13] Both faith and works can be demanded of us, without impairing the doctrine of salvation by God's grace, " if these are look'd upon, as they ought to be, only as the *gracious Terms* and *Conditions*,

---

[10] William Balch, *A Vindication of Some Points of Doctrine* (Boston, 1746), p. 38.
[11] William Balch, *The Apostles St. Paul and St. James Reconciled with Respect to Faith and Works* (Boston, 1743), p. 12.
[12] John Tucker, *The Two Following Sermons . . . were Preached to the First Congregational Church and Society in Newbury-Port, April 9, 1769* (Boston, 1769), p. 13.
[13] Mayhew, *Sermons* (1755), p. 111.

appointed by the Redeemer, without which we shall not be *pardon'd* and *accepted*, because we could not be *happy* without them, if we were." [14]

God might conceivably have required of everyone some positive or arbitrary duty as the condition of his covenant, as he did with Adam. But the actual terms of the covenant are reasonable and consistent. God requires righteousness of men, because morality is necessary to happiness both here and hereafter. " The practice of pure, undefiled religion," said Mayhew, " has a natural tendency to prolong human life, and to render it, in some degree, happy." [15] This argument, of course, derived its strength from the discovery, which the eighteenth century had made, that God's purpose is to make men happy. Beyond the present life, righteousness is necessary for happiness in the world to come. The foundation of eternal happiness " must be laid in ones own Mind, in a personal good Turn and Rightness of Temper, to relish cælestial Joys." [16] In short, the Arminians conceived of salvation as freedom from sin as well as the guilt of sin.

Out of this discussion, there gradually developed the concept of justification as a standard to attain, rather than a specific act of God in pardoning individuals. Jonathan Mayhew stated this position most clearly. The terms of acceptance, he wrote, are laid down in the Scriptures, " so that those who comply therewith, are justified of course, upon such compliance." These terms are stable and fixed, so that every one who meets them is automatically pardoned. We do not suppose " that there is any sentence of absolution, or justification, formally pronounced in heaven, when a man is justi-

---

[14] Samuel Webster, *Justification by the Free Grace of God, through the Redemption there is in Christ* (Boston, 1765), p. 27.

[15] Mayhew, *Sermons* (1755), p. 482.

[16] Lemuel Briant, *The Absurdity and Blasphemy of Depretiating Moral Virtue* (Boston, 1749), p. 21.

fied. . . . There is no *Act* of justification to be conceived of, either as prior, or subsequent to, or different from, the gospel-declarations of mercy." It would probably have prevented confusion " and unintelligible rant, upon the subject of justification," he concluded, " had it always been considered in this light; as being only the sentence which God passes on a man, in, and by his word; instead of being considered as a divine *act*, intirely distinct from, and independent of, it." [17] Mayhew was thinking in terms of an eighteenth-century God of Law, instead of a Calvinist God of inscrutable purposes. He continued to use the traditional vocabulary, but the pattern of his thought had changed significantly.

III

Implicit in the Arminian scheme was the principle that a man's salvation is within his own control, because it depends on the use he makes of his opportunities. The Hopkinsians accused the Arminians of unsound doctrine at this point; this principle was one of the things they had in mind when they taxed the liberals with preaching justification by works. The Arminians were sensitive to the charge that they had exalted man at the expense of the omnipotence and majesty of God, by requiring God to sit idly by while his creatures determined for themselves what their eternal destiny was to be. They protested loudly that they were being misrepresented. All our powers to do good come from God, said Chauncy: " all that we have, and are, we derive from God. Not only our ability, but our very inclination, to every good work, is the free gift of God." [18] William Balch was even more specific: " It is not pretended, that we have any Suffi-

---

[17] Mayhew, *Sermons* (1755), p. 173n.
[18] Charles Chauncy, *Charity to the Distressed Members of Christ* (Boston, 1757), p. 8.

ciency of our own: The Grace of God is acknowledg'd in every Thing, and the Necessity of his special Grace to all the Purposes of Regeneration, Conversion, Sanctification, Perseverance, and eternal Glory." [19]

In the bare assertion that all power comes from God, Arminians did not differ from Calvinists. But by dropping the doctrine of election, the Arminians robbed salvation by grace of the significance it had for the orthodox theologian. In the Calvinist scheme, the special grace of God in redeeming the elect was what mattered. But the Arminian asserted: " The Gospel takes no Notice of different Kinds or Sorts of Grace; — Sorts of Grace specifically different, — one of which may be call'd *special* and the other not so: — one of which, from the peculiar and distinguishing Nature of it, shall prove converting and saving, and the other not." [20] Hence while the grace of which the liberals spoke was not exactly the same thing as common grace, it was equally available to everyone. All that is required of any man is a sincere regard for religious duties, in order to progress in holiness. God will assist him at every step; and if he fails to achieve the goal of salvation, it will not be because he lacks God's grace, but because he resists and counter-strives against the light and grace afforded him. " It is not to be pretended," Balch admitted, " that wicked Men have in fact all that Grace given them that good Men have," or that " God affords at once Grace enough for any Man to go thro', and accomplish the whole Work of his Salvation." But God gives him so much " as may be sufficient to what is *nextly* and *immediately* required of him; on a Man's improving of which, he may

[19] *Letters from the First Church in Glocester to the Second in Bradford, with their Answers* (Boston, 1744), p. 26.

[20] John Tucker, *Observations on the Doctrines, and Uncharitableness, &c. of the Rev. Mr. Jonathan Parsons, of Newbury* (Boston, 1757), p. 5.

from the divine Goodness hope for more, according to his future Needs." [21]

Similarly, when Mayhew urged his congregation to strive to enter in at the strait gate, he was confronted with the objection that a man cannot strive antecedent to a gracious influence of God's spirit on his heart. But Mayhew replied that God's grace is bestowed on every one, not only on those who are finally saved: " God undoubtedly strives with sinful men, by his word, his spirit, and the dispensations of his providence; awakening them to a sense of their guilt, misery and danger, antecedently to their striving, or doing any thing tending to their salvation. . . ." But justification does not always follow automatically; for there are strivings prior to the thorough change of heart which takes place in regeneration, and God's grace is bestowed on many who resist instead of yielding to him, " till they are utterly forsaken of him, and given over to a reprobate mind." [22] As long as the grace of God in salvation made a distinction between elect and non-elect, it was an important doctrine. When this distinction was removed, the doctrine lost its bite, and became a superfluous statement of the obvious fact that God sustains the universe. By the time Arminianism turned into Unitarianism, no one bothered with it any more.

Mayhew's emphasis on striving to enter in at the strait gate was actually no novelty in New England. Generations of Puritan ministers had told their congregations to avail themselves of the means established by God for attaining saving grace. Some men are converted while praying in secret, others while reading the Word, and others while listening to the sermons of the minister. But God ordinarily

[21] *Letters from the First Church in Glocester*, p. 26.
[22] Mayhew, *Striving to Enter*, pp. 21, 22.

works through such means, instead of by sudden direct acts of divine power. Hence every man should pray, read the Bible, and attend public worship. For the unregenerate, these may prove to be the means of grace; for the saints, they are aids to sanctification. Mayhew was not saying anything new when he declared: " Tho' God is omnipotent, yet he seldom or never works wholly without means." [23] His novelty lay in the subtle impression which he left on his hearers that sincere use of the means of grace would inevitably be rewarded with success.

IV

Whether the Lord's Supper should be regarded as one of the means of grace which God has ordained for the conversion of sinners was a question that New England had debated since the days of Solomon Stoddard. Originally, the Supper had been a sacrament for the regenerate only; it was a seal placed on the saved to attest their gracious state. Stoddard regarded it as a means for the conversion of the unregenerate, just as much as preaching of the Word. His theories were most widely accepted by churches in the Connecticut valley, rather than those in eastern Massachusetts where Arminianism was to flourish. But Stoddardeanism, which disregarded the institutional distinction between saints and sinners, was clearly more in harmony with Arminian than with Calvinist patterns of thought. After the Awakening, therefore, with its emphasis on the New Birth, Edwards led the Calvinists back toward regenerate membership, while the Arminians moved toward Stoddardeanism. Edwards' insistence on regenerate membership in Northampton precipitated his dismissal in 1750, and opened the debate which was to root out both Stoddardeanism and the Half-Way Cove-

[23] Jonathan Mayhew, *Practical Discourses* (Boston, 1760), p. 5.

nant in almost all the orthodox churches by the beginning of the nineteenth century.

In the actual debate, Arminians played an inconspicuous role. The Half-Way Covenant was defended chiefly by Old Calvinists, like William Hart, Moses Mather, and Moses Hemmenway.[24] Charles Chauncy's five sermons on the *Breaking of Bread* did appear in 1772, when the discussion was at its height, but this publication was not controversial in tone, nor did it take the form of a reply to any of the followers of Edwards. Why the Arminians contributed so little to the debate is not obvious. Perhaps they were already conscious enough of the gap between themselves and the orthodox to hesitate to interfere in a family row between Old Calvinists and Hopkinsian Calvinists.

Evidence is scanty as to the practice in churches under Arminian ministers. Ebenezer Gay, who was installed in Hingham in 1717, introduced the Half-Way Covenant there and was still following that scheme in 1768.[25] In the First Church in Boston, the Half-Way Covenant had been introduced very late, in 1736. It lasted officially for almost a century, until 1828.[26] Chauncy himself was Stoddardean throughout his ministry. In a sermon preached in 1732, he declared that it is " a mistaken apprehension of the *Lord's Supper* " to suppose it " an Ordinance designed only for Christians of more than ordinary attainments in holiness, and satisfaction about their good estate." [27] Perhaps his views were neutralized by his colleague, Thomas Foxcroft, who was an Old Calvinist. In the West Church, Stoddard-

[24] See Williston Walker, *Creeds and Platforms of Congregationalism* (New York, 1893), pp. 283–287; also Haroutunian, *Piety versus Moralism*, Ch. 5.
[25] Dexter, *Itineraries of Ezra Stiles*, p. 260.
[26] A. B. Ellis, *History of the First Church in Boston, 1630–1880* (Boston, 1881), pp. 200, 273.
[27] Charles Chauncy, *Early Piety Recommended and Exemplify'd* (Boston, 1732), p. 17.

eanism was accepted, but Mayhew had some difficulty in persuading some members of his congregation to abandon the
Half-Way position. There are some, he complained, " who,
in order to obtain baptism for their children, have made a
profession of their faith in Christ, and solemnly bound themselves to observe *all* the laws of his kingdom; and yet turn
their backs upon the Lord's table from year to year, as if
this were no christian institution." He found it hard to
reconcile this neglect with a sincere engagement to obey
God's ordinances. " I have often, and very particularly
shewn what your duty is in this respect," he added, " tho'
with much less success than was desired." He proposed to
continue to remind them of their duty, hoping that the time
would come when baptized persons would no longer habitu-
ally absent themselves " from the fellowship of Christ's
church and people in one of his ordinances." [28]

Chauncy's sermons on the *Breaking of Bread* were the
only extensive discussion by an Arminian of the whole problem. If all Arminians did not agree with him, if some preferred the Half-Way Covenant, Chauncy's treatise nevertheless represented the direction in which the Arminians
were moving. The author rejected the Half-Way system
specifically: " There are no *half members* in the visible kingdom of Christ. Whoever are members at all, are *whole*
members; and, as such, have a right, at mature years, to a
seat at the table of the Lord, unless, by their unchristian
conduct, they have forfeited it." [29] To join in the breaking
of bread is not only the privilege, but also the duty, of all
Christian professors. In the first place, the Lord's Supper
was divinely ordained, as " a visible mark, sign, or badge "

[28] Jonathan Mayhew, *Christian Sobriety* (Boston, 1763), pp. 108, 109.
[29] Charles Chauncy, " *Breaking of Bread*," in *Remembrance of the Dying
Love of Christ, a Gospel Institution* (Boston, 1772), p. 110n.

of the Christian, not only of the regenerate Christian. If we are to obey the distinct command of Christ, there is as much reason why we should break bread as observe the Lord's Day, or pray, or attend the preaching of the Word. In the second place, the Supper is intrinsically valuable. It is not an arbitrary rite, but is intended " to perpetuate, by visible symbols, the memory of a crucified Saviour." [30] When the bread is broken, we are reminded how the body of Christ was wounded for our transgression; when the wine is poured, we have a symbol of the blood that was shed for the remission of sin. " In a word, we have here preached to us with great plainness, though in figurative signs, reconciliation with God through the death of Christ, and complete salvation in eternal Glory, notwithstanding all our past sins. . . ." Since the Supper is an expression of Christian doctrine through symbols, as the sermon is an expression of it through words, often enough both have the same effect. Many in all ages " have been turned from visible christians only, to those who are christians in the real temper of their hearts," by impressions received at the communion table. For those already regenerate, there is nothing " better suited to help forward their growth in the divine life, than their attendance at the sacramental supper in a serious, devout and considerate manner." [31]

Of course Chauncy did not let down the barriers altogether. The " securely wicked, those who live a vicious and ungodly life," obviously could only profane the table of the Lord. The " careless and indifferent " also cannot attend without hypocrisy. Their duty is first to become awakened, to discover a concern for their salvation. Chauncy's sermons were directed at those who, " instead of indulging to vice, are blameless in their lives." To them he declared that at-

[30] *Ibid.*, pp. 21, 29. [31] *Ibid.*, pp. 26, 27.

tendance at prayer and preaching is not enough. " You are as much obliged to 'break bread' at the Lord's-Supper. You may no more omit the one than the other." [32]

The reason for the adoption of the Stoddardean position was quite apparent: there was no longer any way of telling whether a man was truly regenerate or not. " It is not an easie matter for christians, especially christians that are weak in faith, or that are but beginners in religion, to determine concerning their faith, that it is, not of the common, but saving kind." [33]   And if it is hard for anyone to tell of his own estate, how much harder will it be to judge of another!   Not even the apostles, " much less their successors in after ages, who could judge by the outward appearance only, not having it in their power to inspect the hearts of others " could tell " whether the faith they professed was of the saving kind." [34] In many people, Mayhew observed, " there is such a strange mixture of wisdom and folly, virtue and vice, sincerity and hypocrisy, that it is next to impossible for any mortal to determine, whether the good or the bad qualities predominate, so as to constitute the general character." [35]   How can men establish qualifications of which they are not competent to judge, as terms of admission to the church or any of its ordinances?

v

The obedience to the will of God which is required for regeneration is much more than faithful performance of religious duties.   No one can be saved, however regular his attendance at meeting and communion, unless he sincerely tries to obey God's moral commandments.   The Arminians devoted much of their attention to the inculcation of moral-

---

[32] *Ibid.*, pp. 35, 37, 43, 45.   [34] *Ibid.*, p. 106n.
[33] *Ibid.*, p. 119.   [35] Mayhew, *Christian Sobriety*, p. 39.

ity; indeed, they had the reputation of stressing it far more than the orthodox did. Jonathan Mayhew, for example, used special events like the earthquakes of 1755 as occasions for " practical sermons," recalling his people from their idle and sinful ways. In 1763, he published a book with the revealing title *Christian Sobriety*. In this volume he warned his charges against profanity, neglect of public worship, light and irreverent behavior at it, excessive and riotous mirth at other times, sinful diversions such as gambling, excessive expense and pride in apparel, idleness or neglect of business, a disrespectful behavior to superiors, falsehood and lying, rash and immoderate anger, envy, intemperance in eating and drinking, uncleanness, fraud and injustice, a covetous disposition, and finally, enthusiastic notions and superstitious practices.[36]

A moral code of this kind was commonplace enough when Mayhew preached, and all New England could accept such a list of evil ways to be shunned. But the orthodox declared that the Arminians were preaching mere worldly morality, in which the welfare of the creature was exalted above the glory of the Creator. The charge was not without plausibility. While the Arminians considered the chief motive for morality to be a pious regard for the greatness of God, they did not find it easy to subordinate themselves and their concern for their own salvation to his glory. Mayhew did not tell his congregation that they should turn from sin to holiness because holiness is so lovely that nothing can compare with it. Instead, he reminded them of the omnipotence of God, and " how greatly it concerns us to secure to ourselves the good-will and patronage of our Maker, by obeying his commandments; and what a terrible hazard we run, by per-

[36] Mayhew, *Christian Sobriety*, Sermons 4, 5.

sisting in our rebellion against him, and in opposition to his righteous government." [37]   Mayhew did tell them that they should love God because he is good, but what he had in mind was God's past favors to men and his gracious promises to them.   The basis of Mayhew's piety was gratitude, not self-forgetful devotion.   And he was not above appeals to self-interest, reminding his congregation of the esteem and honor which sobriety procures and the temporal advantages which result.[38]   Had the prudent Benjamin Franklin remained in Boston, he would doubtless have attended the West Church.

Righteousness or morality, for the Arminians, was the fruit not so much of a deep religious experience as of education and training.   Our spiritual powers, like our intellectual powers, said Chauncy, must be exercised if we are to be saved. " They are small, and weak, in their beginning; but capable of growth, and naturally tend to it; and will, under the influence of heaven, continually increase in strength, and go on towards perfection, if they are duly exercised." [39]   Since this is true, it is important to begin religious training early, and not expect children suddenly to mend their ways at adolescence as the result of conversion.   In childhood they are freest from a wrong bias, and their natural sense of the indecency of wickedness has not been corrupted by evil habits.   Delay only makes the task more difficult.   " The longer it is put off, the more grief, pain and trouble it will cost the sinner, whenever he turns his feet unto God's testimonies." [40]

The development of character which finally results in regeneration is within reach of every man.   Even the unre-

[37]   Mayhew, *Practical Discourses*, p. 12.
[38]   Mayhew, *Christian Sobriety*, Sermons 6–8.
[39]   Chauncy, *Twelve Sermons*, p. 314; see also Charles Chauncy, *Five Dissertations on the Scripture Account of the Fall; and its Consequences* (London, 1785), p. 30.
[40]   Mayhew, *Practical Discourses*, p. 116.

generate are able to use the means of grace, to consider the promises and threats expressed in God's Word, and to reflect on their wickedness and sin. It follows that we are ourselves to blame if we are not saved: " the Spirit of God, in the work of illumination, so manages his influences, as that men, notwithstanding what he does, have so much to do themselves that it will be properly their fault, and justly chargeable upon them as such, if they remain destitute of the saving truth." [41] While the activity of God and of man are both necessary, God's influence is a constant factor and man's exertions are the variable one. God has placed us in a state of trial, and left it to us to choose death or life. God does not lack the power to regenerate anyone he may choose, by the immediate and violent act of his Holy Spirit, as the Hopkinsians expect. But it is vastly more to his glory to win converts to his kingdom by placing moral motives before moral agents. Man's salvation is in his own control, not because finite man is more powerful than the infinite God, but because God in his wisdom has decreed that those shall be justified who earnestly endeavor to obey him.

VI

The Arminian doctrine of justification and regeneration was completely developed and elaborated by the end of the 1760's — that is, by the generation of which Chauncy and Mayhew were the chief spokesmen. It should be observed that the pattern of this thinking was in all essentials the same as that of the first generation of New England Unitarians. Both stressed man's development rather than his sudden conversion. But the Arminian phase of the liberal theology is particularly interesting because it retained the traditional vocabulary of Christian theology. It spoke of justification

[41] Chauncy, *Twelve Sermons*, p. 310.

by faith, regeneration, sanctification, and perseverance at the same time that it had rebuilt the structure of which those doctrines had been a part. In terms of theological development rather than denominational organization, the point at which Arminianism became Unitarianism was where the old vocabulary disappeared, and the Arminian-Unitarian pattern of thought clothed itself in new language. But that change, striking as it was, is of less real significance than the transformation of Christian doctrine achieved by the early Arminians. It was in the decades immediately following the Awakening that New England crossed the great divide.

CHAPTER SIX

Rationalism

1755–1780

I

At the same time that Arminians were asserting the natural ability of man to do that which is pleasing to God, they were also asserting his natural ability to know what is right. Every man possesses the faculty of reason, which enables him to distinguish between truth and error. By the use of this faculty alone, he can establish the most important doctrines of religion. To be sure, natural religion may have to be supplemented with a special revelation of God's will. But even then, reason is entitled to examine the evidences of any revelation, such as the Christian revelation, which purports to come from God. The combination of natural religion and the Christian revelation may be termed " supernatural rationalism." It must be distinguished from " Deism," which declared that revelation was a needless addition to pure natural religion.

Supernatural rationalism was not an invention of the Massachusetts Arminians. It made its appearance in New England long before there was anyone who could be fairly called an Arminian. John Wise gave the essentials of it in 1717 in two propositions. The first of them was that " reason is congenate with [man's] nature, wherein by a law immutable, enstampt upon his frame, God has provided a rule

for men in all their actions "; and the other was that " revelation is nature's law in a fairer and brighter edition." [1]
The rudiments of a faith in reason may be found even earlier,
in the seventeenth-century Puritans, who never fell back on
a blind reliance on the Bible and a complete distrust of reason. To be sure, they argued that the fall of Adam caused
great confusion in the mind of man, so that a revelation from
God was essential if men were to know what was required of
them. But even after the fall, vestiges of man's original
powers remained, and the Puritans often spoke of conscience
as a guide to right and wrong apart from revelation, and of
man as a rational creature. Departing from Calvin in this
respect, as in many others, the Puritans who settled New
England seemed determined to salvage as much as possible
from the ruins of man's intellectual powers.[2]

A second and doubtless more important source of the rationalism of the New England Arminians was the English
supernatural rationalism stemming from the physics of Newton and the psychology of Locke. Its classic statement was
in Tillotson's sermons, in Locke's *Essay* and especially his
Reasonableness of Christianity, and in Samuel Clarke's two
volumes of Boyle Lectures. The Arminians found it also in
the dissenters, such as Nathaniel Lardner, with whom they
were in touch. Locke's *Essay,* surprisingly enough, was not
prescribed at Harvard until 1743,[3] but Jonathan Edwards
had read it as a youth, and it is hard to believe that it was
not familiar to Harvard students as well. To be sure, when
George Whitefield complained that Tillotson and Clarke
were read at Harvard " instead of *Sheppard, Stoddard,* and

---

[1] John Wise, *A Vindication of the Government of New England Churches,*
(4th ed., Boston, 1860), pp. 28, 30.
[2] Perry Miller, *The New England Mind* (New York, 1939), pp. 183–188.
[3] Benjamin Rand, " Philosophical Instruction in Harvard University from
1636 to 1900," *Harvard Graduates Magazine,* XXXVII (1928), p. 36.

such like evangelical Writers," [4] Dr. Wigglesworth pointed out that Tillotson had not been taken from the library for nine years, and Clarke not for two.[5] But whatever may have been true before the Awakening, these men were read after it. Mayhew quoted from the *Essay* in 1749, when he was concerned to vindicate the certainty and sufficiency of human knowledge; [6] and Chauncy called him "the great Mr. Locke." [7] When engaged in theological studies about 1746, Mayhew compiled a book of extracts, which contained selections from both Locke and Clarke.[8] He praised Clarke in 1747 as an "admirable writer." [9] And Chauncy quoted Clarke at length in the *Benevolence of the Deity*.[10]

If supernatural rationalism was not original with the Arminians, neither was it peculiar to them. In the year 1751, Chief Justice Paul Dudley died in Roxbury, leaving to Harvard College a fund for the establishment of an annual lecture. Two of the prescribed topics were natural religion and revealed religion. Both Calvinists and Arminians were invited to preach on this foundation. To be sure, the Calvinists who delivered Dudleian lectures were moderate or Old Calvinists rather than Hopkinsians or Separatists; they were men like President Holyoke, Professor Wigglesworth, Peter Clark of Danvers, and Andrew Eliot of Boston. These men were all from eastern Massachusetts; but, equally important, they had all been opposers of the revivalists in

[4] George Whitefield, *A Continuation of the Reverend Mr. Whitefield's Journal . . . The Seventh Journal* (London, 1741), p. 29.

[5] Edward Wigglesworth, *A Letter to the Reverend Mr. George Whitefield* (Boston, 1745), p. 31.

[6] Jonathan Mayhew, *Seven Sermons* (Boston, 1749; reprinted London, 1750), pp. 37, 38.

[7] Charles Chauncy, *Five Dissertations on the Scripture Account of the Fall* (London, 1785), p. 139; see also pp. 106, 148, 250, 254.

[8] Alden Bradford, *Memoir of the Life and Writings of Rev. Jonathan Mayhew, D.D.* (Boston, 1838), p. 21.

[9] Mayhew, *Seven Sermons*, p. 14.

[10] Charles Chauncy, *The Benevolence of the Deity* (Boston, 1784), p. iv.

the Great Awakening. To prevent emotionalism and reliance on impulses from stampeding the people into enthusiasm, they had demanded that all private revelations be tested by Scripture and reason. Both moderates and Arminians had been led by their experience in the Awakening to stress the use of reason in religion. Rationalism was not confined to the Arminians, but it was no less typical of them than were the doctrines of grace which distinguished them from the Calvinists.[11]

II

" It is by our reason that we are exalted above the beasts of the field," Jonathan Mayhew told his congregation. " It is by this that we are allied to angels, and all the glorious intelligences of the heavenly world: yea, by this we resemble God himself." [12] However weakened reason may at times be, and inadequate to search out all God's perfections, it is not corrupt. So far as it goes, man may rely on it. Rational powers, furthermore, have been given to all men. There is no doctrine of election which makes the reason of any man corrupt while that of his neighbor is not. There is a doctrine of diversity of gifts: " The whole creation is diversified, and men in particular. There is a great variety in their intellectual faculties." [13] And there is a doctrine of education: " Our intellectual faculties were given us to improve: they rust for want of use; but are brightened by exercise." [14] But when every qualification is made, it still remains true that all men possess the power of reason, and a sufficient capacity to establish the essential truths of religion.

The psychology which the Arminians took for granted was

[11] The treatment of supernatural rationalism in this chapter is based on writings of both Arminians and Old Calvinists.
[12] Mayhew, *Seven Sermons*, pp. 39, 40.
[13] *Ibid.*, p. 30.
[14] *Ibid.*, p. 31.

that of John Locke. It denied innate ideas, and declared that all knowledge comes through sensation and reflection. " I am not convinced," said Chauncy, " that we have any ideas, but what take rise from *sensation* and *reflection,* or that we can have any, upon the present establishment of nature, any other way." [15] The mind has certain other powers, like memory, the ability to distinguish between ideas and to rearrange them, and abstraction. But these powers operate on ideas which come ultimately from sensation. This Lockian psychology was stated clearly by Gad Hitchcock in 1779:

The opinion of innate ideas and principles, which prevailed for so long a time, is now, almost, universally given up; and that of the human mind receiving them afterwards distinct and simple; comparing, compounding and disposing of them, together with the perception of those operations, is adopted in its room, as the original of knowledge.[16]

Since all knowledge comes through the senses, a child is born with mere " naked capacities," unable to discern between his right hand and his left. By use, these faculties may be enlarged: " it is by time, exercise, observation, instruction, and, in short, a due use of the advantages we are favoured with, that we ' gradually ' rise to those attainments our capacities were planted in our nature that we might acquire." [17] This line of argument, which is thoroughly typical of the Arminians, looks forward to the nineteenth century. In place of a static view of man's intellectual abilities, moral attainments, and position in the sight of God, they were substituting a concept of growth and development. The characteristic emphasis of the Unitarians was beginning to appear: man's natural capacity for infinite enlargement of

[15] Chauncy, *Benevolence of the Deity,* p. 99n.
[16] Gad Hitchcock, *Natural Religion Aided by Revelation and Perfected in Christianity* (Boston, 1779), p. 20.
[17] Chauncy, *Five Dissertations,* pp. 33, 34.

the personality and growth of character. " It is in consequence of this progressive capacity," Chauncy declared, in
words that Channing might have used, " that we suppose . . . that all intelligent moral beings, in all worlds,
are continually going on, while they suitably employ and
improve their original faculties, from one degree of attainment to another; and, hereupon, from one degree of happiness to another, without end." [18]

All men do not have equal intelligence, and there are
many problems to which the wisest of men cannot give an
answer. Yet the human mind can be relied on to establish
the basic truths of religion, even if it cannot solve all the
abstruse paradoxes of the metaphysicians. The result is
natural religion, which President Holyoke defined as " that
regard to a Divine Being or God which Men arrive at, by
mere Principles of natural Reason, as it is improveable, by
tho't, consideration & Experience, without the help of Revelation." [19] The essentials of natural religion are three: the
existence of God, the obligations of piety and benevolence,
and a future state of rewards and punishments.

There were two ways, apart from revelation, of proving
the existence of God. One of these was the *a priori* proof,
which Samuel Clarke developed in his Boyle Lectures in
1704. It took the form of a series of propositions: that something has existed from eternity; that there has existed from
eternity some one immutable and independent being; and
that this being must be self-existent. From these initial, self-
evident propositions, he deduced that God is eternal, infinite,
omnipresent, one, free, intelligent, wise, infinitely good, just,
and truthful. This geometrical form of proof of the deity

[18] *Ibid.*, p. 33.
[19] Edward Holyoke, " The First Sermon for the Dudleian Lecture "
(1755), p. 3. Ms, Harvard University Archives. Holyoke was a moderate
Calvinist.

was known in New England, but was not widely adopted. The reason does not seem to be that there was any distrust of the soundness of Clarke's method, but that other arguments were more persuasive. One Dudleian lecturer, the Old Calvinist Andrew Eliot, commented that the *a priori* proof was all right for Dr. Clarke, but most people were simply confused by it. For common understandings, the *a posteriori* proofs were better.[20]

The *a posteriori* proof, or argument from design, saw in the universe the evident marks of a First Cause, and deduced from the nature of that universe the character or attributes of its creator. The light of natural reason, declared Ebenezer Gay,

exercised in the Contemplation of the universal Frame of Nature, or of any Parts thereof; and in the Observation of the general Course of Providence, or of particular Events therein, may convince Men of the Existence and Attributes of God, the alwise powerful and good Maker, Upholder, and Governor of all Things.[21]

This universal frame of nature which declared the glory of God to Ebenezer Gay was a Newtonian universe. In other words, those aspects of the universe which seemed most clearly to reveal its divine origin were its order and harmony. Instead of the unpredictable universe in which Calvin had lived, which taught him the inscrutability of divine providence, Newton offered to theologians a world of law and order, an intricate machine in which every motion was predictable and rational. The kind of God who could produce this kind of universe, argued Mayhew, was necessarily one who combined infinite power with infinite skill and intelligence:

[20] Andrew Eliot, *A Discourse on Natural Religion* (Boston, 1771), p. 7.
[21] Ebenezer Gay, *Natural Religion, as Distinguish'd from Revealed* (Boston, 1759), p. 8.

I hardly need desire you, by way of antidote against the poison [of scepticism] . . . to lift your eyes to the heavens above; to observe the stupendous magnitude, the regular motions, the beautiful order, of the numerous worlds that roll there; or to ask you, how they came there? and by whom they are preserved from age to age in this wonderful order and harmony? . . . It will be sufficient if you consider those microcosms, those little worlds, your own bodies; which are indeed " fearfully and wonderfully made "; — with amazing skill, an art truly admirable and astonishing to every attentive observer. And whose hand formed and fashioned these? Certainly no human one. . . .[22]

The second tenet of natural religion was that reason, without the aid of revelation, can establish the obligations which rest on men, of piety towards their Creator and benevolence towards their fellow-men. For the eighteenth century, this was an intensely important proposition. Morality was losing its former theological sanctions, as the old concept of God as ruler and judge faded behind a system of natural law. What support for morality remained, when many men no longer felt keenly the sense of God speaking to them in a special revelation of his will? If men rejected the Bible, would society crumble, or could some other foundation for ethics be found? Considerations such as these help to explain the preoccupation with ethical theory so characteristic of the Age of Reason, which made religion seem at times little more than an adjunct to ethics.[23]

In their ethical theory, the New England liberals were very eclectic, borrowing at times from every one of the well-known British moralists. Sometimes they argued, after the fashion of Locke and Clarke, that the difference between right and wrong is inherent in the nature of things, and so

---

[22] Jonathan Mayhew, *Christian Sobriety* (Boston, 1763), p. 54.
[23] Leslie Stephen, *History of English Thought in the Eighteenth Century*, 2 vols. (New York, 1876), II, pp. 1–3.

may be deduced by the reason from a knowledge of the relationships necessarily existing between God and his creation. This position is to be contrasted with the supposition that morality depends on the revealed will of an inscrutable God. Mayhew traced out this argument in detail in the first two of his *Seven Sermons* (1748). Let us suppose, he said, that there is a God, who created and governs the world with wisdom and goodness. This being, by the nature of the case, is deserving of our esteem and gratitude: " To treat him with contempt, or disregard, is to treat him as being what he *is not;* which certainly cannot be *right.* *Piety,* therefore, is what we are under obligation to, upon supposition there is any such being as this, existing." Again, if there is such a being, he is perfect in moral excellence. Therefore we are under obligation to imitate him " according to the condition and capacity of our natures, without the consideration of his enjoining it upon us by any express and positive law." [24] To practice moral virtue is our obligation apart from hope of reward or fear of punishment. It may at times be difficult to draw the line between right and wrong, but that is no argument that the distinction does not exist. At this point in the sermon, Mayhew revealed one of the chief influences on his thinking by quoting directly from Samuel Clarke.[25]

Without being quite so explicit as to his sources, Ebenezer Gay presented the same kind of theory in his Dudleian Lecture in 1759. There is an " essential Difference between Good and Evil, Right and Wrong," which the understanding cannot help seeing. This distinction " is founded in the Natures and Relations of Things "; it expresses the will of God as revealed " by his apparently wise and good Constitution of Things, in their respective Natures and Relations."

[24] Mayhew, *Seven Sermons,* p. 12.   [25] *Ibid.,* p. 14.

God publishes it to rational creatures "in making them capable to learn from his Works, what is good, and what is required of them."[26]

If sometimes the Arminians argued that it is by the use of reason that men may know the distinction between right and wrong, at other times they attributed to men a "moral sense" which gives them such guidance. An ethical theory of this kind was in the tradition of Shaftesbury and Hutcheson, who declared that men approve the good and abhor evil, not because the good is accompanied by reward, but because the good is naturally agreeable to them. To be sure, Mayhew distrusted Shaftesbury, whom he regarded as one of "these nominal *Theists*" who were "really *Atheists* at the bottom."[27] But Charles Chauncy, Simeon Howard, and John Adams all read Hutcheson;[28] and for a time in mid-century he was prescribed at Harvard.[29] At a much later date, he deeply influenced William Ellery Channing. If Mayhew did not specifically acknowledge indebtedness to Hutcheson, he clearly did not escape his influence:

Our Creator, besides endowing us with reason to distinguish betwixt moral good and evil, has moreover given us another faculty, which is sometimes called a *moral sense*. . . . By virtue of this faculty, moral good and evil, when they are objects to our minds, affect us in a very different manner; the first affording us pleasure, the other pain and uneasiness: And this, as unavoidably as the eye is differently affected with regular and irregular figures in body; or the ear, with the most grateful harmony, and the most harsh and grating discord. . . .[30]

[26] Gay, *Natural Religion*, pp. 10–11.
[27] Jonathan Mayhew, *Sermons* (Boston, 1755), p. 263.
[28] Chauncy, *Benevolence of the Deity*, p. 207n; Simeon Howard, *A Sermon Preached to the Ancient and Honorable Artillery-Company* (Boston, 1773), p. 11; John Adams, *The Works of John Adams*, Charles Francis Adams, ed. (Boston, 1850), II, p. 4.
[29] Rand, "Philosophical Instruction," *Harvard Graduates Magazine*, XXXVII, p. 37.
[30] Mayhew, *Seven Sermons*, pp. 99–100.

Another source of moral theory for the Arminians was Bishop Butler, who argued that all men have consciences, which mediate between their natural impulses towards benevolence on the one hand and self-love on the other. Mayhew quoted from him several times in his *Seven Sermons,* and called him, like Clarke, " an admirable writer." [31] On a later occasion, he referred to him as " a great ornament of the episcopal order, and of the church of England; the clearness of whose head, the precision of whose language, and the goodness of whose heart, are so conspicuous in all his writings." [32] Thomas Barnard regarded him as " one of the greatest Divines, and truest Thinkers of the present Age." [33]

When men could draw widely from a variety of types of moral theory, as the Arminians did, it is obvious that what really mattered to them was that which was common to the various systems. They found in all the British moralists the assertion that every man, without distinction between elect and non-elect, regenerate and unregenerate, possesses by nature powers enabling him to distinguish between right and wrong. When Jonathan Edwards read Hutcheson, he was led to develop Hutcheson's moral sense into that sense which apprehends holiness which is bestowed by the Holy Spirit on the regenerate soul.[34] But the Arminians found in Hutcheson an assertion of the natural capacity of all men for holiness; it is, said Chauncy, " common to all; as being a power the whole human race come into the world endowed with." [35]

---

[31] Mayhew, *Seven Sermons,* p. 107; see also pp. 105, 125, 126.

[32] Jonathan Mayhew, *Observations on the Charter and Conduct of the Society for the Propagation of the Gospel in Foreign Parts* (Boston, 1763), p. 32.

[33] Thomas Barnard, *A Sermon Preached to the Ancient and Honourable Artillery Company* (Boston, 1758), p. 19.

[34] Clarence H. Faust and Thomas H. Johnson, *Jonathan Edwards* (New York, c. 1935), pp. lxxv–xciii.

[35] Chauncy, *Benevolence of the Deity,* p. 127.

The third doctrine of natural religion was the existence of a future state of rewards and punishments. Generally speaking, the expounders of natural religion acknowledged that it was much more difficult to prove the doctrine of immortality without the assistance of revelation, than to prove the existence of God or the obligations of morality. Jonathan Mayhew, indeed, placed his sole reliance on the Bible: " Mere reason, or the light of nature, suggests no arguments for a happy immortality, which are conclusive and satisfactory, so that we can rest upon them." [36]   Charles Chauncy was willing to show, after the fashion of Bishop Butler, that there are no rational objections to the doctrine, but that was as far as he would dare venture.[37]   The New England rationalists were not even persuaded by the argument that rewards are unfairly allocated in this life and the wicked sometimes go unpunished; hence there must be a future state in which all accounts will be balanced. Thomas Barnard was familiar with this line of reasoning, but he said, " there are so many circumstances to be attended to, before that inequality is proved, that this kind of evidence is not easily or generally seen in a clear and strong light." [38]   On the rational proofs for the doctrine of immortality, then, the New England liberals were much less confident than such English philosophers as Clarke.

III

In this discussion of natural religion, the position of the Arminians was similar to that of the deists. Both had confidence in the power of reason to establish the main points of

[36] Mayhew, *Sermons* (1755), p. 437.
[37] Charles Chauncy, *The Blessedness of the Dead who Die in the Lord* (Boston, 1749), p. 12.
[38] Thomas Barnard, *The Power of God, the Proof of Christianity* (Salem, 1768), pp. 11–12.

religious belief and obligation. But to describe the Arminians as " respectable Deists " [39] and their rationalism as virtually Deism [40] is to indulge in terminology that can only lead to confusion. The essential fact about the Arminians is that they were not merely rationalists; they were supernatural rationalists. They believed in the soundness of natural religion, but they also admitted the claims of revealed religion and the Christian revelation. The abhorrence they felt for infidelity was fully as great as that which they felt for high Calvinism. They believed that their position was a strong barrier against infidelity. Since it has become known that Calvinism is no part of revelation, Samuel Webster explained, " and Ministers have more generally got into a more *solid* and *rational* Way of *Preaching,* some Stop has been put to *Deism* in the Nation." [41]

In their reading, the Arminians encountered both Christian rationalists and deists. They greeted the former with satisfaction and the latter with undisguised disfavor. In 1755, John Adams was trying to decide whether he wanted to enter the ministry, and was busy transcribing passages from Morgan and Bolingbroke. Of the latter he said: " His religion is a pompous folly; and his abuse of the Christian religion is as superficial as it is impious." [42] In writing privately of Voltaire's *Philosophy of History* and *Philosophical Dictionary,* Mayhew balanced blame and praise. " I cannot agree with him in some of his notions relative to Religion," he wrote to Thomas Hollis, " or rather in what appears to be a great part of his Design, viz, the intire subversion of *Revelation;* yet I cannot but think these, as Compositions, to be

[39] G. Adolf Koch, *Republican Religion* (New York, 1933), Ch. 7.

[40] Woodbridge Riley, *American Philosophy: the Early Schools* (New York, 1907), Bk. III, Chs. 1, 2.

[41] [Samuel Webster], *The Winter Evening Conversation Vindicated* (Boston, 1758), p. 114.

[42] Adams, *Works,* I, pp. 43, 44.

very fine Performances." [43]   Mayhew did not recommend
Voltaire to the young men of his church, however.   Instead
he urged them to read Leland's *Review of the Deistical
Writers*,[44] and he emphasized the gulf between Christian rationalists and deists:

Beware of irreligious, deistical books and men; lest you should be deluded by them to your ruin. . . . What profound geniuses? what
enlightened, clarified and sublime souls must these sages have, who
have so clearly detected the imposture, or the folly and gross ignorance of Moses, Solomon and the prophets; of JESUS CHRIST and his
apostles; of all our Boyles, Lockes, Clarkes, Newtons, Butlers, Hoad-
leys, Chandlers, Sherlocks, &c. &c? . . . And how benevolent,
magnanimous and glorious their attempts to undeceive mankind, and
to deliver the world from the errors, the superstitions, and monstrous
notions about religion, taught by such persons! — What an ample
field was here for the heroic exploits, and imaginary triumphs of
vanity in a Collins, a Woolston and a Tindal; in a Shaftesbury and a
Morgan, a Chub and a Bolinbroke? [45]

Mayhew's successor, Simeon Howard, made the same contrast.   He listed a galaxy of believers of the Christian revelation: Clarke, Butler, Chandler, Leland, Lardner, Benson,
Boyle, Locke, Newton, Addison, and Littleton.   Then he
declared triumphantly:

Infidelity has no names to boast of among its advocates, to be com-
pared with these, for learning, penetration, just reasoning and integrity of heart: And if you will be implicit believers, they are as
worthy to be confided in, as any uninspired men that ever lived in the
world; — much more so than a Shaftsbury or a Woolston, a Tindal
or a Collins, a Morgan or a Bolinbroke; or even than the accute and
subtle Hume, or that universal apostle of infidelity, the gay and
sprightly Voltaire.[46]

   [43] Mayhew to Thomas Hollis, Jan. 7, 1766.   Ms, Massachusetts Historical Society.
   [44] Mayhew, *Christian Sobriety*, p. 71n.
   [45] *Ibid.*, pp. 325, 326.
   [46] Simeon Howard, *Christians No Cause to be Ashamed of Their Religion*
(Boston, 1779), pp. 26, 27, 32–33.

It was deistical writers rather than native deists whom the Arminians feared. Certainly, before the Revolution, deists were almost non-existent in New England. John Adams claimed to have encountered a few in Worcester in 1755, where Morgan's *Moral Philosopher* had been circulated, and " the principles of deism had made a considerable progress among several persons, in that and other towns in the county." He drank tea with one man who declared that " the apostles were a company of enthusiasts," and that " we have only their word to prove that they spoke with different tongues, raised the dead, and healed the sick, &c." [47] But such men were not common. New Englanders might accept the tenets of natural religion, but they almost always complemented them with the Christian revelation.

IV

There are, said the great Mr. Locke, three kinds of propositions: those that are according to reason, those that are above reason, and those that are contrary to reason. A revelation may communicate facts or divine commands which are above reason, but it cannot contain anything contrary to reason. " The manifest Absurdity of any Doctrine, is a stronger Argument that it is not of God, than any other Evidence can be that it is." [48] And so, when the supernatural rationalist declared that a revelation is a desirable or essential addition to natural religion, the first thing he stressed was the harmony between the two. To be sure, there are doctrines held by enthusiasts and high Calvinists which can never be reconciled with reason; but that means that they are human additions to Scripture, and no true revelation. We should not suppose that we can advance the cause of revealed religion by depre-

---

[47] Adams, *Works*, I, p. 43; II, p. 13.   [48] Gay, *Natural Religion*, p. 22.

ciating natural religion, said Ebenezer Gay. There is no contradiction between them: " They exist harmoniously together, and mutually strengthen and confirm each other. Revealed Religion is an *Additional* to Natural; built not on the Ruins, but on the strong and everlasting Foundations of it." [49] The very existence of God must be proved by reason, so the argument ran, before men will be ready to believe that he has provided them with a revelation; and only by use of the reason can they know the meaning of a given revelation.

Natural and revealed religion are so inseparable that the existence of unadulterated natural religion is a myth. As Ebenezer Gay remarked, the gospel of Christ has been " *a Light to lighten the* modern deistical *Gentiles*," who hold juster notions of the divine attributes and moral duties than did the ancients because they have drawn from that Christian revelation which they decry.[50] It is because of the improvements that later ages have made in general science and literature, said Gad Hitchcock, that the deists know more than their forerunners among the ancient philosophers. " But this is chiefly to be attributed to the advantage of the christian revelation, which has been a rich blessing, even to those who do not believe in it." [51]

The whole question of the advantage of a divine revelation could be brought to a focus on the first man, Adam. As good sensational psychologists, the supernatural rationalists denied that he was created with any innate ideas. All his knowledge was acquired in the same way that we acquire ours, through sensation and reflection. Granted that Adam's intellectual powers were unweakened by sin, it still would have taken a long time for him to discover the ordinary techniques of living, let alone engage in deductions about the attributes of the

---

[49] *Ibid.*, pp. 19–20.   [51] Hitchcock, *Natural Religion*, p. 30.
[50] *Ibid.*, p. 30.

deity. Gay reached the conclusion, therefore, that Adam had always had the benefit of revelation:

Had Man, with all his natural Endowments in their perfect Order and Strength, been placed in this World, and no Notice given him of it's Maker, might he not have stood wondring some Time at the amazing Fabrick, before he would have thence, by Deductions of Reason, argued an invisible Being, of eternal Power, Wisdom and Goodness, to be the Author of it and him; to whom he was therefore obliged to pay all Regards suitable to such glorious Excellencies? Would he so soon and easily have made those Discoveries, which are necessary to the Perfection of natural Religion . . . ? [52]

But why, one might ask, is there now any need of special revelation? Why is not the continual revelation of God's power and attributes in the universal frame of nature sufficient? The answer was that while a revelation is not absolutely necessary, it is extremely desirable because of men's failure to make full use of their rational powers. The confidence of the supernatural rationalists in reason was not unlimited. They granted its theoretical ability, but saw only too well how men could misuse it. Standing as they did midway between the deists and the " enthusiasts," the color of their argument depended on who was, for the moment, their opponent. Against the former they stressed the failures of unassisted reason and the importance of revelation; against the latter, they urged in glowing terms the powers of reason and the sufficiency of natural religion. Samuel Clarke and John Locke had set the fashion that was followed in New England. " There was plainly wanting a *Divine Revelation*," Clarke said, " to recover Mankind out of their universal corruption and degeneracy; and without such a Revelation, it was not possible that the World should ever be effectually reformed." [53] In New England, Thomas Barnard

---

[52] Gay, *Natural Religion*, p. 24.
[53] Samuel Clarke, *A Discourse Concerning the Unchangeable Obligations of Natural Religion* (5th ed., London, 1719), p. 198.

declared simply that " every Rule of right Conduct is better explained than unassisted Nature can do it, and pressed on Men with infinitely superior Motives than mere Reason offers." [54]

v

But it was not enough for the supernatural rationalists to prove the theoretical possibility and the practical desirability of a revelation. They also had to establish that Christianity was a true revelation, and that the Bible was really the word of God. For Calvin and the Puritans, of course, this had been no problem. The witness of the Holy Spirit in the hearts of true believers was sufficient to fix the authority of Scripture. This would never do for disciples of Locke; rationalists wanted evidence, not enthusiasm. To lead a truly Christian life of course meant something more than to give intellectual assent to revealed truths. But Christianity was first and foremost a system of propositions, either susceptible of rational proof, or accepted because its author was demonstrably a divinely inspired messenger. Or to use the traditional terminology, belief in Christianity was made to rest on an examination of both its internal and external evidences.

The first step was to show that the Bible contains nothing contrary to reason. A revelation may not only republish the Law of Nature, but also require certain positive duties, such as rites and ceremonies. It is no argument against revelation that unassisted reason cannot discern the ground for positive acts required by God. The only requirements are that the positive duties be not arbitrary, and that they commend themselves to reason; and these tests are met by the Jewish and Christian ceremonials. Is there anything irrational in the rites of Baptism and the Supper? For Simeon Howard, these sacraments were no more irrational than the initiation

[54] Thomas Barnard, *The Christian Salvation* (Boston, 1757), p. 19.

ceremonies of human organizations; and if there was any incongruity in judging the Christian church by the standard of what is appropriate for a fraternal society of Boston merchants, Howard showed no awareness of it: " Is it not proper that persons should in a public, formal manner be initiated into the society of christians; and, that after they are members, they should by some significant rite distinguishing them from other persons, commemorate the love and goodness of their *founder?* " [55] And though the mediatorial scheme of salvation is above reason, does it not bear an analogy with what we know of God's method of acting? He generally makes use of means in the distribution of his favors, restoring health by means of the physician, feeding the poor by the liberality of the rich, and instructing the ignorant by means of the learned. This interpretation of the mediatorial work of Christ was doubtless persuasive to the members of the West Church, who did not have to be told who the rich and the learned were.

Some Arminians regarded such internal evidences as sufficient. Dr. Howard was among them: " The superior, the unrivaled excellency of the institution, the sublimity, the perfection and consistency of its doctrines; the reasonableness, the extent, and unmixed purity of its precepts are, in my apprehension, sufficient to prove its divine original, to an honest candid mind, without any external arguments." [56] Doubtless many of his colleagues would have agreed with him. In England, however, discussion of the external evidences was necessary to confute some deists of a lower type, who insinuated that the Scriptures were only " a cunningly devised fable." If there were few such deists in Massachusetts, the Christian rationalist nevertheless took his cue from the books he was reading, and argued almost as vigorously

[55] Howard, *Christians No Cause*, p. 17.   [56] *Ibid.*, p. 20.

as though infidelity had already taken possession of Harvard College. Without the slightest sense of irreverence, he called on Christ and the Apostles to produce their credentials, prove their sincerity, establish their reputation for veracity, show that they were not impostors, and convince the world at large that they were fit to associate with respectable people. " When the Almighty *mediately* uses instruments, like ourselves, to convey his light and truth to us, they must be able to give convincing evidence, that they received their message from God, and were ordered by him to publish them." [57]

The chief external proofs of Christianity were that Christ fulfilled prophecies and worked miracles; that the record of his ministry was set down by reliable witnesses; and that the remarkable spread of Christianity, despite its humble beginnings, bears witness to its divine origin. John Barnard, the second Dudleian lecturer, dealt most fully with the fulfillment of prophecies. By examination of the Old Testament, he showed " that there was a certain Person, stiled the MESSIAH " who was spoken of " as one to be sent from GOD " for our salvation. He demonstrated further by examination of the New Testament that " this promised MESSIAH has long since made his Appearance in our World." Then by comparing the prophecies with the life of Christ, he reached the triumphant conclusion that " All those *Characteristicks*, by which the MESSIAH was to be distinguished from every other Person, do exactly agree in our Lord JESUS CHRIST, and in no other Person whatever." [58]

That extraordinary gifts of the Holy Spirit and the power to work miracles attest the truth of revelation, was a

---

[57] Barnard, *Power of God*, p. 14.
[58] John Barnard, *A Proof of Jesus Christ His Being the Ancient Promised Messiah* (Boston, 1756), pp. 9, 27. Barnard was a moderate Calvinist.

familiar doctrine in New England long before the Dudleian lectures. At the time of the Awakening, Chauncy had written: " It was necessary the Christian Revelation should be *approved of GOD, by Signs, and Wonders, and Miracles, done in the midst of the People.*" Since he was trying to discourage speaking with tongues by the revivalists, he hastily added: " there is no Need of the like *extraordinary* Influence of the DIVINE SPIRIT, *now* that Christianity has received its Confirmation and been establisht, in the World, as a Religion coming from GOD." [59] A decade later, Mayhew pointed to the resurrection of Christ as " the great argument, by which the truth of the gospel is established." [60] John Adams remarked in his diary that heathen peoples, sunk in gross opinions and practices, " could not be made to embrace the true religion till their attention was roused by some astonishing and miraculous appearances." The reasoning of philosophers alone could not overcome superstition. " But when wise and virtuous men, commissioned from heaven, by miracles awakened men's attention to their reasonings, the force of the truth made its way with ease to their minds." [61] And Thomas Barnard said miracles are " the capital proof in the case." [62]

David Hume had indeed attempted to prove that even if miracles had occurred, they would be worthless as a support for revelation. The chances for mistake or fraud on the part of witnesses were so great that their testimony is not acceptable. His objections were noted in New England, but given scant consideration. Thomas Barnard, who called him " a subtle enemy of our faith," pointed out that the miracles of

[59] Charles Chauncy, *Ministers Cautioned Against the Occasions of Contempt* (Boston, 1744), p. 16.
[60] Mayhew, *Sermons* (1755), p. 160.
[61] Adams, *Works*, II, p. 8.
[62] Barnard, *Power of God*, p. 22.

Christ were many in number, were clearly beyond human power, and were performed before numerous spectators. To complete them, he rose from the dead, in accordance with his own prediction. Considering the opposition to Christianity, its spread " must have been an infinitely greater miracle than any on which it professed to be founded; and therefore, according to the doctrine of Mr. *Hume,* the reality of these miracles must be assuredly believed." [63] Benjamin Stevens quoted at length from Hume's essay, enumerating the various items that are necessary to establish the authenticity of miracles: the number and education of the witnesses, their integrity, a reputation which they would be careful to protect, the necessity for having the miracles performed in such a public manner that delusion would be impossible. Stevens admitted that the apostles were not men of learning, but they made up with good sense their lack of a Harvard A.B. In other respects, he insisted, their testimony was adequate even according to Hume's standards. [64]

But the limits of scepticism had not been reached. Perhaps Jesus Christ never existed, and the whole record of his ministry was an elaborate forgery. Perhaps the apostles had invented the story with a desire for power; perhaps they or later Christians conspired to corrupt the sacred history for their own advantage. Such doubts had been raised, if covertly, by English deists, and had inspired Nathaniel Lardner's many volumes of the *Credibility of the Gospel History.* Mayhew read the early volumes of the series, more than once. [65] But of the Dudleian lecturers, it was David Barnes who gave the fullest summary of Lardner's researches. In-

---

[63] *Ibid.,* p. 20.

[64] Benjamin Stevens, " Mr. Stevens's Sermon at the Annual Dudleian Lecture, May 13th, 1772." Ms, Harvard University Archives. Stevens was a moderate Calvinist.

[65] Bradford, *Mayhew,* p. 98.

dependent historians agree that Jesus Christ actually lived and was crucified, and that soon afterwards a new sect called Christians made its appearance. These are " facts as well authenticated as any in history." [66] The story of the life of Christ, found in the gospels, was written soon after the events which it records, " by persons who enjoyed peculiar advantages for ascertaining the truth of the facts which they relate." [67] The early date of the gospels appears from several considerations. Other ecclesiastical writers in the first and second centuries quote them or mention them, " as every one may see if he has not time to consult the originals, by looking into Dr. Lardner's credibility of the gospel history, — A writer of great learning and of an approved character." [68] Even enemies of the gospel in early times bear witness to the fact, since some of their objections were evidently based on passages taken from the New Testament. Furthermore, some of the writers claimed to be eyewitnesses, a claim which would have been exploded then had it been false. Their manner of writing shows they were well acquainted " with the customs usages & manners of the augustan age." [69] The writers were reliable witnesses, being neither enthusiasts nor impostors: " Their writings do not appear to be the effects of a disordered brain, nor do carry with them any marks of forgery and deceit." [70] They did not address themselves to the passions of their hearers, as it is customary for enthusiasts to do. They conducted themselves " with openness and candor, and were wholly free from those little mean arts, shiftings and inconsistencies which mark the conduct of im-

[66] David Barnes, " Revealed Religion," Dudleian Lecture (1780), p. 7. Ms, Harvard University Archives.
[67] *Ibid.*, p. 8.
[68] *Ibid.*, p. 9.
[69] *Ibid.*, p. 12.
[70] *Ibid.*, p. 13.

postors." [71]   They were free from self-seeking, and bore themselves with dignity even amid severe trials. The miracles which attested their preaching were not performed in the dark, as one would expect of impostors, but in the open, in the presence of multitudes. The gospel was first preached by " illiterate men, bro't up in obscurity, ignorant of the charms of eloquence and of the force of oratory, nor did they pretend to captivate the heart or engage the attention by harmonious sounds and well turned periods." [72]   Yet despite these handicaps, and the opposition of powerful enemies, the gospel spread and prospered.[73]   Finally, Barnes insisted, the evidence from prophecy is now more conclusive than ever, since the predictions of Christ, especially as to the destruction of Jerusalem, have been fulfilled.

VI

It is hard to find any novelty in discussions by American supernatural rationalists of the evidences of Christianity. Their position was almost wholly derivative. Hence their argument is less interesting for its details than for the assumptions on which it rests.

It was the psychology of John Locke which gave these questions the special urgency they had for the Arminians. Admittedly, the proposition that Christ's mission was attested by miracles long antedates the eighteenth century; one version of it may be found in St. Thomas. But it had never been the sole proof of the truth of the Christian revelation. The real reliance of the Puritan had been on the inner conviction which forced itself on him when he read the Bible,

[71] *Ibid.,* p. 15.
[72] *Ibid.,* p. 22.
[73] This remarkable spread of Christianity, despite its many enemies, was the topic of Hull Abbot's " Sermon at the Dudleian Lecture at Harvard College in Cambridge August 29, 1764. P.M." Ms, Harvard University Archives.

that this was truly the voice of God speaking. But Locke shifted the whole issue of Christian faith, from inner conviction to external testimony. " Faith " for the Puritan had meant an experience in which the whole inner being of a man was poured forth in trust in God and submission to his will. " Faith " for James Dana was " an assent of the mind to any truth or matter of fact, upon *testimony;* in other words, 'tis admitting for truth what *another* declares to us, from a confidence in his veracity." If it is a man who testifies, then our faith is human faith; if it is Christ or his apostles whose word we are willing to accept, the result is Christian faith. " In every view faith depends on testimony." [74]

The supernatural rationalists stressed the miracles, because this was the point which distinguished them from the deists. In terms of bare logic, supernatural rationalist and deist had much in common, just as today, the Marxian Socialist and the Communist have much in common intellectually. But the emotional and social gulf between the two was enormous, and miracles were the symbol of it. The result was that the Arminians and later the Unitarians became so emotionally involved in belief in miracles that they found it hard to outgrow it. In 1821, William Ellery Channing was still taking his stand on the proposition that " Christianity is not only confirmed by miracles, but is in itself, in its very essence, a miraculous religion." [75]

Little wonder, then, that a shudder passed over the older members of the congregation when, on a warm evening in July of 1838, a slender young man stood before the graduating class of the Harvard Divinity School, and quietly dismissed what had long been the foundation of Christian faith,

[74] James Dana, *Two Discourses Delivered at Cambridge, May 10, 1767* (Boston, 1767), p. 10.
[75] William Ellery Channing, *The Works of William E. Channing, D.D.* (One vol. ed., Boston, 1889), p. 221.

the last bulwark against infidelity, and the main reliance when Unitarians were denied the name of Christian. Jesus spoke of miracles, said Emerson, because life is itself a miracle. " But the word Miracle, as pronounced by Christian churches, gives a false impression; it is Monster. It is not one with the blowing clover and the falling rain."

CHAPTER SEVEN

The Benevolence of the Deity

1763–1784

I

When the Arminians denied the doctrine of election, they said that God could never behave in so cruel and arbitrary a manner. When they denied original sin, they argued that a benevolent deity would not damn innocent infants. When they asserted that man is a free moral agent, they said that God would not create a being which lacked the power to do what was required of it. When they made regeneration a doctrine of development, they insisted that God's holy spirit is always striving with men for their salvation. In short, throughout their discussion of Christian doctrine, the Arminians were gradually reshaping their concept of the nature of God. They had become profoundly convinced that God is a benevolent deity, whose first concern is the happiness of his creatures.

In debate over religious doctrine, men commonly argue about superficial differences. The assumption that God is beneficent and benevolent was so fundamental that it almost escaped notice. It entered into the argument over election, original sin, and justification; but only on two occasions was it examined critically. The first of these was a brief and undignified spat between Jonathan Mayhew and John Cleaveland (Yale, 1745), a revivalist from Connecticut, settled over the Separatist church in Ipswich; the other was the publication of Charles Chauncy's *Benevolence of the Deity.*

In 1763, Mayhew published two Thanksgiving sermons on the nature, extent, and perfection of the divine goodness. These sermons not only exalted God's benevolence above his wisdom and justice, but also made slurring remarks about orthodoxy. If any man actually believes in reprobation, Mayhew said, his views cannot be reconciled with the goodness of God, for it is " most false and unscriptural, horrible to the last degree, to all men of an undepraved judgment, and blasphemous against the God of heaven and earth." [1] Cleaveland replied that the logical conclusion of Mayhew's position was universalism; that if God is benevolent to every creature, he must save even the devils in Hell. He declared that Mayhew was evidently trying to represent the goodness of God in such a light as to make the atonement of Christ wholly superfluous.[2] Mayhew took offense at Cleaveland's " defamatory libel," and replied in an ill-tempered *Letter of Reproof to Mr. John Cleaveland of Ipswich.* He accused Cleaveland of vanity, ignorance, prevarication, profaneness, misrepresentation, falsehood, wickedness, malice, and many other sins of the same sort. Cleaveland's fault was the more inexcusable, he argued, because he himself was engaged at the time in defending the congregational churches against episcopal encroachments. " You have joined your slanders to those of my anonymous *episcopal* defamers; you have brought the like accusation against me, and made use of the like dishonest arts to hurt my reputation." [3] Mayhew even insinuated that Cleaveland was in league with the episcopal party: " And what reward do you expect from that quarter,

---

[1] Jonathan Mayhew, *Two Sermons on the Nature, Extent and Perfection of the Divine Goodness* (Boston, 1763), p. 66.

[2] John Cleaveland, *An Essay, to Defend Some of the Most Important Principles in the Protestant Reformed System of Christianity* (Boston, 1763).

[3] Jonathan Mayhew, *A Letter of Reproof to Mr. John Cleaveland of Ipswich* (Boston, 1764), p. 43.

for this furious attack upon me? — Perhaps to be made a
BISHOP *in America!* " [4] The chief ground for complaint that
Mayhew advanced was that of misquotation. Cleaveland replied that some of the mistakes were errors of the press, and
others paraphrases, which he supposed would be apparent to
every intelligent reader.[5]

This unmannerly episode was the only occasion when Arminian formally clashed with Calvinist over the nature of
God. And the only extended analysis of the God of the
Arminians was Chauncy's *Benevolence of the Deity.* This
little volume was remarkable for the way in which it mir-
rored all the most popular eighteenth-century concepts: the
sensational psychology, benevolence, optimism, the great
chain of being, the theories of the British moralists, and religious liberalism. It would be hard to find in New England
a more complete surrender to the Age of Reason. It was
one of those books which Chauncy wrote in the 1750's, but
did not publish for over twenty years. In 1768 he wrote to
Ezra Stiles: " I have still another piece, which, when I have
leisure, I will publish with all freedom. . . . It is upon
the benevolence of GOD, its nature, illustration, and consistency with evil both natural and moral. This was written
many years ago. It will make a moderate octavo volume." [6]

II

In most respects, the God of the Arminians was similar to
the God of the Calvinists. In both cases, the concept was of
a being infinitely powerful, wise, and just. In both cases,
God was the creator and sustainer of the universe, and the

---

[4] *Ibid.*, p. 44.
[5] John Cleaveland, *A Reply to Dr. Mayhew's Letter of Reproof to
Mr. John Cleaveland of Ipswich* (Boston, 1765).
[6] Charles Chauncy, " A Sketch of Eminent Men in New England," *Collections of the Massachusetts Historical Society*, X (1809), pp. 163–164.

ruler of mankind. The immensity, variety, and complexity of the physical universe were customarily advanced as evidence of the power and wisdom of the Creator. Beyond our world are the other planets of the solar system, and beyond them a " stupendous army of fixed stars," each with its own choir of planets, comets and satellites. " God, whose almighty fiat first produced this amazing universe, had the whole plan in view from all eternity; intimately and perfectly knew the nature and all the properties of all these his creatures." [7] He retains complete control over his creation: " Yea, he could invert the course of nature, stop the sun in its course. . . ." [8] There is no withstanding his almighty power. Ordinarily, however, he does not rule the world by sudden interpositions in the course of nature. He is a God of law: " The settled, uniform course of things, no less than particular, striking interpositions, demonstrate the uncontroulable power and providence of him, who ' siteth on the circle of the earth, and counteth the inhabitants of it as grasshoppers.' " Indeed, the purpose of special interpositions seems to be " to rouse the attention of unthinking mortals to those general evidences of his being and providence, which they have every day before their eyes." [9]

God's power over the souls of men is as complete as his power over the universe of nature; he is " the righteous Sovereign of the world, as well as the Creator of it, and the Lord of nature." [10] He can judge men guilty, and doom them to everlasting destruction, or he can admit them to the everlasting bliss of heaven. Two earthly prototypes were

[7] John Adams, *The Works of John Adams*, Charles Francis Adams, ed. (Boston, 1850), II, p. 20.

[8] Charles Chauncy, *Trust in God, the Duty of a People in a Day of Trouble* (Boston, 1770), p. 27.

[9] James Dana, *A Century Discourse* (New Haven, 1770), pp. 9, 10.

[10] Jonathan Mayhew, *A Discourse on Rev. XV. 3d, 4th, Occasioned by the Earthquakes in November 1755* (Boston, 1755), pp. 17–18.

the basis for the Arminian concept of God: the king and the father. Mayhew observed: " the great and blessed God is pleased, in his word, to represent himself to us very often under the character both of a *Father* and of a *King*." [11] As a king, God has the same powers over men that earthly kings have — with this difference, that kings are fallible, but God's judgment is sure, and his decrees irresistible. His wisdom and power are infinite. But the Arminians patterned their God on good princes, not on tyrants: " when these titles are given to God in his word, the design is, to represent him under the character of the *wisest* & *best* Father, the *wisest* & *best* King; not that of an *unreasonable, unnatural,* and *cruel* parent; not that of an *unwise* and *unreasonable,* a *cruel* and *unmerciful* king." [12] God is not a stern and unyielding monarch; if he has despotic power, he is at least a benevolent despot. It is more agreeable to the word of God, as well as more honorable to him " to conceive of him as the universal Father, who in this World tempers the Severity of a Judge, with the Tenderness of a Parent." [13] This concept of God was, of course, the product originally of a monarchical age. After the American Revolution, monarchy fell into disrepute in liberal theology as well as in politics, leaving the Unitarians with the pure concept of the universal Fatherhood of God.

In the moral realm as in the physical world, God is a God of law. He is theoretically omnipotent, possessing the power to regenerate men without the use of means, just as in the physical world he possesses the power to cause miracles. But this power he no longer uses, preferring to work his will through second causes, even when the salvation of souls is at

[11] Mayhew, *Sermons on the Divine Goodness*, p. 23.
[12] *Ibid.*, p. 23.
[13] Thomas Barnard, *A Sermon Preached to the Ancient and Honourable Artillery Company* (Boston, 1758), p. 10.

stake. God is a " moral governor," and men are subjects of his moral government. God's moral law is " agreeable to moral fitness in the relation of things; in perfect conformity to which the rectitude, and happiness of the creator himself consists." Happiness for moral agents results " from acting according to certain rules prescribed by the creator, and made known to them by reason or revelation." [14] To make men obey his moral government, God uses moral means only; no man can be forced to be good against his will. Rational motives and encouragements to righteousness are placed before him — the hope of reward and the fear of punishment. God will not subvert this moral government by arbitrarily saving a favored few in defiance of eternal justice, or condemning others through mere caprice. For if the God of the Arminians was a monarch, he was a constitutional monarch; his was a government of laws, not whim.

The concept of God as Creator, combined with the concept of God as Ruler of mankind, produced the theory of divine providence. This had long been standard doctrine in New England. [15] Towards the end of the seventeenth century it had become especially prominent in the writings of Increase and Cotton Mather. The Arminians accepted it without significant change. Even a scientist, Professor John Winthrop, insisted that " the operations of nature are conducted, with a view, *ultimately*, to *moral* purposes; and that there is the most perfect coincidence, at all times, between GOD's government of the *natural* and of the *moral* world." [16] The Arminians always took it for granted that " all the outward privileges and advantages, whether natural, civil or religious,

---

[14] Daniel Shute, *A Sermon Preached . . . May 25th, 1768. Being the Anniversary for the Election* (Boston, 1768), pp. 6, 7.

[15] See Perry Miller, *The New England Mind* (New York, c. 1939), pp. 228–235.

[16] John Winthrop, *A Lecture on Earthquakes* (Boston, 1755), p. 29.

that any person or people enjoy, are not casual events, but proceed from the righteous disposal of our heavenly Father." [17]   Or, as Mayhew put it, there is " a kind of agreement, or some correspondence, between the natural, the civil and moral world," so that extraordinary occurrences in the former may be considered as " the prognostications and forerunners of some commotions, equally uncommon and surprising in the latter; and as designed to give us warning of them." [18]

In 1755 there occurred one of these providences that was not quickly forgotten.   On November 18, about quarter past four in the morning, the ground was shaken by an earthquake, accompanied by a noise as of the rumble of thunder. This lasted, it was estimated, for a full four minutes, and was followed by other minor tremors.   Chimneys were broken or damaged, the roofs of the houses were injured, and pewter dishes thrown from the shelves.   The quake was felt as far north as Nova Scotia, as far south as Philadelphia, and out to sea as well.   The impression made upon the people was greatly heightened when news came of the destructive shocks in Spain and Portugal on the first of the month.   The New England clergy, orthodox and liberal alike, believed that this was intended as an awful warning of the terrible consequences of provoking God's wrath.   More than a score of sermons and pamphlets drawing this moral appeared within a few months, by such distinguished ministers as Mather Byles, Chauncy, Mayhew, Thomas Foxcroft, and Thomas Prince.

There was no disagreement on the two fundamental points: that the quake was caused by God and was an expression of his wrath, and that he worked by means of second

---

[17] Henry Cumings, *A Thanksgiving Sermon Preached at Billerica, November 27, 1766* (Boston, 1767), p. 9.
[18] Jonathan Mayhew, *Practical Discourses* (Boston, 1760), pp. 370, 371.

causes. Though we cannot explain the secret workings of an earthquake, said Chauncy, "yet we have no reason to think, but that it takes rise from sufficient *second Causes,* in common with the other phænomena of nature." [19]   Professor Winthrop attempted to explain the shocks as the result of an explosion of combustible matter or fumes in caverns in the earth, but he too supposed that they "may justly be regarded as the tokens of an incensed DEITY." [20]   New England ministers were not quite sure what it was that had made God angry, but they were able to list innumerable sins, on the assumption that the true object of divine wrath was somewhere among them.   "He visiteth them in his Displeasure for all their prevailing Sins, of Prophaneness, Unrighteousness and Intemperance," John Rogers declared.   More specifically, his people have been guilty of "various Acts of Irreligion, Avarice, Pride, Prodigality and Luxury, Injustice, Falsehood, Deceit, Malignity, Extortion, &c." [21]   Charles Chauncy listed uncleanness, pride, unrighteousness, and drunkenness. But he observed that many of the serious earthquakes that had been felt in New England had occurred Saturday night or Sunday morning.   He therefore deduced that sabbath-breaking was the chief ground of God's displeasure. [22]   The application of all these earthquake sermons was an exhortation to repent.   "If we do not reform," said John Rogers, "I say, we have all the Reason in the World to expect more and greater Calamities." [23]

But God's providence was sometimes seen in a more friendly mood, encouraging and aiding the projects of men,

---

[19] Charles Chauncy, *Earthquakes a Token of the Righteous Anger of God* (Boston, 1755), p. 8.

[20] Winthrop, *Lecture on Earthquakes,* p. 27.

[21] John Rogers, *Three Sermons on Different Subjects* (Boston, 1756), p. 53.

[22] Chauncy, *Earthquakes,* pp. 16–19.

[23] Rogers, *Three Sermons,* p. 60.

rather than admonishing and reproving them. The successes of British arms over the French were clearly the result of God's favor, and many a Thanksgiving discourse enumerated the various coincidences and circumstances by which God had ingeniously accomplished his purposes. The greatest generals are dependent on God for victory, Chauncy declared.

> He gives them Presence of mind, or confounds their Tho'ts; he directs their Counsels, or suffers them to be led aside by a Spirit of Infatuation; he renders their Projections prosperous, or frustrates their best concerted Measures: He gives Courage to their Armies, or strikes them with Surprise; And if he intends to render them victorious, he will order such a concurrence of Circumstances in their Favour, as that they shall have the Advantage of their Enemies, and tread upon their High Places.[24]

This was no mere theory; it was tested by experience in 1745 when the expedition from New England to Cape Breton was successful beyond all expectations. The weather was uniformly favorable to the English while they were attacking Fort Louisburg, but the very afternoon they entered the town it began to rain. Had the victory been delayed, the trenches would have filled with water, perhaps forcing the English to raise the siege. God protected them while they were preparing their batteries, so that scarcely a man was lost. When Commodore Warren was at sea, bound for Boston from the West Indies, a vessel " is accidently cast in his Way at Sea, accidentally to Men, but *intentionally* by God, giving him certain Information, that the *New-England* Forces had been some time on their Voyage. . . ."[25] Changing his course, he arrived at Louisburg just in time to capture the French ship *Vigilant*, which otherwise might have frustrated the designs of the English.

---

[24] Charles Chauncy, *Marvellous Things Done by the Right Hand and Holy Arm of God in Getting Him the Victory* (Boston, 1745), p. 7.
[25] Chauncy, *Marvellous Things*, p. 18.

III

This general concept of God was shared by Calvinists and Arminians. The parting of the ways came when the attempt was made to define what God's purposes are, to explain his end in the creation of the universe. How will God exercise his powers towards men? the Arminians asked. Does he seek their happiness, or is he concerned solely with his own glory?

The strict Calvinist replied without hesitation that the only motive in God's acts is his own glory. " Whatever that be which is in itself most valuable," said Edwards, ". . . *that* must be worthy to be God's last end in the creation; and also worthy to be his highest end." [26]   Obviously, God himself is infinitely the greatest and best of beings, and his glory is most worthy to be the end of creation. " God gives to himself what is his own proper due, by making the manifestation of his own glory, his truly great end." [27]   Some of God's moral attributes are wisdom, holiness, justice, goodness, and truth; and God manifests his glory by exercising these attributes in due proportion. God's goodness towards men is shown in the creation of them as moral agents, and his promise to them that if they obey and love him they shall be saved. If men obey the terms of the covenant, God will make good his part of the agreement, and in this way he shows his truth and faithfulness. But it should be observed, according to John Cleaveland, that by so doing,

he manifests and maintains his moral character in justice to himself; it is not for their sakes, but for his own name sake, that he makes good his promise. . . . Moreover, God would do himself great injustice, if he should make any thing his great end, but his own glory: If such deny the God that is above, who serve the creature more than

[26] Jonathan Edwards, *The Works of President Edwards* (New York, 1843), II, p. 200.
[27] Cleaveland, *Essay*, p. 19.

the creator; would not God deny himself, if he should make the creature's happiness, his great end? [28]

When God acts, he displays all his moral attributes — justice, holiness, and truth, as well as wisdom and goodness. His justice in the damnation of sinners is just as important as his mercy in the salvation of the saints.

In contrast with this Calvinist argument, the Arminians placed benevolence first in the rank of God's moral attributes. Mayhew showed that the goodness of God is the most amiable of his perfections: " God may be loved on account of it, without particularly taking his other attributes into consideration, in a manner in which he cannot be loved for any of the rest, without the consideration of this." [29] His other attributes, apart from this one, inspire men with terror and amazement rather than with hope and joy. " Knowledge and power, detached from goodness, afford at le[a]st as much reason for fear and suspicion, as for hope and confidence." [30] Wisdom and power without benevolence are the equivalent of craft and cunning. But even guilty creatures may adore the justice of God when they recall that his benevolence is inseparable from it. " If it were proper to make any comparison betwixt the divine attributes," Mayhew wrote, " or to say that one of them is more glorious than another, mankind in general, to besure, would not hesitate much at calling this the most glorious." [31]

In defining benevolence, Chauncy took pains to insist that the word has exactly the same meaning when ascribed to God as when applied to man. Here he was combating the tendency of high Calvinism to make the gulf between God and

[28] *Ibid.*, pp. 19, 20.

[29] Mayhew, *Sermons on the Divine Goodness*, p. 17.

[30] James Dana, *A Discourse Delivered at Kensington* (New Haven, 1775), p. 9.

[31] Mayhew, *Sermons on the Divine Goodness*, pp. 17–18.

man so wide that human concepts, when applied to the deity, lose their familiar meaning. If the Bible says that God is good, then benevolence in God will produce the same kind of benevolent act that it does in man. " Every Being, in heaven and earth, to whom this attribute may be applied, partakes of the *same quality,* though not in the same *manner,* nor in the same *degree* and *proportion.*" [32]   But divine benevolence is not an impulsive principle, " a sort of blind instinct, or good-nature, detached from reason and right, or a regard for fitness and propriety." [33]   God is infinitely wise as well as infinitely good, and divine benevolence is always under the guidance of divine wisdom. Otherwise the most appalling disorder and confusion might result:

. . . a principle of benevolence, though of *infinite propelling force,* if not guided in its operations by *wisdom* and *intelligence,* instead of producing *nothing but good,* might, by blindly counteracting itself, produce, upon the *whole,* as the final result of its exertions, infinite confusion and disorder. [34]

The effects of unguided benevolence may be as serious as those of positive malevolence; parents can do great injury to their children with too much kindness. Benevolence, finally, is expressed freely, not under compulsion; the benevolent acts of God are acts of choice.

Chauncy defined benevolence as " a principle disposing and prompting to the communication of happiness." [35]   And in saying that God is benevolent, he meant above all that he is benevolent towards men and seeks their happiness. Samuel Osborn told his congregation in 1743 that " God did not create or give Men Being for his own Sake, but for their Sakes, that he might communicate Happiness to them." God

[32] Charles Chauncy, *The Benevolence of the Deity* (Boston, 1784), p. 14.
[33] Mayhew, *Sermons on the Divine Goodness,* p. 14.
[34] Chauncy, *Benevolence of the Deity,* p. vii.
[35] *Ibid.,* p. 11.

is already infinitely happy; his creation of men could not increase his own happiness, and so it must have their happiness as its end.[36] Mayhew argued that by promoting the happiness of the creature, God was promoting his own glory. But, he added, if any prefer to say that

. . . God's view is, to promote his *own glory* by *doing good*, making the latter the *means*, and the former the *end*; I have no objection, except that it may, perhaps, seem to represent him rather as an ambitious Being, who desires the praise & homage of his creatures, than an infinitely good One, who aims at making them happy without any *selfish* end. . . .[37]

The proofs of divine benevolence were of two kinds, *a priori* and *a posteriori*. As with the corresponding proofs of the existence of God, both kinds were acceptable to the Arminians, but the latter was their chief reliance. " Some have endeavoured to prove, by metaphysical reasoning, that the Deity is perfectly and infinitely benevolent," Chauncy declared; and he admitted that such reasoning seemed sound to him. But, he went on to say, " as this method of arguing may appear to some abstruse, and not so well adapted to carry conviction with it, I shall leave it, and go on to another that is more easy and familiar, and, it may be, at the same time, more strikingly conclusive." [38] He proposed to demonstrate the divine benevolence from God's works themselves. This line of argument, which came to be known as Natural Theology, had already made its appearance in New England, es-

[36] Samuel Osborn, *The Case and Complaint of Mr. Samuel Osborn* (Boston, 1743), p. 10. Osborn's position is similar to William King's: " Since God . . . can neither be profited nor incommoded by his Works, nor affected by their Good or Evil; it follows, that he made these things for no Advantage of his own, and that he neither receives nor expects any Benefit from them. For by creating things without himself, he must necessarily have sought either their Benefit or his own; but what Benefit can God seek for himself, who possesses all Good? " William King, *An Essay on the Origin of Evil*, translated by Edmund Law. (1st ed., London, 1731), p. 52.
[37] Mayhew, *Sermons on the Divine Goodness*, p. 77.
[38] Chauncy, *Benevolence of the Deity*, pp. 51, 52.

pecially in Cotton Mather's *Christian Philosopher,* which drew largely on such English writers as Ray, Derham, Cheyne, and Grew.[39] It was to become even more popular both in England and America in the nineteenth century, and may be found in Paley, in the *Bridgewater Treatises,* and in Edward Hitchcock's *Religion of Geology.*[40]

God's works reveal his benevolence in two ways. In the first place, inanimate nature is so ordered and arranged as to serve the needs of the men who inhabit it; and in the second place, animate creatures are endowed by nature with powers and abilities qualifying them for happiness. Under the first heading Chauncy mentioned the sun, whose composition, size, and location is admirably suited to convey light and heat to the earth " without which it would have been an unfit habitation for any of those *animated,* and *intelligent* beings, who now exist happy on it." [41] The earth itself shows the mark of divine goodness in its annual and daily revolutions, which grant us the gifts of the seasons and day and night. Not all parts of the world are equally favored with light and heat, but God has made compensation in the cold countries by supplying men with wood for fuel, and animals with an increase of fur when it is needed. The earth shows God's goodness in the distribution of its surface into sea and land. Such varying conditions make possible a greater variety of creatures, and a greater manifestation of good. Do some complain that the seas are too wide? They are of precisely the right proportion to supply the moisture necessary to make the land fruitful. Do some complain that the water in the sea is salt? That is necessary to prevent putrefaction.

[39] See Kenneth B. Murdock, ed., *Selections from Cotton Mather* (New York, c. 1926), pp. xlviii–liv.

[40] See Conrad Wright, " The Religion of Geology," *New England Quarterly,* XIV (1941), pp. 335–358.

[41] Chauncy, *Benevolence of the Deity,* p. 74.

" The proper reflection from all which is, that the *benevolent Deity* could not have better adapted *inanimate nature* for the diffusion of good. It is visible wherever we cast our eyes." [42]

Chauncy was able to discover such marks of divine benevolence in the most unlikely spots. The same sermon which described the earthquake of 1755 as a testimony of divine wrath, found God's goodness in it as well:

The *goodness* of God has likewise been wonderfully manifested in this event of providence. To what else can it be ascribed, that, when he so awfully shook our houses, he so proportion'd the force with which he did this, as that they should not be shattered to pieces, and bury us in their ruins. [43]

This kind of argument was stressed by Chauncy more than by his colleagues, but others also found it useful. John Adams, for example, pointed out that if the projectile force in the planets were different, men could not survive on the earth. " *Ergo,* an intelligent and benevolent mind had the disposal and determination of these things." [44] And Mayhew referred his readers specifically to one of the classic statements of this argument, Cheyne's *Philosophical Principles of Religion,* " where there are many curious observations on the seasons." [45]

The goodness of God is also apparent in the intellectual and moral constitution of man. Chauncy listed all man's natural endowments, and showed how each of them is a mark of divine benevolence. His nature is compound, partly material and partly rational. He is allied both with the lower animals and with the angels, and is able to enjoy both sensitive and rational pleasures. God has made man with bodily senses, to be an inlet of knowledge; and he has wisely pro-

---

[42] *Ibid.,* p. 77.
[43] Chauncy, *Earthquakes,* pp. 10, 11.
[44] Adams, *Works,* II, p. 19.
[45] Mayhew, *Sermons on the Divine Goodness,* p. 56n.

vided that the sensation of pain should accompany that which is harmful to him, thereby guarding him from danger. He has assured his moral happiness by making him a moral agent, possessing a moral sense, self-determination, and a conscience. Finally, the most striking evidence of all the marks of kindness is the redemption of man through Jesus Christ.[46]

IV

The insistence of the Arminians that God's moral government exists for the happiness of his creatures had implications for political theory as well. Theology might be termed the political theory of God's moral government. Politics and theology both involved assertions about the relationships between men and their rulers, the law of nature, the capacities of men, and the object of government. As the American Revolution approached, there was constant interplay between political and religious ideas. Thus the concept of an agreement between ruler and subject appeared in one form as the contract theory, and in another as the covenant theology. God's government, like that of earthly rulers, is restrained by inherent rules of justice and benevolence; the belief in the binding force of law pervaded theology as it did political theory. Repeatedly, ministers argued points in theology by analogy with civil government. And in their election sermons, they reversed the process, expounding natural rights, the social compact, the contract theory, and the right of revolution, as part of the law of God, in harmony with his methods of government.[47]

Such parallels were used by ministers of varying shades of religious belief; liberalism in political theory was not a mo-

[46] Chauncy, *Benevolence of the Deity*, pp. 85–173.
[47] See Alice M. Baldwin, *The New England Clergy and the American Revolution* (Durham, N.C., 1928).

nopoly of the religious liberals. But certain of the prevailing political ideas were especially congenial to the Arminians. The concept of man as a free moral agent, endowed with reason, open to persuasion, and capable of voluntary obedience to the laws of nature, was as basic to Locke's *Second Treatise* as it was to Arminian preaching. The obedience God requires of us, said John Tucker of Newbury, is not that of slaves to a tyrannical master. " It must be *free*, — a matter of choice, and not of force, driving us on against a reluctant mind." Then, translating this doctrine into political terms, he added: " Like to this, is the obedience we owe to civil government." [48] Furthermore, that the end of all government is the welfare and the happiness of the governed was the common assumption of the Arminian theology and of the philosophy of the Declaration of Independence. In 1749, William Balch told the General Court that God wills the happiness of his creatures; therefore to promote " the Happiness of all around us, is to be *like* him: It is to copy after the divine Pattern. . . ."[49] Thirty years later, on a similar occasion, Simeon Howard declared the business of " rulers in general " to be " to promote and secure the happiness of the whole community." [50]

[48] John Tucker, *A Sermon Preached at Cambridge . . . May 29th, 1771.* Election Sermon (Boston, 1771), p. 37.

[49] William Balch, *A Publick Spirit, as Express'd in Praying for the Peace and Seeking the Good of Jerusalem.* Election Sermon (Boston, 1749), p. 8.

[50] Simeon Howard, *A Sermon Preached . . . May 31, 1780.* Election Sermon (Boston, 1780), p. 13.

Arminians were prominent in the leadership of the Revolutionary movement. Mayhew delivered in 1750 a *Discourse Concerning Unlimited Submission* (Boston, 1750), which received wide attention for its bold assertion of the moral duty to resist tyrannical rulers. Both Mayhew and Chauncy were active in opposing the movement for Anglican bishops in the colonies, as a threat to American liberties. See Arthur L. Cross, *The Anglican Episcopate and the American Colonies* (New York, 1902). John Lathrop was the author of a most inflammatory sermon occasioned by the Boston Massacre, which he entitled: *Innocent Blood Crying to God from the Streets of Boston* (London, 1770, reprinted Boston, 1771). In smaller towns also, men like Samuel West

V

The Arminians had discovered in God's works the marks of benevolence. But pain, injury, disappointment, and death are as common in human experience as success and happiness. How can the benevolence of God be reconciled with the existence of moral and physical evil? Here was a problem which the Arminians recognized, but they were confident it could be solved without much trouble. In any event, they observed, it was one which confronted all religious people, whether Jews or heathens, deists or Christians.

If the confidence of the New England Arminians on this score seems naïve today, at least they were in good company. The Age of Reason was an age of optimism; its philosophers had decided that whatever is, is right. The New England liberals merely repeated what they had been taught by distinguished British divines. One of these was William King, Archbishop of Dublin, whose most important work was *De Origine Mali* (1702). This was translated into English by Edmund Law, and published in 1731; there were several later editions in the eighteenth century, the fifth appearing in 1781. Law's translation was voluminously annotated, many quotations from other authors being cited in support of King's thesis. Directly or indirectly, the book influenced Bolingbroke and Pope. Chauncy read it; and indeed parts of the *Benevolence of the Deity* are little more than a restatement of it. There seems to be no evidence that other New

---

of Dartmouth, Jeremy Belknap of Dover, New Hampshire, and Henry Cumings of Billerica took the lead in local protests against the Stamp Act and other provocative measures of the British government. (Baldwin, *New England Clergy*, p. 94n.)   Exceptions of course there were: Ebenezer Gay long continued to pray for the King and the royal family, and was criticized in the press for his indifference to the colonial cause. (Baldwin, *New England Clergy*, p. 132n.)   But Gay was the exception; more typical were patriots, of whom Jonathan Mayhew and John Adams were the leading figures.

England liberals read it, but its influence could have reached them indirectly through many channels.

Archbishop King's chief reliance in proving that evil is consistent with divine benevolence was the concept of the great chain of being.[51] This concept arranged all creation in a continuous chain, each link of which contained a little bit more of existence than the link below. At the bottom was non-existence; next came matter; then the various forms of life, ranging from vegetables through animals to rational moral agents. Above man were the hierarchies of angels; God himself was at the top, possessing the greatest fullness of being. There were two assumptions latent in this concept: gradation and plenitude. Gradation means that the difference between one link and the next is infinitely small; plenitude means that God is bound to create every link in the chain, on this planet or on some other, in order to reveal his perfections. There must be no missing links, or chasms, or voids in the ranks of creation.

The concept of the great chain was used by Chauncy, both in the *Five Dissertations* on the Fall, and in the *Benevolence of the Deity*. He declared that it is from the " diversity of beings, duly subordinated to each other, that the *plenitude* of nature arises." In this way, the creation is " filled up," all the classes of creatures forming " links in the chain of existence," and concurring " to constitute *one whole* without *void* or *chasm*." [52] God's creation then demonstrates " the riches and glory of the Creator's goodness, far beyond what it could have done, if the *continuity* had been broken, by the *non-existence* of any of the ranks of creatures, which now make it an *absolutely full and well-connected universe*." [53] No other Arminian made so rounded a statement of the con-

---

[51] See Arthur O. Lovejoy, *The Great Chain of Being* (Cambridge, 1936).
[52] Chauncy, *Benevolence of the Deity*, p. 191.
[53] *Ibid.*, p. 193.

cept, yet it was familiar to the rest of them also. Daniel
Shute said that the whole plan of creation is adjusted to promote the benevolent purpose of God, " to which the immense
diversity in his works; the gradation in the species of beings
that we know of, and many more perhaps than we know of,
and the somewhat similar gradation in the same species, arising from their make, their connections, and the circumstances
they are placed in, are happily subservient." [54]   In producing
such an almost infinite variety of worlds and creatures, said
Mayhew, it is supposable that " the infinitely wise Author of
all, had a view to the general, common good of his creation;
and consequently, that this variety itself may contribute
thereto." [55]

There are three kinds of evil, said Chauncy, taking his cue
from Archbishop King: evil of imperfection, moral evil, and
physical evil.   Men are not created perfect, either in respect
to their moral or physical capacities.   They are more nearly
perfect than the creatures below them, but they are inferior
to the angels in power, wisdom, holiness, and all other attributes.   But to say that God is not benevolent because he
has favored some of his creatures more than others would be
to take a very narrow view of God's purposes.   In discussing
divine benevolence, " we ought not to consider its *displays* as
they affect *individual beings only*, but as they relate to the
particular system of which they are parts." [56]   It is certainly
better that God's power should be displayed by the creation
of every link in the chain of being than that there should be a
void in the creation.   The different creatures do not interfere
with one another; it is possible to have birds in the air and
fish in the sea at the same time.   By creating them both, God

[54] Shute, *Election Sermon* (1768), p. 6.
[55] Mayhew, *Sermons on the Divine Goodness*, p. 29.
[56] Chauncy, *Benevolence of the Deity*, p. 57.

has made possible a greater sum of happiness in the universe, because a greater variety of faculties is possible:

. . . the capacity for happiness, in the universe, is enlarged by means of the diversity of beings that have existence in it. And if the capacity is enlarged, it is, from hence, demonstrably certain, that the *quantum* of good *may* be *greater* than it could have been, if, instead of this *diversity*, fewer orders of beings, or a single one only, had been made.[57]

A diversity of creatures also makes it possible for them to be variously useful to one another, increasing the sum of happiness by acts of beneficence.

But if the benevolence of God is shown in the variety of his creation, then the imperfections of man are not inconsistent with it. Somewhere in the scale there had to be such a creature, endowed with his precise abilities and imperfections. Any level of existence is better than non-existence. Imperfection, furthermore, is inseparable from creation; for a creature derives its being from another, and is necessarily finite in its powers. " Absolute perfection therefore is an incommunicable glory of the only true God." [58] If imperfection is an argument against the benevolence of the creator, then a benevolent God could have created nothing that was not perfect; that is, he could have created nothing at all.

So much for the argument based on the fact that God made men men, and not angels. The second objection to the doctrine of divine benevolence was based on the moral disorders prevalent among men. A benevolent God, it was argued, would not have placed his creatures in circumstances where, by perverting their powers, they would involve themselves in ruin. Moral evil, Chauncy pointed out, implies two things: " *irregularity* in the beings chargeable with it, and

[57] *Ibid.*, p. 191.   [58] *Ibid.*, p. 184.

consequent unhappiness as the *fruit* thereof, either by the *constitution of nature,* or *positive infliction* from the *Deity.*" [59] The possibility of irregularity in the beings is inseparable from their being free moral agents. They themselves are responsible for it, not God. He could have prevented it only by doing one of three things. He might have failed to create moral agents, or he might have made them so perfect that they could not have sinned, or he might have interposed to prevent agents from abusing their liberty. Not to have given free agents a place in the scale of being would have been to lessen " the *quantum* of good, capable of being communicated." [60] God would have made impossible the highest form of happiness, which is the result of virtuous acts by free and intelligent creatures. If, in the second case, God had made all men perfect in their moral powers, there would have similarly been " an unavoidable bar to that *diversity* in the creation " which affords the fullest communication of good.[61] The third objection, that God might have interposed to prevent moral agents from abusing their liberty, is equally specious. That would have destroyed their character as moral agents. It was better for God to create them, frankly recognizing the risks, than to omit them from the great chain or destroy their essential character.

The second part of moral evil is the unhappiness that arises from immoral conduct. Chauncy was ready to maintain that " *unhappiness* may be the fruit of *benevolence,* and an argument in proof of it, rather than an objection against it." A great part of such unhappiness " is of the medicinal kind, and strongly tends to the cure of its patients." [62] Pain resulting from wickedness is a motive to repent. It teaches by example also: the punishments inflicted on the guilty serve as warn-

---

[59] *Ibid.,* p. 207.
[60] *Ibid.,* p. 209.
[61] *Ibid.,* p. 212.
[62] *Ibid.,* pp. 236, 237.

ings to their neighbors. It is true that sometimes the innocent suffer with the guilty, but this is inevitable while they live mixed together. " So that, if this objection proves any thing, it is that such an order of beings ought not to have been created." [63] Besides, the evils which the innocent suffer may prepare them for future happiness in the world to come, by schooling them in patience and forgiveness. In any case, they make possible the display of such divine attributes as holiness, pity, mercy, and pardon.

The third kind of evil is natural evil. Here Chauncy forsook the concept of the great chain, and used another equally dear to the Age of Reason. Natural evils are the effects of established laws, whose purpose and tendency are beneficial. Such pre-established general laws " are preferable to immediate, unrelated exertions of the Divine agency; and inconveniences may have been lessened, rather than increased thereby." [64] Pain will result from disregard of the laws of nature, but it keeps creatures on guard against what is hurtful to them. Hunger and thirst are evils which are wisely contrived to prevent men from forgetting to eat. Toil and labor are evils which are necessary to prevent the earth from being a wilderness. Death is an evil, but if no one died, the number of individuals who could be happy on this planet would be fewer.

VI

It should be observed that Chauncy's argument contrasts sharply with that of Edwards, but much less sharply with that of certain other Calvinists, such as Joseph Bellamy. Chauncy admitted freely that God created a system in which evil might occur as incidental to a greater good. He defined that greater good in terms of the happiness of the creature,

[63] *Ibid.*, p. 248.   [64] *Ibid.*, p. 274.

instead of the glory of the creator. But Joseph Bellamy, though a follower of Edwards, was partway seduced by the optimism and humanitarianism of the Age of Reason; like the Arminians he sometimes, if not consistently, spoke as though God's end in creation had been to make the elect " more humble, holy, and happy." Like the Arminians, too, he spoke of man as " a noble creature, an intelligent free agent, capable of moral action, and a proper subject of moral government." [65] When Bellamy wrote in this vein, the chief difference between him and Chauncy was in the latter's rejection of God's eternal decrees, by which some men are free to choose only that which is sinful. There is a real difference, the Arminians insisted, between the proposition that God permits evil and the proposition that he specifically decrees that a particular individual must inevitably sin. The first statement is compatible with divine benevolence, the second is not.

These speculations on the origin of evil are to be found, in all their range and elaboration, only in Chauncy's writings. Yet the argument is Arminian in the sense that it is the product of Arminian assumptions, even if few of the Arminians explored the logic of their assumptions very far in this direction. Chauncy's solution of the problem of evil was the kind of solution that his colleagues would find congenial. For if one doctrine were to be chosen as the heart of their position, it was the paternal character of God. It is sometimes said that the great discovery of the Unitarians was the dignity of human nature. It is quite as true that the great discovery of the Arminians was the benevolence of the deity.

[65] Quoted in Joseph Haroutunian, *Piety versus Moralism* (New York, c. 1932), p. 32.

CHAPTER EIGHT

The Salvation of All Men

1763–1790

I

God's goodness is shown most clearly in the salvation of human souls. Should any man be condemned to eternal punishment, God would have to be regarded as less than infinitely benevolent. The salvation of all men, then, was the conclusion to which the Arminian concept of divine benevolence unmistakably pointed.

For a long time, the Arminians drew back from this conclusion. They argued instead that a benevolent God may punish men when discipline is for their own good and for their happiness in the long run; and that he may condemn men to eternal punishment if that sentence, serving as a warning to others, will increase the sum of happiness enjoyed by mankind as a whole. The Arminians disputed the notion that God punishes men vengefully because his justice must be satisfied. Punishment is for discipline; and if moral progress can be achieved without exacting the last measure of retribution, God will remit the penalty which men deserve on the score of strict justice. God's justice is really an expression of his goodness.

Mayhew used an analogy with paternal and civil government. Why does a wise and good parent correct his children? " Is it not in order to reform, and do them good? — or at least with a view to the benefit of his other children, or those of the household; that they may be kept under due subjection, and restrained from the like evil and hurtful practices? " Such punishment is really a form of kindness. Similarly in civil government, the most absolute sovereign, if he is wise and good, will not " inflict any punishments, but what he considers as needful for the support of his government; — if not for the particular good of those that suffer, as in capital cases, yet for the good of his people in general, by way of example and terror, that good order may be preserved." [1] And so we may rest assured that God, who is good to all, has some benevolent end in view when he permits anyone to suffer.

The argument here revealed inner tensions and inconsistencies. Mayhew himself could say that God would punish men with eternal damnation for the good of the whole, yet assert in the very same sermon that " God is likewise good and kind to all the *individuals* of which these species consist." The whole is made up of parts, and he could hardly care for the whole and neglect the parts which compose it. " There is no medium betwixt his being actually kind and merciful to all, and his being positively cruel and unmerciful to some." [2] John Cleaveland pounced gleefully on this inconsistency. According to the Doctor's scheme, he said, God's purpose in punishing devils and wicked men is either to make them happy, or make them miserable, " without any view to his own glory in either." But if God's purposes terminate on the creature, their effect on the creature will define God's nature: " if his aim terminates in their everlasting happiness, his end is good, and God is good: But if it terminates in their eternal misery, his end is positively bad & evil, and God is positively evil." Therefore, if all reasonable creatures are not eternally happy, God is not kind

---

[1] Jonathan Mayhew, *Two Sermons on the Nature, Extent and Perfection of the Divine Goodness* (Boston, 1763), pp. 20, 21.

[2] *Ibid.*, pp. 34, 35.

to all, but cruel to some. Mayhew must therefore prove that "God will aim at making them happy, in punishing them eternally," or else admit that God is both good and evil.[3] Mayhew was caught very neatly; he replied with a torrent of invective, as though Cleaveland's accusations of heresy were too plausible for comfort.[4]

Charles Chauncy was confronted with the same dilemma at about the same time. But where Mayhew struggled and protested, Chauncy calmly surrendered. One fruit of his intensive study of the Bible in the 1750's was the conclusion that all sinners must ultimately be reconciled to God. Using the methods of textual analysis he had learned from John Taylor of Norwich, Chauncy prepared a full-length treatment of the subject. The manuscript remained on the shelf for more than twenty years; finally it was published anonymously in 1784, under the title, *The Mystery Hid from Ages and Generations, Made Manifest by the Gospel-Revelation; or, the Salvation of All Men the Grand Thing Aimed at in the Scheme of God.*

II

There seems to be no single explanation for the long delay in the publication of Chauncy's book. The approach of the Revolution had something to do with it: energies that might otherwise have been devoted to theology were absorbed by politics, and it might be argued that few people would be interested in such a book at such a time. Samuel West's *Essays on Liberty and Necessity* remained in manuscript for twenty years because the author supposed "the public were

---

[3] John Cleaveland, *An Essay, to Defend Some of the Most Important Principles in the Protestant Reformed System of Christianity* (Boston, 1763), pp. 59, 60.
[4] Jonathan Mayhew, *A Letter of Reproof to Mr. John Cleaveland of Ipswich* (Boston, 1764).

too much interested in disputes of a political nature to attend to the subject." [5]   Similarly, Chauncy argued " that the present is the worst time which could ever happen, for men's minds are too much absorbed in politics to attend unto anything else." [6]   A practical consideration was the fact that, so long as the war lasted, the book could not be printed, since it required certain fonts of Greek and Hebrew type which were not available in Boston. [7]   The manuscript was finally sent to London to be printed.

Chauncy was a prudent man as well as a practical one, and there were also prudential reasons to restrain him from hasty publication.   The doctrine of universal salvation ran counter to traditional Christian theology, and Chauncy realized that broaching the matter might well mean a controversy.   The gospel truths which are necessary to salvation, he felt, must be preached regardless of the consequences; but there are many less crucial doctrines which need not be insisted on at a time when the world is not in a mood to understand.   In 1768, he wrote to Ezra Stiles: " The materials for one design I have put together, and they have lain by in a finished quarto volume for some years.   This is written with too much freedom to admit of publication in this country." [8]   Certain of Chauncy's intimates, in particular John Eliot of the New North Church, encouraged him in his caution.   In 1779, Eliot declared:

It will not do to publish it at once, if proper to expose it at all.   It is too sublime for the soaring of vulgar imaginations, & would dazzle, if

---

[5] Samuel West, *Essays on Liberty and Necessity*, Part I (New Bedford, 1795), p. 3.

[6] John Eliot to Jeremy Belknap, Feb. 1781.   *Collections of the Massachusetts Historical Society*, Ser. 6, Vol. IV (1891), p. 207.

[7] Belknap to Ebenezer Hazard, Dec. 19, 1782.   *Ibid.*, Ser. 5, Vol. II (1877), p. 172.

[8] Charles Chauncy, " A Sketch of Eminent Men in New-England," *Coll. Mass. Hist. Soc.*, X (1809), p. 163.

not blind, the eyes of the populace. It would be like the rays of the noonday sun to persons who had never before seen the light. Our Saviour said to his followers: " I have many things to tell you, but ye cannot bear them now." And this Dr. C. quotes to excuse his own conduct in concealing his sentiments from the people under his charge, as well as the world in general.[9]

But there was a third factor involved in Chauncy's decision, which finally tipped the scales in favor of publication. It was the appearance in New England in 1772 of an itinerant preacher, John Murray, who taught a doctrine of the universal redemption of all souls through Christ. The chief influences on Murray's thought were his Calvinistic upbringing, his later contact with Wesley and Whitefield, and his discovery of universal salvation in the writings of James Relly. From Relly's *Union*, Murray learned that Christ is so united with all mankind that our sins are his as well, and the punishment that he bore is our punishment. Christ, then, has already atoned for the sins of all mankind, so that there is no more debt to be paid to God, and no punishment for sinners to endure.[10] The pattern of this argument, though not the conclusion, was closer to Calvinism than to Arminianism. So if Murray reached a conclusion similar to that of Chauncy, he did so by a fallacious argument; and Chauncy and his friends were unanimous in their disapproval. John Eliot reported: " He has made a great noise in Boston, & most of the libertines of the day attended him. I heard him once. . . . I can't find he has any seriousness at bottom." [11]

---

[9] Eliot to Belknap, July 31, 1779. *Coll. Mass. Hist. Soc.*, Ser. 6, Vol. IV, p. 145.
[10] Later American Universalists, like Hosea Ballou, were not Calvinistic in their assumptions as Murray was, but shifted to Arminian grounds. Even before his death, then, Murray was left outside the main line of Universalist development. See Richard Eddy, " History of Universalism," Ch. 4, in Joseph Henry Allen and Richard Eddy, *A History of the Unitarians and Universalists in the United States* (New York, 1894).
[11] Eliot to Belknap, Feb. 28, 1775. *Coll. Mass. Hist. Soc.*, Ser. 6, Vol. IV, p. 85.

Jeremy Belknap found Antinomianism in his doctrine, and dismissed it as " detestable." [12] Furthermore, Murray seemed to the clergy of the Standing Order to be merely another exhorter to the uneducated, of the kind that had been familiar ever since the Great Awakening. John Eliot described Murray's audiences as " the promiscuous herd who attend wherever they can get their passions roused & inflamed." Murray was but one of the numerous " sectaries," who " however they may spat one another, agree in this one thing, to pull down the standing clergy." [13]

The spread of Murrayism posed a problem for Chauncy. On the one hand, he was tempted to demolish the false assumptions in Murray's preaching; on the other hand, there was the danger that the casual observer would suppose that his doctrine of universal salvation and that of Murray were the same thing, and that he was abandoning scripture " for the sake of gratifying the humours of Murray." [14] John Eliot in Boston explained the situation to his country correspondent in Dover, New Hampshire:

Murray has tended to irritate the passions of those whom we call worthy men, rather than to mollify their minds with ointment to receive a doctrine any ways similar to what he hath propagated. They are not able to distinguish between the restitution of all things upon his plan, and the other scheme which employs the attention & arrests the assent of so many of the wise & learned of the modern New England clergy.[15]

Though Chauncy was reluctant to publish his manuscript, he did allow some of his friends to read it. John Eliot saw part of it in 1779, and read the whole text early in 1780.[16]

[12] Belknap to Hazard, July 2, 1784. *Ibid.*, Ser. 5, Vol. II, p. 364.
[13] Eliot to Belknap, May 23, 1780. *Ibid.*, Ser. 6, Vol. IV, pp. 186–187.
[14] Eliot to Belknap, Feb. 1781. *Ibid.*, Ser. 6, Vol. IV, p. 202.
[15] Eliot to Belknap, Dec. 10, 1780. *Ibid.*, Ser. 6, Vol. IV, p. 201.
[16] Eliot to Belknap, July 13, 1779; Jan. 26, 1780; April 14, 1780. *Ibid.*, Ser. 6, Vol. IV, pp. 144, 174, 183.

By December of that year, the inner circle of Chauncy's acquaintances were referring to it as " the pudding," so that they might talk about it without revealing their secret to outsiders. Thus on one occasion, when he wanted to find out whether an absent gentleman was in sympathy with his views, Chauncy inquired, " Doth he relish the pudding? " [17] Before long, too many people were in on the secret to have it remain a secret much longer. There was one episode at an ordaining council for Oliver Everett, who had been called to the New South Church, when it looked as though the pudding would be out of the bag for fair. The discussion began when the candidate was asked his views on the Trinity. " At last Dr. Chauncy grew mad, told Deacon Jeffres he was a fool, & Deacon Greenough that he knew nothing, & was fit only to lift up his hand, which was all any body expected from him." Angry words were spoken in reply, and the argument went on for an hour, until Dr. Cooper of the Brattle Street Church succeeded in quieting the storm. " It was lucky the dispute turned upon the article of the trinity & exhausted the patience of the Council, for this was only a prelude to other matters which would have set us all aghast. We might have been obliged to eat the pudding, bag & all." [18]

After much discussion, Chauncy resolved to send out " a scouting party, to make discoveries and try the temper of the public." [19] His colleague, John Clarke, compiled a series of Scripture texts and quotations from learned divines in support of universal salvation. Chauncy added a preface, in which he asserted that Murray's version of the doctrine was " an *encouragement* to *Libertinism*," with the result that many of the young people " by means of it, have lost all sense of religion, and given themselves up to the most crimi-

[17] Eliot to Belknap, Feb. 1781. *Ibid.*, Ser. 6, Vol. IV, p. 207.
[18] Eliot to Belknap, Feb. 1, 1782. *Ibid.*, Ser. 6, Vol. IV, pp. 225–226.
[19] Belknap to Hazard, Dec. 19, 1782. *Ibid.*, Ser. 5, Vol. II, p. 172.

nal excesses! " [20]   The pamphlet was called *Salvation for All Men*, was signed by " One Who Wishes Well to All Mankind," and appeared in August, 1782.   Certain of Chauncy's friends were not pleased with this particular pamphlet, evidently feeling that it would have been better to publish nothing rather than to issue " a meer castrated edition of the whole work," without its extensive critical apparatus.[21] Jeremy Belknap felt that the pamphlet had not put Chauncy's argument on the strongest ground, but seemed " to be an attempt to recommend the doctrine by the force of human authority." [22]   Murrayites were pleased, but they showed no signs of being converted from their Calvinistic universalism to Chauncy's variety.   " They are bold to say that [Chauncy and Clarke] will be Murrayites soon, that they have given up the main point & are coming over as fast as they can." [23]

A war of the printing press immediately broke out.   Samuel Mather wrote an essay in which he analyzed Clarke's pamphlet point by point, and accused its author of advocating " the *Popish* doctrine of *purgatory*, though not in plain and explicit terms, yet in truth and reality." [24]   Clarke's reply was not so much a refutation of Mather as a counterattack on him for the " *unprovoked abuse* " and " *sly insinuations* " in his pamphlet.   Clarke reprimanded him for trying " to confound the doctrines set forth in that pamphlet with the strange assertions of a certain *preacher* "; and he accused him of saying one thing in private and writing another in public in interpretation of certain critical passages of the

[20] [Charles Chauncy], *Salvation for All Men, Illustrated and Vindicated as a Scripture Doctrine* (Boston, 1782), p. iii.   A second edition appeared later in the same year.

[21] Eliot to Belknap, Aug. 14, 1782. *Coll. Mass. Hist. Soc.*, Ser. 6, Vol. IV, p. 233.

[22] Belknap to Hazard, Dec. 19, 1782. *Ibid.*, Ser. 5, Vol. II, p. 171.

[23] Eliot to Belknap, Sept. 30, 1782. *Ibid.*, Ser. 6, Vol. IV, p. 237.

[24] Samuel Mather, *All Men Will Not Be Saved Forever* (Boston, 1782), p. 8.

Bible.[25]   Before the local clergy tired of this pastime, contributions had been made by the Reverend Joseph Eckley of the Old South Church,[26] the Reverend William Gordon of the Third Church in Roxbury,[27] and the Reverend Peter Thacher of Malden, who afterwards became minister of the Brattle Street Church.[28]   From Rhode Island, Samuel Hopkins of Newport also wrote against Chauncy.[29]

The results were necessarily inconclusive, so long as the pudding remained concealed.   Jeremy Belknap called the controversy " only the skirmishing of light infantry, while the main body lies still, and nothing decisive will come of it." His fear was that passions would become so embittered, and prejudices so aroused, that the pudding itself would not get a fair reception.[30]   The situation had developed to a point where the pudding would have to be placed in general circulation.   In October, 1783, Dr. Eliot reported: " 'Tis probable the Pudding will be boiled in England." [31]   The following summer, the first copies finally appeared in Boston.

III

Chauncy's universalism seemed new and heretical to many Arminians, just as it did to the Calvinists.   Yet it rested on assumptions which Arminians had long taken for granted. It is perhaps more important to stress the familiar premises of the argument than its novel conclusion.

[25] John Clarke, *A Letter to Doctor Mather* (Boston, 1782), pp. 1, 3, 6.

[26] [Joseph Eckley], *Divine Glory, Brought to View, in the Condemnation of the Ungodly* (Boston, 1782).

[27] William Gordon, *The Doctrine of Final Universal Salvation Examined and Shewn to Be Unscriptural* (Boston, 1783).

[28] Peter Thacher, *That the Punishment of the Finally Impenitent Shall Be Eternal* (Salem, 1783).

[29] Samuel Hopkins, *Inquiry Concerning the Future State of Those Who Die in Their Sins* (Newport, 1783).

[30] Belknap to Hazard, Dec. 19, 1782. *Coll. Mass. Hist. Soc.*, Ser. 5, Vol. II, p. 172.

[31] Eliot to Belknap, Oct. 22, 1783. *Ibid.*, Ser. 6, Vol. IV, p. 265.

In the first place, Chauncy insisted that only the Bible can be the source of truth in a matter of this kind. What will become of the soul after death is a question to which reason gives no certain answer; it is precisely the kind of question which calls for revelation to supplement reason. The light of reason may tell us that there is an existence beyond the grave. " But does it discover, with *clearness* and *certainty*, what our *condition* will be in *that state?* " [32]   The Scripture doctrine, of course, must harmonize with reason; it may be above reason, but it cannot be contrary to it. Chauncy went to the Bible, therefore, not to find texts to corroborate a preconceived idea, but to compare, interpret, and harmonize various parts of Scripture. From this process his conclusions emerged, not at once, but only as he had been " gradually and insensibly let into them by a long and diligent comparing of *scripture with scripture.*" [33]

Chauncy's second assumption was supported both by the Bible and by natural religion. It was that God is infinitely benevolent, wise, and powerful. He expresses his benevolence towards his creation by forming human souls for happiness. Since he is wise and powerful, his purposes cannot be frustrated, and his goal must at last be achieved. " It would be hard to suppose, that infinite wisdom should finally be outdone by the obstinacy and folly of any free agents whatsoever." [34]

Chauncy assumed with respect to men that they are free moral agents, which means that God's ends will be attained, not by mechanical force, but by men's voluntary response to motivations set before them. He assumed further that in this life, men are possessed of both sinful and virtuous tend-

[32] Charles Chauncy, *The Mystery Hid from Ages and Generations . . . or, The Salvation of All Men* (London, 1784), p. 359.
[33] *Ibid.*, p. vi.
[34] *Ibid.*, p. 2.

encies; hence they sometimes behave sinfully and sometimes virtuously. But he also believed that the inner disposition of the heart is not a fixed and unalterable thing; that men's sinful impulses can be brought under control, their tendencies to do justly and to love mercy strengthened, and the temper of their souls drawn to God. But in the present life this goal is seldom reached; hence the actual state of man is that of a being limited by weakness and sin.

And finally, Chauncy assumed that salvation means reconciliation with God — both God to man and man to God. God's pardon of the guilty is only half of the process of reconciliation. The other half is the development in man of the ability truly to love God and to place service to him above all selfish desires. Salvation is from sin itself, as well as from the guilt of sin. Without an altered temper of the heart and soul, God's pardon would not mean happiness for the creature. That comes only when " they are all cured of their moral depravity, and formed to a meetness for heaven, by being brought back to a virtuous temper of mind." [35]

For Chauncy, then, all of life and part of life after death is a process of trial and discipline, by which sin is conquered and virtue triumphs in the soul. The future, stretching out into eternity, may be divided into several stages. The present one will come to an end when Christ returns to sit at the right hand of the Father and judge the quick and the dead. Then the righteous will forthwith be translated to heaven, there to reign in life and glory, while the wicked shall be sent " by the Lord Jesus Christ, in execution of his mediatory trust, to the place of *weeping, and wailing, and gnashing of teeth.*" [36]

But Christ does not yet resign his role as mediator. Another state now commences, or perhaps a series of states,

[35] *Ibid.*, pp. 10–11.   [36] *Ibid.*, p. 220.

which may be of long continuance: " during the whole of this
state, the *righteous* shall be *happy*, under the government of
Christ, and the *wicked miserable*." [37] The torments of the
sinful may well be quite as dreadful as anything the orthodox
clergy could imagine. But they are designed by God for
reformation, not for vengeance. Hence the souls of men will
suffer " in proportion to the number and greatness of their
vices." [38] Or, if you will, men will suffer in proportion to
the tenacity of the grip which their own moral depravity has
on them. Ultimately the last rebellious heart will be subdued, the last unwilling soul will have become the obedient
subject of God, and the last miserable sinner " fixed in the
possession of compleat and everlasting happiness." [39] Only
then will death, the second as well as the first death, be swal-
lowed up in victory. Only then will the Son of God and
Saviour of men " deliver up his trust into the hands of the
Father, who committed it to him," [40] so that God is finally
all in all. " Then cometh the end, when he shall have delivered up the kingdom to God, even the Father; when he
shall have put down all rule, and all authority, and power.
For he must reign till he hath put all enemies under his
feet." [41]

IV

The orthodox reaction to Chauncy's book was less violent
than might have been expected. The most ambitious reply
was the younger Edwards' *Salvation of All Men Strictly*

[37] *Ibid.*, p. 221.
[38] *Ibid.*, p. 10.
[39] *Ibid.*, p. 3.
[40] *Ibid.*, p. 13.
[41] 1 Cor. 15:24, 25. This passage was crucial in Chauncy's thinking. " It
was this indeed that first opened to me the present scheme, serving as a *key* to
unlock the meaning of many passages in the sacred writings, which before I
could never understand." Chauncy, *Salvation of All Men*, p. 197.

Examined (1790), which proved chiefly that its author was not the skilled controversialist his father had been. Two of the orthodox arguments against Chauncy deserve mention. The first was the traditional one, that sin committed against an infinite God is an infinite evil which deserves infinite punishment. Chauncy called this a " metaphysical nicety "; he retorted that sin committed by a finite creature under the sway of finite passions and appetites is a finite evil. On this point there was never any chance for accommodation or compromise. Both arguments were logical; both were equally plausible and implausible; both were stated with admirable dogmatism — and neither had the slightest effect on the opposing party.

The second point made by the orthodox hinted at more trouble to come. " If no other than a disciplinary punishment be consistent with the divine goodness," said Edwards, " surely the requirement of an atonement in order to pardon is unaccountable." [42] If men are punished in accordance with their deserts, then they can claim a release from further suffering as theirs of right, once amendment of character has taken place. " What need then have they of Christ, of his obedience and death, or of his mediatorial intervention, to be brought into the account? " [43] Of course Chauncy firmly believed in Jesus Christ as the mediator " *through whom,* and *upon whose account,* happiness is attainable by any of the human race." [44] He argued that the mediatorial role is greatly exalted when Christ is regarded as the Saviour of all men, rather than of a small group of the elect. But whether the role is altered as well as exalted was a matter to which he

---

[42] Jonathan Edwards, Jr., *The Works of Jonathan Edwards, D.D.* (Boston, 1854), I, p. 64.
[43] *Ibid.*, I, p. 13.
[44] Chauncy, *Salvation of All Men*, p. 17.

gave little attention. The emergence of anti-Trinitarianism after the Revolution gave the question an urgency which it had not had at the time the book was written.

Among the Arminians, there were very few who accepted the pudding without hesitation. Even Chauncy's intimates, who were predisposed in its favor, were somewhat reluctant converts. John Eliot speculated that the lot of the stubbornly impenitent might be annihilation, rather than final restitution. " Annihilation is not the punishment inflicted on human creatures. It is only a departure from being to those who are not equal to the purposes of existence." [45] Nevertheless, he hoped to be convinced by the Doctor's arguments. " I am much pleased with what you have written against my scheme of Annihilation," he wrote to Belknap. " I had rather believe the other doctrine, because it is more congenial to the disposition of my soul, which is benevolent upon the whole; and had I only a rational view of the matter I should adopt it." [46] His final judgment was that Chauncy's scriptural interpretations were unanswerable, but that this was, nonetheless, a highly speculative matter about which one might be skeptical. " Perhaps I may be said to believe it. There are degrees of faith. Mine is not so strong but that I something doubt at times." [47]

Jeremy Belknap's initial reaction was more favorable than Eliot's, but as time went on, he too became less positive. In 1787, he received a call to the Church in Long Lane in Boston, which had originally been organized by Scotch Presbyterians under John Moorehead, and which afterwards became a Unitarian church under William Ellery Channing. A deacon of the church received an anonymous letter, signed

---

[45] Eliot to Belknap, March 29, 1780. *Coll. Mass. Hist. Soc.*, Ser. 6, Vol. IV, p. 180.
[46] Eliot to Belknap, Jan. 26, 1780. *Ibid.*, Ser. 6, Vol. IV, p. 175.
[47] Eliot to Belknap, April 14, 1780. *Ibid.*, Ser. 6, Vol. IV, p. 183.

" Moorhead's Ghost," which accused Belknap of universalism. Belknap immediately denied any sympathy with Murray's doctrine. As for Chauncy's, he admitted that he had doubts about " the immortality of the wicked in a state of future punishment," though he " had no doubt of the certainty of the punishment." But whether the second death which is in store for the wicked is " an utter extinction of being," or whether it will be followed by another resurrection " are points which I cannot determine, nor do I think the Scriptures afford us full satisfaction on these subjects." [48]

Uncertain whether universalism is a doctrine clearly taught in the Bible, the Arminians refused to make it a central theme of their preaching. Chauncy's book appealed to them more for its emphasis on the process of reformation of character than for its conclusion. Yet in a negative way, they accepted that conclusion; for the opposite doctrine of the eternal torment of the wicked dropped out of their sermons entirely. They finally put behind them the argument of Mayhew, that the everlasting punishment of a few may be to the advantage of mankind as a whole. Before them, though they knew it not, was Emerson's doctrine of the infinity of the soul, whose latent powers are gradually unfolded as it is reshaped by the influx of the divine energy of the Oversoul. Meanwhile, the Arminians could only reiterate prosaically that life is a time of trial and discipline and gradual transformation of character, by which man is fitted for eternal happiness hereafter.

[48] Jane B. Marcou, *Life of Jeremy Belknap, D.D.* (New York, 1847), pp. 144, 145.

CHAPTER NINE

Anti-Trinitarianism

1755–1805

I

There was no inevitable connection between Arminianism
and anti-Trinitarianism. Full-fledged Arminians were to be
found in New England when Unitarianism was no more than
a rumor discussed in ordaining councils. John Tucker was
termed " a Corypheus among the Arminians " by one of his
successors in the Newbury church. Yet this biographer,
orthodox though he was, attested that " there is no proof that
he deviated any farther from the accredited standards of the
day." [1] Even in the nineteenth century, it was possible to find
a few ministers who were at once Arminian and Trinitarian.[2]

But the orthodox commonly assumed that Arminianism
led invariably to Arianism, and then to Socinianism and even
more horrible errors. There was much to justify their suspicions. For if Arminianism and anti-Trinitarianism were
logically two different things, temperamentally and histori-
cally they went together. As Joseph Bellamy (Yale, 1735)
wrote to Ezra Stiles: " till the infinite evil of sin is seen, an
incarnate God dying on the Cross, is an incredible story." [3]

[1] Leonard Withington in William B. Sprague, *Annals of the American
Pulpit* (New York, 1857–1869), I, p. 453.

[2] Preserved Smith became a Unitarian in 1820. Up to that time, "though
he held Arminian sentiments on some points, yet, he did not reject the trinity.
He might be termed a trinitarian Arminian. . . ." [Preserved Smith], *A
Biographical Sketch of the Rev. Preserved Smith, late of Rowe, Mass.*
(Greenfield, Mass., 1852), p. 15.

[3] Isabel M. Calder, ed., *Letters and Papers of Ezra Stiles* (New Haven,
1933), p. 21.

The identification of anti-Trinitarianism with Arminianism was the more plausible because the two were found together in the writings of many English philosophers and divines. Samuel Clarke was perhaps the most influential of them. His *Scripture-Doctrine of the Trinity* (1712) was a pervasive influence, spreading anti-Trinitarianism in the Church of England and dissenting circles alike for two generations after its publication. Second only to Clarke was Thomas Emlyn, the author of *An Humble Inquiry into the Scripture-Account of Jesus Christ* (1702). The whole group of dissenters with whom Mayhew corresponded — Benson, Lardner, and Foster — were as unsound on the Trinity as they were on the doctrines of grace. So was Richard Price, whose *Sermons on the Christian Doctrine* (1787) influenced many Arminians at the end of the century.

The variety of anti-Trinitarianism which was most common throughout the eighteenth century was Arianism.[4] This term was loosely applied to the doctrine that Christ is inferior to God the Father, yet more than mere man, having been created before the beginning of the world. Clarke, Emlyn, and Price were Arian or semi-Arian. Clarke's book was a collection, with commentary, of all the Biblical texts bearing on the subject. It came to the conclusion that there is but one supreme cause existing from all time. With it have existed from the beginning the Son and the Holy Spirit; but " What the proper Metaphysical *Nature, Essence,* or *Substance* of any of these divine Persons is, the Scripture has no where at all declared; but describes and distinguishes them always by their PERSONAL *Characters, Offices, Powers,* and *Attributes*." [5] Supreme honor, therefore, is due only to the Creator, and whatever honor is paid to Christ must be

---

[4] See J. Hay Colligan, *The Arian Movement in England* (London, 1913).

[5] Samuel Clarke, *The Scripture-Doctrine of the Trinity* (3rd ed., London, 1737), p. 234.

understood as redounding ultimately to the glory of the Father.

Arianism is to be distinguished from Socinianism, which made of Christ a man, though one whom God created wholly perfect, and endowed with special authority and a faithful revelation of his will. The roots of Socinianism may be traced back from England to Holland, and ultimately to Poland and Transylvania in the sixteenth century.[6] It was a major irritant of the Trinitarian controversy which began in the Church of England in the 1690's. It was less widespread and held by less influential thinkers in England than Arianism in the first half of the eighteenth century; but as the decades passed, it tended to supplant the unstable compromise which was Arianism. By the end of the century, English Unitarianism was perhaps best exemplified in the Socinianism of Joseph Priestley.

It was the Arminianism of men like Samuel Clarke that first appealed to the New England liberals. Their Arianism made its way much more slowly. Anti-Trinitarianism in New England before the Revolution was in a stage comparable to Arminianism before the Great Awakening. There was enough of it to alarm the orthodox, but its exact nature and extent remained uncertain. Probably no one would have been more astonished than Jonathan Mayhew, had it been revealed to him that a controversy over the Trinity, rather than over the doctrines of grace, would finally split the churches of the Standing Order.

II

Throughout the first half of the century, then, incidents revealing unsoundness on the Trinity were rare. It was

---

[6] See Earl Morse Wilbur, *A History of Unitarianism: Socinianism and its Antecedents* (Cambridge, 1945); also H. John McLachlan, *Socinianism in Seventeenth-Century England* (London, 1951).

said of Benjamin Kent in 1735 that he " held and vented unsound and dangerous opinions with respect to the great and
important Scripture doctrine of the Trinity "; [7] and at about
the same time, Robert Breck was accused of denying the
genuineness of 1 John 5:7.[8] Later generations looking back
have observed that the Arminians failed to mention the Trinity, and this omission has sometimes led to the suspicion that
they were concealing their heresy. But it should be recalled
that the Unitarian Controversy brought to the fore a doctrine
which up to that time had not been particularly stressed in
New England. The Trinity was a part of Puritan theology,
but it never took up much of the attention of the first settlers.
Neglect of it was an established custom long before any
Arians appeared on the scene.

About mid-century, the orthodox showed signs of increased uneasiness. In 1750, Aaron Hutchinson (Yale,
1747) was settled in Grafton, and soon afterwards the covenant was altered to recognize specifically the doctrine of one
God in three persons.[9] In 1743, when John Rogers was settled in Leominster, the church declared: " We dedicate ourselves to the Lord Jehovah, (to the Father, Son and Holy
Spirit,) and take Him for our eternal portion." Seventeen
years later, the covenant was revised so as to avoid all possible ambiguity: " We do avouch the Lord to be our God,
whose name alone is Jehovah, Father, Son and Holy Spirit
three persons in one God. . . ." [10] One reason for this increased doctrinal awareness was that the Leominster church
had just gone through the unpleasant business of dismissing

[7] Levi A. Field, *An Historical Sketch of the First Congregational Church
in Marlborough, Mass.* (Worcester, 1859), p. 26.
[8] *A Narrative of the Proceedings of those Ministers of the County of
Hampshire. . . .* (Boston, 1736), p. 4.
[9] Frederick C. Pierce, *History of Grafton* (Worcester, 1879), p. 181.
[10] Rufus P. Stebbins, *A Centennial Discourse Delivered to the First Congregational Church and Society in Leominster, September 24, 1843* (Boston,
1843), pp. 82, 96.

Mr. Rogers, one of the charges being unsoundness on this very point. A majority of the council which dismissed him agreed that " the aggrieved brethren had just ground of suspicion, that the Rev. Mr. Rogers did not hold or believe the essential Divinity of Christ as it is revealed in the Divine Word." [11]

There was another cause for alarm at about the same time. In 1755, Jonathan Mayhew appeared in print with ridicule of the Athanasian version of the doctrine. He seemed to be blurting out, in characteristically blunt fashion, something which his more discreet colleagues only whispered among themselves. He spoke of the importance of the unity of God, " the not sufficiently preserving of which *Unity* and *Supremacy* amongst Christians, has long been just matter of reproach to them; and a great stumbling-block both to *Jews* and *Mahometans*." Then he added a footnote:

With the metaphysical abstract nature, or essence of the Deity, I am not bold enough to meddle. Disquisitions of this kind, and denunciations of God's vengeance against those who do not affect to be *wise,* or are not willing to believe, *above what is written,* are left to the unaccountable Temerity of the Athanasians.[12]

One can imagine the annoyance of the orthodox ministers when they read these oblique criticisms. Their feelings were not soothed when they found later, in the same volume, a criticism of " hot religious zealots " and " great sticklers " for what is supposed to be orthodoxy: " Some contend, and foam, and curse their brethren, for the sake of the *Athanasian Trinity,* 'till 'tis evident they do not love and fear the ONE living and true God as they ought to do." [13]   But Mayhew was merely goading them for the final thrust. Toward the end of the volume, he commented on the passage from the

[11] *Ibid.,* p. 84.
[12] Jonathan Mayhew, *Sermons* (Boston, 1755), p. 269n.
[13] *Ibid.,* p. 403.

New Testament which declares " to us there is but one God, the Father ":

The scripture informs us that the *Logos* had a *body* prepared for him, and that he partook of *flesh* and *blood*, that he might " thro' death destroy him that had the power of death, that is the *devil*." But that he took into *personal union* with himself, an human *soul*, my Bible saith not; nor that there is any other true God, besides " his Father and our Father, his God and our God." Indeed some who call themselves Christians, have exalted even the *Virgin Mary* above all that is called God in *heaven*, and that is worshipped *there;* saying that she is more *kind* and *merciful* than God himself; and praying her to *command* her Son to befriend them; styling her the *Mother of God*, &c. It would be no great surprize to me to hear that the *Pope* and a *general Council*, had declared the *B. Virgin* to be the *fourth*, or rather the *first Person*, in the *Godhead*, under the title of *God*, or *Goddess* THE MOTHER; adding that neither the *Persons* are to be *confounded*, nor the *substance divided;* that the Mother is eternal, the Father eternal, the Son eternal, and the Holy Ghost eternal; but yet that there are not *four* Eternals, but *one* Eternal; that this is the *catholic faith*, which except a man *believe* faithfully, he cannot be *saved*. . . . But neither *Papists* nor *Protestants* should imagine that they will be understood by *others*, if they do not understand *themselves:* Nor should they think that nonsense and contradictions can ever be too *sacred* to be *ridiculous*.[14]

This passage was something of a scandal in its day. Was this not confirmation of what the orthodox had so long suspected? Obviously some sort of action was called for. There is reason to believe that Dr. Sewall and Dr. Prince of the Old South Church wanted to deprive Mayhew of his seat on the Harvard Board of Overseers, but nothing came of that suggestion.[15] Several of the Boston ministers began to stress the doctrine of the Trinity in sermons and lectures; and in 1756, Sewall, Prince, and Foxcroft joined to sponsor the publication of *All Power in Heaven, and in Earth Given*

---

[14] *Ibid.*, p. 418n.
[15] Alden Bradford, *Memoir of the Life and Writings of Rev. Jonathan Mayhew, D.D.* (Boston, 1838), p. 26n; Josiah Quincy, *The History of Harvard University* (Boston, 1840), II, p. 67.

unto Jesus Christ, by Ebenezer Pemberton. This sermon was accompanied by an appendix giving some of the scriptural evidences for the " eternal essential Divinity of our blessed Saviour "; and the three sponsors expressed the hope that this compilation would guard its readers " from those most dangerous and pernicious Suggestions against his adorable Deity which have been of late unhappily publish'd, to the great Grief and Offence of many among us." [16]

Jonathan Edwards was alarmed by the new turn of events, and wrote to Thomas Foxcroft urging that an open defence of the doctrine of the divinity of Christ be made.[17] Joseph Bellamy was equally disturbed. Come to Boston, he wrote, " and see there a celebrated D.D. the head of a large party! He boldly ridicules the doctrine of the Trinity, and denies the doctrine of justification by faith alone, in the sight of all the country, in his book of sermons." [18] Jonathan Parsons (Yale, 1729) of Newburyport was more upset than any of the others. " Perhaps *Arminianism* and *Arianism* were never propagated with *more openness* and *resolution,* nor with *less opposition,* in our land than at this day," he lamented. " Men of figure are bold enough to deride and banter the sacred doctrines of christianity, and despise our orthodox confessions of faith. . . ." He hoped that when they prayed, serious Christians would, as it were, call God's attention to what was going on, " especially in their closets, where they can freely mention their name, character, office, and the influence they are likely to have upon others." Parsons himself had no doubt as to where Mayhew would end:

[16] Ebenezer Pemberton, *All Power in Heaven, and in Earth Given unto Jesus Christ* (Boston, 1756), pp. 21, iv.

[17] Joseph S. Clark, *A Historical Sketch of the Congregational Churches in Massachusetts* (Boston, 1858), p. 181.

[18] Joseph Bellamy, *The Works of Joseph Bellamy, D.D.* (Boston, 1853), I, p. 610.

" I see no reason to expect that such haughty, blaspheming bablers, will, without deep repentance of this as well as other sins, be found in the last day, among those whom Christ saves. . . ." [19]

Mayhew's book appeared in 1755. The following year, the dismay of the orthodox was increased by the re-publication at Boston of Thomas Emlyn's *Humble Inquiry*. It was dedicated to the clergy of New England by its anonymous sponsor, who affirmed that in his opinion it contained " the true, plain, unadulterated doctrine of the gospel." [20] James Freeman long afterwards reported that Mayhew was the " principal means " of the re-publication of this book, and that he was aided by his parishioners and several friends.[21] Mayhew, if Mayhew it was who wrote the dedication, expressed the hope that the clergy of New England would agree with him that the piece was " rationally, spiritually and candidly " written, and should be recommended to the people under their charge. But if, he added, they should find that its doctrine was heresy, at least they would have a fair opportunity to refute it. Edwards wrote again, this time to Professor Wigglesworth of Harvard, urging that he accept the challenge; but Wigglesworth replied that a better plan would be to reprint the best English answer to Emlyn that could be found. This would do all the good that a new refutation could, and at the same time " it would avoid giving any occasion, which some of the adverse party seem to wish for, of setting the controversy on foot among ourselves; a thing

---

[19] Jonathan Parsons, *Good News from a Far Country* (Portsmouth, N. H., 1756), pp. iii, 76n.

[20] Thomas Emlyn, *An Humble Inquiry into the Scripture-Account of Jesus Christ . . . Now Re-published, with a Dedication to the Reverend Ministers of All Denominations in New-England* (Boston, 1756), p. viii.

[21] James Freeman, *Sermons on Particular Occasions* (3rd ed., Boston, 1821), pp. 235, 236.

which I would avoid as much as possible consistent with a due concern for such an important truth." [22]   So it was Edwards' son-in-law, Aaron Burr of the College of New Jersey, whose *Supreme Deity of our Lord Jesus Christ, Maintained* (1757) accepted the challenge of Emlyn's anonymous sponsor.[23] Other trinitarians soon began to make a point of insisting on the importance of the divinity of Christ, even when they did not specifically refute Emlyn.[24]

A few years of quiescence followed; then, in 1767, Simeon Howard was installed at the West Church as successor to Mayhew.   He was believed to hold theological views similar to those of the distinguished doctor whose pulpit he occupied and whose widow he married.   No doubt Andrew Croswell had his installation in mind when he admonished his colleagues not to participate in the ordination of Arians.   Those "who have fellowship in such undertakings," he said, "if they are not *Arians* themselves, they are next door to *Arians*."   Such men "can carry on the cause of *Arians* for them, better than they themselves can. — These have been the chief instruments of promoting it thro' the land in general, and especially, in the *Metropolis*." [25]   Samuel Hopkins also prepared a sermon especially to be preached in Boston, "under a conviction that the doctrine of the divinity of Christ was much neglected, if not disbelieved" by a number of the ministers there.[26]

[22] Clark, *Congregational Churches*, p. 184.   The English refutation of Emlyn chosen by the orthodox to be reprinted was an anonymous tract: *That Jesus Christ is God by Nature, of the Same Essence with the Father, Proved to be the Doctrine of Christianity.*   (Reprinted Boston, 1756).

[23] [Aaron Burr], *The Supreme Deity of Our Lord Jesus Christ, Maintained* (Boston, 1757).

[24] Joseph Bellamy, *Works*, I, pp. 417–441; John Barnard, *The True Divinity of Jesus Christ* (Boston, 1761).

[25] Andrew Croswell, *Comfort in Christ* (Boston, 1767), p. 14n.

[26] Samuel Hopkins, *The Works of Samuel Hopkins, D.D.* (Boston, 1854), I, p. 199; see also III, pp. 501–517.

Although Mayhew and Howard were accused of Arianism, neither of them accepted that name openly. But it is clear that the tendency of the first generation of Arminians was towards Arianism rather than Socinianism. Chauncy usually referred to Christ as " the Son of God," to emphasize his subordination to the Father. Mayhew, indeed, protested because many theologians, instead of using this title, " chuse commonly to change it into, *God the Son;* an expression which never once occurs in the holy scriptures." Then he added, in a manner typical of him: " With how fair, candid and pious an intention they do this, others may *conjecture,* but themselves doubtless *know.*"[27] Mayhew clearly rejected Athanasianism, and he specifically denied that he was a Socinian.[28] He denied further that he had " treated in a bold or ludicrous manner, the divinity of the Son of God, as revealed in scripture," while acknowledging that he had expressed disbelief, " and even contempt of certain metaphysical and scolastic, unscriptural and ridiculous definitions or explications of the *trinity,* which some men have given."[29] The closest he came to a positive statement of belief was that Christ possessed a " glory which he had with the FATHER before the world was." But as to the incarnation, or " mode of the divine inhabitation in Christ," he declared that " it is neither revealed, nor to be comprehended by mortal men; who cannot even comprehend the manner in which their own spirits dwell in their bodies."[30] On this issue, Mayhew and Chauncy alike retreated to Bible language and refused to be more explicit.

[27] Jonathan Mayhew, *Christian Sobriety* (Boston, 1763), p. 59.
[28] Mayhew, *Christian Sobriety,* p. 57; Mayhew, *A Defence of the Observations on the Charter and Conduct of the Society for the Propagation of the Gospel in Foreign Parts* (Boston, 1763), pp. 110, 111.
[29] Mayhew, *Defence,* p. 111.
[30] Mayhew, *Christian Sobriety,* pp. 57, 60.

III

Arianism continued to be the commonest form of Unitarianism in New England until well into the nineteenth century. The liberals long considered a Socinian or " humanitarian " Christology to be as unscriptural as Athanasianism. Two ministers among them, however, were receptive to Socinianism: James Freeman and his college classmate, William Bentley. There was enough difference between these two and their colleagues for many of the Arians to show a certain degree of coolness towards them.[31]   This lack of cordiality was not a matter of theology alone: Freeman was minister of the Stone Chapel, or King's Chapel, with its Anglican traditions; and Bentley, of the East Church in Salem, was a Jeffersonian when most of his colleagues were Federalists. But for some years the Boston ministers were reluctant to exchange with Freeman, while Bentley had no hesitation in doing so.[32]   The story of New England Socinianism, then, is chiefly the story of these two men.

Freeman's background was congregationalist; and after graduation from Harvard in 1777, he read theology with the usual expectation of installation over a congregational church. But in September, 1782, the Wardens of King's Chapel invited him to serve for the time being as lay reader, there being no immediate prospect of securing a candidate with episcopal orders. They authorized him to use the Athanasian Creed or not, at his discretion. He accepted their offer, and even began to speculate that he might be the first minister ordained in America by the Episcopalians on a basis

---

[31] " Unitarianism in America," *Monthly Repository of Theology and General Literature*, VII (1812), p. 56; William Bentley, *The Diary of William Bentley, D.D.*, 4 vols. (Salem, 1905–1914), *passim*.

[32] Bentley, *Diary*, I, p. 107.

of complete independence from the Church of England.[33]

Freeman soon came to like the Anglican liturgy, though he continued to regard congregational polity as the best in the world.[34] Before long, however, he developed scruples about trinitarian phrases in the Book of Common Prayer. Unlike the other Boston ministers, who could skirt the issue by withdrawing to a vague Arianism couched in biblical phrases, Freeman had to meet it directly. Even if he discarded the anathemas of the Athanasian creed, there remained the milder Trinitarianism of the Nicene embedded in the order of worship. He explained his difficulty to the congregation; and rather than lose his ministrations, they agreed to changes in the liturgy. On June 19, 1785, the proprietors voted, twenty to seven, " that the Common Prayer, as it now stands amended, be adopted by this church as the form of prayer to be used in future by this church and congregation." [35]

The most important alterations were the omission of the Nicene Creed and the Thirty-nine Articles, and revision of trinitarian formulas in the prayers and collects; but alterations were also made in the services for special occasions, the Catechism, and the Psalter.[36] Most of the revisions followed those of Theophilus Lindsey, which were based in turn on recommendations by Dr. Samuel Clarke. Freeman would have been willing to make more radical changes, and suggested the adoption of Lindsey's revised liturgy *in toto*. But " the people of the chapel were not ripe for so great a

[33] Henry Wilder Foote, *James Freeman and King's Chapel* (Boston, 1873), pp. 6, 7; reprinted from *The Religious Magazine and Monthly Review*, XLIX (1873), pp. 505–531. See also Foote, *Annals of King's Chapel* (Boston, 1881, 1896), II, Ch. 21.
[34] Foote, *James Freeman and King's Chapel*, p. 9.
[35] Foote, *Annals*, II, p. 381.
[36] *Ibid.*, II, pp. 381–383.

change." He therefore accepted some " defects and impro-
prieties " for the sake of being rid of Athanasianism, and with
the hope that further alteration might be possible at a later
date.[37]

Meanwhile, Freeman and his congregation were anxious
to secure ordination for him so that he would be competent
to administer the sacraments. In March, 1786, a committee
from the Chapel waited on Bishop Samuel Seabury, but he
demurred because of the unusual circumstances of the case,
and stated that he would have to consult with the clergy.
The following June, therefore, Freeman appeared before
the Episcopal Convention, meeting at Stratford, Connecticut.
He was examined with particular reference to his views on
the Trinity, was urged to go home and reconsider, and was
encouraged to return should deliberation lead him to alter
his opinions. Instead he went to New York to request ordination of the Bishop-elect, Dr. Samuel Provoost, who was
not unsympathetic, but was no more anxious to get himself
involved than Seabury had been. Finally, the Society decided to proceed with lay ordination, which took place on
Sunday evening, November 18, 1787.[38] It should be noted
that the method followed was not that which then prevailed
among the congregational churches, since no council was
called, neighboring ministers did not participate, and the congregation acted quite autonomously. No one was more
pleased at the outcome than William Bentley: " This moment I have received by the Salem Gazette the glorious news
of your Triumph over an oppressive enemy. It has raised
me into a transport." [39]

---

[37] Freeman to Lindsey, July 7, 1786, in Thomas Belsham, *Memoirs of the
Late Reverend Theophilus Lindsey, M.A.* (London, 1812), p. 239n.

[38] Detailed accounts are to be found in Foote, *Annals*, II, pp. 383–394,
and Foote, *James Freeman and King's Chapel*, pp. 16–29. See also Bentley,
Diary, I, pp. 81–82.

[39] Bentley, *Diary*, I, p. 80.

In both of these serious steps — rewriting the liturgy and accepting lay ordination — Freeman was much influenced by the Reverend William Hazlitt, an English Socinian or Unitarian, and a friend of both Price and Priestley.[40] He had sailed for America with his family in 1783, expecting to find a vacant pulpit somewhere and stay permanently. He preached first in the middle states, particularly in Philadelphia, where he was active in publishing some of Priestley's tracts. Finding no satisfactory opening there, he journeyed to Boston, with his eye on the vacancy at the Brattle Street Church caused by the death of Dr. Samuel Cooper, and bearing a letter of introduction to the Reverend John Eliot. On May 15, 1784, the very day he arrived, the Boston Association of Ministers was meeting at Dr. Chauncy's house, and Eliot presented him to the assembled brethren. When the question of ordination came up in the course of the discussion, Hazlitt expressed the view that lay ordination was scriptural. Freeman was impressed by his argument, and a friendship immediately developed between the two men. Hazlitt was soon busy supporting Freeman with letters printed in the gazettes; and Freeman afterwards declared, " I bless the day when that honest man first landed in this country." [41]

Hazlitt preached many times in Boston and nearby towns during a period of a year or more, but was no more successful in finding a permanent settlement than he had been in Philadelphia. Doubtless his Socinianism, which he did not conceal,

---

[40] This account of Hazlitt in America draws heavily on a letter, signed "An Old Unitarian," in Thomas Belsham's *Monthly Repository*, III (1808), pp. 302–307. The information in the letter is so detailed and circumstantial, that it seems probable that Hazlitt himself wrote it. Additional details may be found in W. Carew Hazlitt, " The Hazlitts in America a Century Since (1783–87)," *The Antiquary*, X (1884), pp. 113–119, 137–143; W. C. Hazlitt, *Lamb and Hazlitt* (London, 1900), pp. 11–17; and two letters from Hazlitt to Richard Price, Oct. 19, 1784 and Nov. 15, 1785, in *Proc. Mass. Hist. Soc.*, Ser. 2, Vol. XVII (1903), pp. 322–324, 334–336.

[41] Belsham, *Lindsey*, p. 240n.

was too extreme for many of his listeners; certainly he always attributed his failure to the bigotry of the orthodox. But it is very clear that his personality was an obnoxious one. His contemporaries liked and respected him up to a point; yet they nicknamed him " Paddy " on account of the three years he had lived in Ireland, and described him as intolerant, conceited, and a bore. Jeremy Belknap recorded that he criticized everyone but Price, Priestley, and Dr. Ewing of Philadelphia, " so as to disgust people who might have been pleased with him." [42]   With reference to the failure to receive a call to Brattle Street, John Eliot commented:

He was buoyed up with such an idea, and flattered himself that there were no difficulties at all in the way. It was only to hear him, & they would be much too captivated to let him go. In short, he is the most conceited & most imprudent man I ever met with, & yet hath many good qualities both of head and heart.[43]

Belknap said of him: " I think I never met with a person who was really a man of sense, and a scholar, whose company was so disgusting to me." [44]   He persuaded Dr. Lathrop to let him use his meetinghouse for a series of lectures, but they were poorly attended. " No wonder," wrote Eliot; " he spins out the subject, proposes to have 30 lectures. They are good solid discourses, but not adequate to the expectations of them who wish to serve him. I wish he was in Ireland." [45]

While in Boston and nearby, he preached from several of the Boston pulpits, and in such towns as Salem, Dorchester, Jamaica Plain, Weymouth, Marshfield, and Scituate. In Hingham he preached as many as forty times, and seems to

[42] Belknap to Hazard, June 19, 1784. *Coll. Mass. Hist. Soc.*, Ser. 5, Vol. II, p. 358.
[43] Eliot to Belknap, Aug. 26, 1784. *Ibid.*, Ser. 6, Vol. IV, p. 274.
[44] Belknap to Hazard, Aug. 16, 1784. *Ibid.*, Ser. 5, Vol. III, pp. 168, 169.
[45] Eliot to Belknap, Feb. 24, 1785. *Ibid.*, Ser. 6, IV, p. 285.

have hoped for a settlement there; but old Dr. Gay, in his eighty-ninth year, refused either to die or to retire. In the fall of 1785, he began to preach in the remote frontier settlement of Hallowell, on the Kennebec; but after a winter in Maine, he reached the conclusion that America was not the land of promise after all, and returned to England, where his family joined him soon after.

With everyone save Bentley and Freeman, Hazlitt quickly wore out his welcome; and so in the last analysis, it was his influence on them that mattered. He represented a living link with the leaders of English Unitarianism, and with Priestley in particular. While he did not introduce Priestley's writings to them, by his enthusiasm he stimulated theirs. In 1785, both Freeman and Bentley encouraged local publication of extracts from Priestley's catechism; the Boston edition appeared in the same volume as the new liturgy.[46] That same year, Hazlitt gave Bentley six copies of Priestley's *Appeal*, which he distributed to various proprietors of the East Church, except for one copy which he saved to lend.[47] In 1788, Bentley gave some of Priestley's smaller tracts to his friend, Captain Hodges, to take with him when he sailed; they contain, he declared, " all you may want to know of the simple doctrines of Christianity."[48] In 1795, Freeman sponsored the printing in Boston of Priestley's *Discourses on the Evidence of Revealed Religion;*[49] and the following year, when five hundred dollars was put into his hands for printing Unitarian books, Priestley's *History of the Corruptions of Christianity* was the first title that came to his mind.[50] In 1794, Priestley's son, William, visited Boston where he

---

[46] Bentley, *Diary*, I, p. 68.
[47] *Ibid.*, I, p. 19.
[48] *Ibid.*, I, p. 111.
[49] " Selections from Dr. W. Bentley's Correspondence," *New England Historical and Genealogical Register*, XXVII (1873), p. 352.
[50] Bentley, *Diary*, II, p. 202.

called on Freeman, who passed him along to Bentley for a personally escorted tour of the sights of Salem.[51]   In contrast with the eagerness with which they promoted Priestley, both Freeman and Bentley denied having anything to do with the re-publication of Emlyn's *Humble Inquiry* in 1790.[52]

There is some evidence that these activities encouraged the spread of Socinian doctrine, but the results were not spectacular.   Freeman gave credit to Hazlitt for having persuaded many of the Boston ministers to omit the trinitarian doxology: " Since his departure, the number of those who repeat only scriptural doxologies has greatly increased, so that there are now many churches in which the worship is strictly Unitarian." [53]   In March, 1792, a Unitarian congregation was formed in Portland, Maine, by the Reverend Thomas Oxnard, who had been an Episcopalian minister there.   He had been influenced by the writings of Priestley and Lindsey, which Freeman had given him.[54]   At about the same time a similar group organized in Saco, Maine.[55]   Neither became permanently rooted, however.   Freeman also reported to Lindsey in 1794 of the spread of Unitarianism in Plymouth, Barnstable, and Bristol counties.   But despite his optimism, even he was forced to admit, in a letter dated May 24, 1796, that the movement might be " losing ground in one quarter while it is gaining it in another." [56]

The safest conclusion is that Socinianism was far less important than Arianism; but the example of Freeman and the dissemination of Priestley's writings made it easier for a later

[51] *Ibid.*, II, pp. 112, 113; *New England Hist. and Gen. Reg.*, XXVII (1873), p. 356.
[52] Bentley, *Diary*, I, pp. 158, 187.
[53] Belsham, *Lindsey*, p. 240n.
[54] *Ibid.*, p. 245.
[55] *Ibid.*, p. 246.
[56] *Ibid.*, pp. 250–254.

generation to outgrow Arianism. That development was a slow process, made even slower by the attempts of the orthodox after 1805 to prove that the liberals were all of them Socinians in disguise. The liberals were slow to accept the label " Unitarian " on that account. In a letter written to an English Unitarian in 1812, Francis Parkman insisted that Freeman was the only " Unitarian " minister in Boston. " You say they are all Arians or Unitarians," he wrote, " as if these were very nearly the same. But I assure you, they would contend for a very great distinction, and *holding, as I believe they do, high and exalted views of the person and mediation of Jesus Christ . . . they would, I think, be very unwilling to be confounded with the followers of Dr. Priestley.* Some of them, I know, are utterly opposed to the sentiments and spirit of Unitarianism." [57]

IV

Parkman's protest serves as a reminder that there were really two problems with which the Arminians had to deal as they worked out their Christology. One was the nature of Christ: was he one person of a triune God? was he a subordinate being who nevertheless existed before the beginning of the world? or was he simply a specially favored man? The other problem was Christ's functions; and in particular, in what way does he serve as mediator between God and sinful man? Their emphasis on Christ's death, as well as his life, was one of the things which made the Arminians hesitate about Socinianism.

The Arminian emphasis on God's benevolence, quite as much as the spread of anti-Trinitarianism, forced a reconsideration of the doctrine of the atonement. When John

[57] Francis Parkman, " Letter to the Rev. Mr. Grundy, of Manchester," *Monthly Repository*, VII (1812), p. 201.

Cleaveland replied to Mayhew's two Thanksgiving sermons on the divine goodness, the crux of his complaint was that Mayhew had explained the goodness of God in such a way as to make the atonement of Christ superfluous. His evident design, Cleaveland charged, was " to represent the divine goodness in such a light as to shew, there was no absolute necessity of the sacrifice of Christ to make atonement, or to satisfy divine justice in order to God's forgiving the sins of men consistently with his moral goodness." [58]   The issue which divided them can be stated very simply. Cleaveland's view of the atonement was Anselmic; Mayhew's was Grotian.

The Anselmic theory of the atonement rests on the assumption that God will require satisfaction for every transgression. Man owes obedience to God; if he disobeys, he dishonors his creator. But God is an infinite being, and a sin against his law is an infinite one, which demands an infinite atonement. This is beyond the power of finite man; hence the necessity for Christ, the God-man. By taking on himself the sins of men, and giving his life freely for them, Christ has balanced the infinites in this moral equation. His righteousness is then imputed to the elect, so that God may display his mercy and goodness in the salvation of sinners.

The Anselmic theory made the relationship between God and man one between creditor and debtor. The Grotian or " governmental " atonement made it one of ruler and subject. A ruler inflicts punishment for the purpose of maintaining order and preventing crime. He wishes to ensure obedience to his government. He may remit the penalty if his purpose can be achieved in some other way. Christ's death serves as an example to sinners, warning them of the horrible nature and consequences of sin. His sacrifice there-

---

[58] John Cleaveland, *An Essay, to Defend Some of the Most Important Principles in the Protestant Reformed System of Christianity* (Boston, 1763), p. 9.

fore upholds the dignity of God's moral government, even without the punishment of every individual transgressor.

Mayhew's position was unmistakably Grotian. Infinite goodness and wisdom require, he said, that " the highest veneration for the majesty of God, his laws and government, should be preserved amongst all his reasonable creatures." The sacrifice of Christ secures this end, not because God " is in his own nature deficient in goodness, or not perfectly merciful," but because this method tends " to beget and preserve in the minds of reasonable creatures, a just sense of God's authority, the dignity of his laws and government: Which, as was intimated before, is evidently best even for themselves." [59]

Cleaveland protested that what Mayhew had done was to make the atonement simply the most convenient or expedient means for saving sinners, instead of something inherently essential. " The common supposition of divine justice," he insisted, " is, that it is so absolute in God . . . that he cannot consistently with his justice, righteousness or moral rectitude, forgive the sins of men, without satisfaction for sin or an atonement." But " Christ made no atonement by his sacrifice or sufferings, if his sacrifice or sufferings were without any kind of reference to such divine justice in God. . . ." [60] In short, Cleaveland regarded the governmental atonement as no atonement at all.

Mayhew was not the only Arminian who adopted the governmental atonement — or, at least, rejected the Anselmic theory and retreated to ambiguous generalities. Chauncy said of Christ that he " both did and suffered every thing that was necessary in order to a WORTHINESS, a RIGHTEOUS-

---

[59] Jonathan Mayhew, *Two Sermons on the Nature, Extent and Perfection of the Divine Goodness* (Boston, 1763), p. 64.
[60] Cleaveland, *Essay*, p. 11.

NESS, on account of which God might, in consistency with the honor of his perfections, and the authority of his law and government, manifest his mercy towards sinners." [61]   And Henry Cumings of Billerica regarded it reasonable to suppose that when God " restores sinners to favour upon repentance, he will do it in such a way, as shall keep in view his wrath against sin, and thereby preserve an awe and reverence of his government, among the rest of the subjects of his moral kingdom." [62]

Some Calvinists, to be sure, also adopted the governmental theory.   Edwards did not, but he was deserted by some of the most prominent of his followers.   In various forms the theory appeared in the works of Joseph Bellamy, Samuel Hopkins, and the younger Edwards; and indeed it was regarded as one of the hallmarks of the " New England Theology."   But it was especially congenial to the Arminians. It enabled them to reject the imputation of the righteousness of Christ and to emphasize the benevolence of God, without making Christ superfluous.   It fitted well with the Arianism to which they were turning, as the Anselmic atonement did not.   To be sure, many Arminians never went beyond such statements as that " *without shedding of Blood there was no Remission,*" [63] or that " we needed him to make *Atonement* or *Reconciliation* for *Iniquity*, and to bring in everlasting Righteousness; which none other could do." [64]   They were less concerned about the manner of operation of the atonement than they were about the danger of assuming that Christ's obedience makes ours unnecessary.   But the govern-

---

[61] Charles Chauncy, *Twelve Sermons* (Boston, 1765), p. 151.
[62] Henry Cumings, *A Sermon Preached at Bolton, at the Ordination of the Rev. Phineas Wright, October 26, 1785* (Boston, 1785), p. 14.
[63] Thomas Barnard, *The Christian Salvation* (Portsmouth, 1757), p. 13.
[64] Samuel Webster, *Justification by the Free Grace of God, through the Redemption there is in Christ* (Boston, 1765), p. 22.

mental atonement was the kind of theory to which they gave their assent when forced to take a stand.

But the function of Christ was not merely to make atonement by his obedience for the disobedience of men. Centuries of devout Christians had produced a much richer interpretation of his mission than that, and the Arminians had no reason to reject most of the traditional doctrine. They described him, in familiar terms, as prophet, priest, and king. As prophet, he is the chief source of our knowledge of God's revealed will. He teaches both by his doctrine and by his example: " He came to give mankind the most perfect and engaging example of obedience to the will of God; of all piety and righteousness, humility and charity, temperance and patience; — a living example in frail human flesh." [65] Since " examples teach more effectually than precepts," he has " set us the most shining example of that holy religion, which he came to preach and establish in the world." [66] As priest, Christ intercedes for men before the throne of grace. Samuel Webster spoke of him as " a Mediator between God and us, and a powerful Advocate at the Father's right Hand." [67] As king, Christ is the ruler of his church, its sole lawgiver and the judge of transgressions. It was he who " sent forth ministers to propagate it," and " fixed constitutions and ordinances, to derive on it all the advantages of religious society." [68]

It must be admitted that this kind of elaboration of the functions of Christ was derived from traditional Christian doctrine and reading of the Scripture, rather than from the inner logic of the Arminian position. As the decades passed,

[65] Mayhew, *Christian Sobriety*, p. 65.
[66] Samuel West, *A Sermon Preached at the Ordination of the Rev'd Jonathan Newell* (Boston, 1775), p. 6.
[67] Webster, *Justification*, p. 12.
[68] Thomas Barnard, *The Power of God, the Proof of Christianity* (Salem, 1768), p. 18.

bit by bit it was abandoned. Christ finally became simply the source of revelation from God, who inspires men by his example. His life of spotless purity counted most; his death became only a dramatic incident of perfect obedience:

> By his instruction he dispels the errours, which overshaded the human mind; by his precepts and exhortations he imparts new energy to the commands of reason, assisting it to regain its lost dominion over animal nature; and by his sufferings and death he proves the inherent and unchangeable mercy of God, moves sinful men to penitence and reformation, and thence expiates their guilt, and procures them the pardon of sin, and a title to celestial felicity.[69]

The Grotian atonement had now become as outdated as the Anselmic — the only difference being that while the earlier Arminians rejected the Anselmic atonement, the next generation simply forgot the Grotian.

But the figure of Christ continued to be the chief focus of religious emotions. Despite their changing Christology, men like Chauncy, or John Clarke, or William Emerson still regarded Christ as central to Christianity. A later Emerson could serenely condemn historical Christianity for dwelling " with noxious exaggeration about the *person* of Jesus." But for his father, a universe without Christ to perform his unique function would have been a universe empty and cold, devoid of all hope.

[69] William Emerson, *A Sermon, Delivered March 2, 1803, at the Ordination of the Rev. Thomas Beede* (Amherst, N.H., 1803), p. 16.

CHAPTER TEN

The Right of Private Judgment

1745–1805

I

Had Jonathan Mayhew vented his abominable heresies a century earlier, his stay in Massachusetts would have been a brief one. Even if he had escaped the fate of the Quakers who were executed in 1659, it is probable that the measure meted out to Roger Williams, Anne Hutchinson, and William Pyncheon would have been his portion also. The first settlers of Massachusetts Bay were not interested in religious toleration, which they regarded as an admission of insincerity. They had braved toil and danger to establish on these shores a Bible Commonwealth in accordance with their own interpretation of the Word of God, and they granted to those who disagreed with them full liberty to stay away.

But as the second half of the seventeenth century wore on, various factors conspired to blunt the persecuting spirit of the leaders of the Puritan theocracy. The most basic was the increasing maturity of the colony itself, marked by more complex social organization and the rise of activities and interests over which the church order found it hard to maintain control. For the clerical leaders of Massachusetts, of course, this change was not progress but deterioration. One of its symptoms was the appearance of dissenting groups, Baptists and Episcopalians as well as Quakers. In 1665, the First Baptist Church in Boston was organized. Its members were subjected to fines and imprisonment, and various types of persecution were practised until the 1680's. Eventually, however, the majority became reconciled to the fact that there were minorities in their midst. By 1718, Christian charity had made sufficient headway for both Increase and Cotton Mather to participate in the ordination of a Baptist minister in Boston.[1]

This drift toward toleration was reinforced by pressure from the Crown. The execution of the Quakers was rebuked by the home government, which also attempted to secure freedom of worship for members of the Church of England. Although the local authorities fought against such pressure as long as they could, the Massachusetts Charter of 1691 provided " that for ever hereafter there shall be a liberty of Conscience allowed in the Worshipp of God to all Christians (Except Papists) Inhabiting or which shall Inhabit or be Resident within our said Province or Territory." [2]

A third factor was the importation from England of the doctrine of toleration. There, it had first been accepted as an imperious necessity at the time of the civil wars, when the existence of innumerable conflicting opinions made it obvious that the ideal of uniformity was an impossible one. By the end of the century, religious liberty had become an ideal to be embraced, rather than a necessity to be reluctantly accepted. The arguments advanced by Chillingworth, Jeremy Taylor, Tillotson, and Locke finally penetrated the New England mind as well. For though Roger Williams had long since denied the power of magistrates to compel belief, the time was not ripe when he spoke, and in the final triumph

---

[1] A. H. Newman, *A History of the Baptist Churches in the United States* (New York, 1894), pp. 174–196.

[2] Sanford H. Cobb, *The Rise of Religious Liberty in America* (New York, 1902), Ch. 5, *passim*. The Charter of 1691 is reprinted in *Publications of the Colonial Society of Massachusetts*, II (1913), pp. 7–29.

of religious freedom in Massachusetts, his *Bloudy Tenent of Persecution* was probably much less important than Locke's *Letter Concerning Toleration.*

As a result, Mayhew stood in no fear of the gallows, or even of being ridden out of town on a rail. In an Election Sermon in 1747, Charles Chauncy expressed the prevailing view of religious liberty. The magistrates, he declared, must not " exert their authority in *settling articles of faith*, or *imposing modes of worship*, so as that all must frame their *belief*, and order their *practice*, according to their decisions, or lie exposed to *penalties* of one kind or another." Penal laws are not adapted to enlighten men's minds; only reasonable arguments can do that. The rulers, therefore, should leave " every member of the community, without respect of persons, freely to choose his own religion, and profess and practice it according to that *external form*, which he apprehends will be most acceptable to his maker: Provided, his religion is such as may consist with the public safety. . . ." Furthermore, those in authority should protect every man from abuse on account of his religious beliefs, " so far as he keeps within the bounds of decency, and approves himself a peaceable member of society." [3] By the time that Chauncy spoke, few would have dissented.

II

To be sure, complete separation of church and state did not prevail in Massachusetts. A law passed in 1692 provided that every town should maintain an " able, learned and orthodox " minister, supported by taxation. Although later acts of the General Court exempted Quakers, Baptists, and Episcopalians from contributing to the support of Congrega-

[3] Charles Chauncy, *Civil Magistrates Must be Just, Ruling in the Fear of God* (Boston, 1747), pp. 36, 37.

tional worship, yet the churches of the Standing Order were in a favored position. Inhabitants of a town who could prove that they belonged to one of the exempted groups were allowed to pay their tax money for the support of their own minister, but the indifferent and those not numerous enough to organize a society of their own in any given town had no relief.[4]

By the ministers of the Standing Order, Calvinist and Arminian alike, this scheme of state-supported religion was considered to be no infringement of religious freedom. The attack on it came from without, led especially by the Baptists. So consistent a supporter of liberty as John Tucker of Newbury defended it in 1774. To have to pay for the support of a minister with whom one disagreed, and to be obliged by law to listen to him, are two different things, he argued. " Were any obliged to this latter, by the laws of the province, they might justly complain of spiritual tyranny." In both towns and parishes, that which is approved by the majority is binding on all, since all enjoy the protection and privileges of the province laws. And the province " has the same right to provide for the support of a public ministry, as it has for the support of schools, or to enact any thing which it judges beneficial to civil society." In short, a tax-supported ministry is not tyranny and slavery in matters of conscience, whatever it may be with respect to the pocketbook.[5]

Jonathan Mayhew likewise defended the Massachusetts form of establishment. He considered it " perhaps, the most generous and catholic one that was ever made in any country," since at the same time that it favors one denomination

---

[4] Jacob C. Meyer, *Church and State in Massachusetts from 1740 to 1833* (Cleveland, 1930), Ch. 1.
[5] John Tucker, *Remarks on a Discourse of the Rev. Jonathan Parsons, of Newbury-Port* (Boston, 1774), pp. 11, 14.

" it countenances and encourages *all* others, and puts them in a legal method to support the public worship of God, according to their inclinations and consciences respectively." [6]   Indeed, Mayhew interpreted the law of 1692 so broadly that he supposed any Protestant minister would qualify as orthodox. " So that if any particular town in the Province should legally chuse, settle and support a protestant minister of *any* denomination, whether episcopalian, presbyterian, congregational, baptist, or lutheran, this would be looked upon as satisfying the said law." [7]

Such an establishment, Mayhew insisted, was a very different thing from the privileged position of the Church of England in the mother country. He saw no inconsistency, therefore, in approving the one and condemning the other, and in opposing Anglican bishops as the first step toward the wrong kind of establishment in the colonies. He feared the application of a sacramental test to exclude non-conformists from office, and the imposition of taxes on all without exemptions, for the maintenance of the episcopal clergy. [8]   Charles Chauncy similarly believed that no American bishop would be content to be deprived of the civil powers exercised by his colleagues at home — powers over the probate of wills, letters of guardianship and administration, and so on. [9]   Authority of this kind was what he had in mind when he argued that the state has no right to make religious establishments. " We are, in principle, against all civil establishments in religion," he declared; " and as we do not desire any such es-

---

[6] Jonathan Mayhew, *A Defence of the Observations on the Charter and Conduct of the Society for the Propagation of the Gospel* (Boston, 1763), p. 60.

[7] *Ibid.*, p. 58.

[8] Jonathan Mayhew, *Remarks on an Anonymous Tract, Entitled an Answer to Dr. Mayhew's Observations* (Boston, 1764), p. 63.

[9] Charles Chauncy, *The Appeal to the Public Answered* (Boston, 1768), p. 148.

tablishment in support of our own religious sentiments, or practice, we cannot reasonably be blamed, if we are not disposed to encourage one in favor of the Episcopal Colonists." [10]

The Massachusetts Standing Order was perpetuated, and indeed made a part of the fundamental law, by the Constitution of 1780. The provisions of Article III of the Bill of Rights were less liberal, even, than the old province laws had been. Previously, Baptists and Quakers who supported their own worship were exempted from taxation; now they were assessed as usual, and their ministers had to apply to the town for an appropriate share of the taxes. Many groups found that it was not easy to gain a recognized status which the town officials would respect. These provisions of the new constitution were bitterly criticized, the chief attack being made by the Baptists under the leadership of Isaac Backus. [11]

Arguments in favor of a more thoroughgoing separation of church and state had little effect on the Arminians. Their comments on the Massachusetts establishment followed a regular pattern: they proclaimed their devotion to freedom of conscience, but insisted that rights of conscience were not involved in the matter. [12] Aaron Bancroft of the Second Par-

[10] *Ibid.*, p. 152. On the whole question of American Bishops, see Arthur L. Cross, *The Anglican Episcopate and the American Colonies* (New York, 1902).

[11] S. E. Morison, " The Struggle over the Adoption of the Constitution of Massachusetts, 1780," *Proc. Mass. Hist. Soc.*, L (1917), pp. 368–381.

[12] It is usual today to condemn the supporters of the Standing Order, and to praise the Baptists for advocating separation of church and state. Yet we think nothing of taxing the whole community for support of public schools, even though various minority groups are profoundly out of sympathy with the kind of intellectual and moral training which the schools afford. We do not even grant tax-exemption to dissenters, as the Massachusetts Constitution of 1780 did to religious minorities.

Actually, the past century and a half has seen the school supplant the church as the chief institution (apart from the family) by which social norms are transmitted to the new generation. As the church declined in importance, society relinquished control over it, a process which we call " the triumph of the

ish in Worcester was regarded by his contemporaries as a conspicuous advocate of religious freedom. In an election sermon in 1801, he declared:

Religion, as a transaction between God and the souls of men, is too sacred for human regulation. Civil government may not intermeddle with this holy subject. But it clearly falls within the province of a christian legislature, to support institutions, which facilitate the instruction of people in the truths and duties of religion. . . .[13]

Similarly, Enos Hitchcock asserted that religious establishments are " the just abhorrence of freemen." Yet he insisted that all groups in the community should assent to public encouragement of religion, because all benefit from " the air of respectability which elegant churches give a town." [14]

III

Although there was no longer any persecution of heresy or dissent by the civil authorities, the Arminians had to confront a subtler form of intolerance among the congregational churches themselves. Alarmed by the spread of Arminianism, the orthodox began to smoke it out by means of creeds and confessions of faith, and to draw the party line in various acts of fellowship among the churches. To be sure, not all the Calvinists joined in the heresy-hunts which increased in frequency as the threat of Arminianism and Arianism became

---

principle of separation of church and state." At the same time, the school gained in importance and society subdued it, a process which we call " the triumph of the principle of free public education." The right of the teacher to free expression in the classroom, even though his salary is paid by the state, he calls " academic freedom." Similarly, the right of the minister to preach the truth as he saw it was one of the things the Arminians meant by " religious freedom." Now, of course, it is textbooks rather than sermons that must be orthodox. Perhaps we are in no position to chide our ancestors for " illiberality."

[13] Aaron Bancroft, *A Sermon, Preached . . . May 27, 1801, the Day of General Election* (Boston, 1801), p. 21.

[14] Enos Hitchcock, *A Discourse Delivered at the Dedication of the New Congregational Meetinghouse in Providence* (Brookfield, 1795), p. 6.

greater. Many moderate Calvinists had read Locke, just as the Arminians had, and welcomed Archdeacon Francis Blackburne's *Confessional* (1766) as eagerly.[15] Andrew Eliot, for example, wrote: " Dr. B-----n's Confessional is one of the most valuable performances of the age. . . ." [16] Such men were willing to tolerate those who disagreed with them on doctrine, and refused to use creeds as devices for excluding other Christians — or at least Protestants — from fellowship.[17]

As early as 1756, John Adams was acutely conscious of this determination of the orthodox to deny fellowship to Arminians, and it was one reason why he became a lawyer instead of a minister. Following his graduation from Harvard, he

---

[15] Blackburne was a friend of Theophilus Lindsey, but unlike him never left the Church of England, despite a gradual realization that he could no longer subscribe to the Thirty-Nine Articles. His change of views cut him off from preferment within the Church, however. His book, *The Confessional*, was a landmark of the continuing struggle for the right of private judgment. Thomas Hollis promoted a correspondence between Blackburne and Mayhew, which was soon cut off by the latter's untimely death. Blackburne's book was read by various members of Mayhew's congregation; Harrison Gray praised it highly in a letter to Hollis, and Mayhew's widow said of its author: " This excelent Man is greatly venerated among us. His name is never mentioned but with honor." Ezra Stiles wrote to Charles Chauncy: " I have not seen, tho have heard much of, the Confessional." *Cf.* Mss in Massachusetts Historical Society: Hollis to Mayhew, June 23, 1764, June 19, 1766; Mayhew to Hollis, April 8, 1766; Harrison Gray to Hollis, December 15, 1767; Elizabeth Mayhew to Hollis, Nov. 17, 1768; Ezra Stiles to Chauncy, March 19, 1770.

[16] Eliot to Hollis, Nov. 14, 1766. Ms, Mass. Hist. Soc.

[17] One might cite President Edward Holyoke, whose orthodoxy and tolerance both were attested by John Barnard: " I think Mr. Holyoke as orthodox a Calvinist as any man; though I look upon him too much of a gentleman, and of too catholic a temper, to cram his principles down another man's throat." See Clifford K. Shipton, *Sibley's Harvard Graduates* (Boston, 1937), V, p. 271. Ezra Stiles's *Discourse on the Christian Union* (Boston, 1761) was an important and widely-read expression of this tolerant spirit among moderate Calvinists. It frankly recognized that differences of opinion existed among Congregationalists over the Great Awakening, Calvinism, and Arminianism, and the authority of ecclesiastical councils. But it also enumerated the many points on which all were agreed, and urged union and good fellowship among all Congregationalists. Other tolerant Calvinists, among many who might be named, were Simon Bradstreet, Samuel Mather, Edward Wigglesworth, and Andrew Eliot.

taught school at Worcester, at the same time reading theology with a view to entering the ministry. In a letter to a classmate, dated April 1, 1756, he expressed the opinion that a divine could " do more good to his fellow-men, and make better provision for his own future happiness in this profession than in another." But he added a significant postscript: " There is a story about town that I am an Arminian." [18] He had already begun to realize what he would have to face. His diary for February 18, 1756, contains this entry:

Spent an hour in the beginning of the evening at Major Gardiner's, where it was thought that the design of Christianity was not to make men good riddle-solvers, or good mystery-mongers, but good men, good magistrates, and good subjects, good husbands and good wives, good parents and good children, good masters and good servants. The following questions may be answered some time or other, namely — Where do we find a precept in the Gospel requiring Ecclesiastical Synods? Convocations? Councils? Decrees? Creeds? Confessions? Oaths? Subscriptions? and whole cart-loads of other trumpery that we find religion encumbered with in these days? [19]

By the following summer, he had abandoned the idea of the ministry, terrified by " the frightful engines of ecclesiastical councils, of diabolical malice and Calvinistical good-nature." [20] A fragment of autobiography reveals what lay behind his decision. He had followed with care the controversy in which Lemuel Briant was involved, since Briant was his own minister. Indeed, some of the meetings of the councils that sat on the case met at his father's house. The thorny theological questions confused him; and at the same time, he recalled, " I saw such a spirit of dogmatism and bigotry in clergy and laity, that, if I should be a priest, I must take my side, and pronounce as positively as any of

[18] John Adams, *The Works of John Adams* (Boston, 1850), I, pp. 30, 32.
[19] *Ibid.*, II, pp. 5–6.
[20] *Ibid.*, I, p. 35.

them, or never get a parish, or getting it must soon leave it." He then resolved that he was not made for the pulpit in such times, since such a life promised only " endless altercations " with little chance of doing good to his fellow-men.[21]

Soon many of the New England church covenants were rewritten in such a way as to lay down a doctrinal standard for admission. The earlier covenants had been simple statements of a purpose to walk together in Christian fellowship. No doctrinal test had been included, since doctrinal uniformity could be taken for granted. The action of the church in Leominster following the dismissal of John Rogers revealed the new spirit of the times. The new covenant was not only more explicit on the doctrine of the Trinity, but it condemned a long list of Arminian errors.[22] Similarly, when the South Church in Ipswich was organized in 1747, its members declared: " As to Matters of Faith we cordially adhere to the Principles of Religion (at least the Substance of them) contained in the shorter Catechism of the Assembly of Divines, wherewith also the New England Confession harmonizeth. . . ." Lest there be any lingering doubt as to what they meant, they went on to explain: " And we moreover adhere to these in the Calvinistical, which we take to be the genuine or natural Sense, hereby declaring our utter Dislike of the Pelagian, Arminian Principles, vulgarly so called." [23]

The process of revision of church covenants continued throughout the century. One episode which attracted a great deal of attention occurred in the church in Plymouth in 1794. Chandler Robbins (Yale, 1756), a native of Connecticut,

---

[21] *Ibid.*, I, pp. 41, 42.

[22] Rufus P. Stebbins, *A Centennial Discourse Delivered to the First Congregational Church and Society in Leominster* (Boston, 1843), pp. 95–97.

[23] Thomas Franklin Waters, *Ipswich in the Massachusetts Bay Colony* (Ipswich, 1917), II, p. 469. Much the same wording was used the following year when the Linebrook Church in Ipswich was organized.

had been installed there in 1760. In 1770, he urged the church to abandon the use of the Half-Way Covenant, which he had hitherto accepted with some misgivings. The question was discussed heatedly at several church meetings, extending over a year and a half. Finally the majority voted to drop the question without taking any action;[24] but since Robbins was opposed to the practice of baptizing the children of Half-Way members, the procedure of owning the covenant lapsed anyway.[25] As time went on, Robbins became more and more clearly identified with the New Divinity group, while the liberals became increasingly restive, and some of them talked of a separation.[26] Robbins eagerly welcomed a revival in 1793, which produced more than fifty conversions.[27] The following year, the question of admission to church membership came up for discussion once more. A precinct committee urged a very liberal policy, and proposed a confession of faith so inclusive that, according to Robbins, " *any Denomination* of Men called christian except *Deists,* could & would readily subscribe such a *Confession* & *Covenant.*" [28] A church committee insisted instead on an explicitly Calvinistic confession, which was adopted by the church on June 17, 1795.[29] The liberals were unhappy at the outcome, but they bided their time until the death of Robbins; on the first day of January, 1800, they installed one of their own kind, James Kendall (Harvard, 1796).[30] The Calvinists, who were in the minority in both church and precinct,

---

[24] " Plymouth Church Records," *Publications of the Colonial Society of Massachusetts,* XXII (1920), pp. 335–345. See also John Cuckson, *A Brief History of the First Church in Plymouth, from 1606–1901* (Boston, 1902), Ch. 8.
[25] " Plymouth Church Records," *op. cit.,* XXII, p. 384.
[26] *Ibid.,* XXII, p. 383.
[27] *Ibid.,* XXII, p. 378.
[28] *Ibid.,* XXII, p. 384.
[29] *Ibid.,* XXII, pp. 388–389.
[30] *Ibid.,* XXIII (1923), pp. 538–543.

then withdrew and formed a new church and society.[31]   After time had elapsed for the wounds to begin to heal, the Calvinistic confession was dropped, and the church reverted to its earlier simple and undogmatic covenant.[32]

Nathanael Emmons (Yale, 1767), an acknowledged leader of the Hopkinsians, gave the rationale of the exclusive policy which the high Calvinists were adopting, in his Convention Sermon in 1804.   This was the sermon characterized by William Bentley as " the most illiberal discourse I ever heard." [33]   The title was: *Unity of Sentiment among Christians, Necessary to Unity of Affections*.   It asserted two very good reasons why " Christians should be required to think alike upon religious subjects." [34]   One is that in the Bible we are given a complete and perfect system of religious truth, so there can be no excuse for diverging from it.   The other is that the doctrines the Bible presents, such as Moral Depravity, the Decrees, the Atonement, and the Trinity are " plain and intelligible to all." [35]   It is true that some men have greater intellectual powers than others; but " their difference in knowledge will not create any diversity of opinions respecting the same subjects." [36]   It is true that we are given the right of private judgment, but we do not have the right to form an opinion " contrary to the dictates of reason and the declarations of scripture." [37]   It follows that " Christians who are united in the belief of the truth, have a right

[31] *Ibid.*, XXIII, pp. 545–548.
[32] *Ibid.*, XXIII, pp. 573–575.
[33] William Bentley, *The Diary of William Bentley, D.D.* (Salem, 1905–1914), III, p. 89.
[34] Nathanael Emmons, *Unity of Sentiment among Christians, Necessary to Unity of Affection* (Boston, 1804), p. 5.   Although the Arminians rejected Emmons' doctrine, they were not his chief target in the sermon.   He was actually condemning the proposal of the moderate Calvinists, especially Jedidiah Morse, for closer organization in the form of a General Association.
[35] *Ibid.*, p. 7.
[36] *Ibid.*, p. 9.
[37] *Ibid.*, p. 10.

to blame those, who think differently from them, upon religious subjects." [38]　Finally, there is " no propriety, nor prospect of success, in attempting to unite the professed friends of Christ in brotherly love, without first uniting them in the belief of the same essential doctrines of the gospel." [39]

The Arminians, on the other hand, persistently fought the use of creeds and confessions of faith as tests of orthodoxy. They warned men constantly to " keep close to the Bible," not to be " wise above what is written," and to avoid " metaphysical additions " to the revealed truth.　Simeon Howard put it to a newly ordained minister in these terms: " As much as possible, he will lay aside all attachment to human systems, all partiality to names, councils and churches, and honestly inquire, ' what saith the scriptures? ' " [40]

In vain the orthodox protested that their creeds and confessions were scriptural, that they represented the true sense of the word of God.　In that case, the liberals retorted, why not use the words of scripture themselves?　" Why may not I go to the Bible to learn the doctrines of Christianity as well as the Assembly of Divines? " [41]　If a confession is needed to explain the meaning of the Bible, will not another confession be needed to explain the first and so on *ad absurdum?*　Are we to suppose that " divine truths, are, some how better, or more important, cloathed in *human expressions,* than when uttered in the words of the *Holy Ghost?* " [42]

The liberals took it for granted that on many abstruse points of theology no two men would interpret scripture in

[38] *Ibid.,* p. 15.
[39] *Ibid.,* p. 18.
[40] Simeon Howard, *A Sermon, Preached in Boston, November 18, 1791; at the Ordination of the Rev. Thomas Adams* (Boston, 1791), p. 9.
[41] Belknap to Hazard, April 11, 1784, *Coll. Mass. Hist. Soc.,* Ser. 5, Vol. II, p. 324.
[42] John Tucker, *A Sermon Preached at the Ordination of the Rev. Mr. Amos Moody* (Boston, 1766), p. 23.

exactly the same way. Who gave one man, therefore, the right to impose his interpretation on another? Who gave a Christian society or an ordaining council the authority to demand assent to some human explication of scripture doctrines as a condition of ordination? Certainly the New Testament does not; for can anything be found there " made necessary to the enjoyment of christian priviledges, farther than a profession of the christian faith or doctrines, as *there* revealed, and a practice conformable to the rules of the gospel? " [43] The liberals considered the right of each man to read the Bible, and interpret it as God gave him light, to be the basic doctrine of Protestantism, and they did not propose to surrender it.

A few doctrines clearly stated in the Bible were regarded as fundamental; the others, elaborated at length in creeds and confessions, were non-essential. The liberals complained persistently that the orthodox were multiplying the number of essentials beyond all reason. It is a pity, John Rogers remarked, " they can't be content with that number of articles which the Head of the church hath assigned; but needs be adding, till they have swell'd their creed to an enormous size, the weight of ' which both we and our fathers have been unable to bear.' " [44] Some, John Tucker complained, " have made a multitude of fundamentals in religion," and so opened the way for uncharitable bickering. " But how many of these must fall before this plain question, or be entirely stript of their fundamental nature: — Shall not every one who believes in Jesus Christ, and sincerely repents of his sins, be saved? . . . And if so, what is there farther that is fundamental to religion, or absolutely necessary to salva-

[43] John Tucker, *A Reply to the Rev. Mr. Chandler's Answer* (Boston, 1768), p. 42.

[44] John Rogers, *The Nature & Necessity of Spiritual Conversion* (Boston, 1757), pp. 18–19.

tion? " [45]   The lesson of Christian charity deduced from these facts was that only God knows whether certain errors are truly fatal, and men should not presume to judge prematurely.

IV

The orthodox could not believe that their opponents were sincere. Many supposed that the liberals were using a backhanded way of attacking the faith once delivered to the saints. Few of the Arminians " dare openly and directly to attempt it," complained James Chandler, " but they are labouring for it *artfully* several ways." One is " by testifying against creeds, confessions of faith, and every thing of that sort. . . ." In reality, it is " the doctrines confessed, and not merely the using of confessions, that their aim is against." Another artifice is " to represent them as matters of controversy, and so, of indifference in religion." [46]

Such accusations were made countless times against the Arminians, and with even greater bitterness against the later Unitarians. They seemed plausible because of a position which the Arminians took quite without apology on many occasions. The minister is obliged to preach fearlessly and without equivocation everything he thinks essential to eternal life. But " truths of a secondary consideration he may keep within his own breast, when the publication of them will tend to disturb the minds of men, and impede the usefulness of his ministry." [47]   On these grounds, Charles Chauncy prudently postponed publication of his book on universal salvation. " The Truth in it's clear and full Light, may not bear to be spoken at *all Times*, and in *all Circumstances*," John

[45] John Tucker, *A Minister's Appeal to his Hearers, as to his Life and Doctrine* (Boston, 1767), p. 9.
[46] Quoted in John Tucker, *A Letter to the Rev. Mr. James Chandler, Pastor of the West Church in Rowley* (Boston, 1767), pp. 4, 5.
[47] Aaron Bancroft, *A Discourse Delivered . . . at the Ordination of the Rev. Samuel Shuttlesworth* (Worcester, 1790), pp. 12–13.

Tucker advised. " Wrong Impressions are sometimes to be remov'd by Degrees; and the Light to be let in gradually, as the Mind is *prepar'd* to receive it." [48]

The orthodox were infuriated by this argument, which involved, they felt, a lack of candor verging on dishonesty. They found it hard to believe that the liberals really preferred Christian fellowship to doctrinal correctness. No doubt there were times when Arminians exalted prudence above principle. But at least they were consistent enough never to exclude Calvinists from fellowship on doctrinal grounds. There is no record of a Calvinist duly ordained and installed in one of the churches of the Standing Order, who was forced to endure the kind of ostracism that Aaron Bancroft encountered in his first seven years in Worcester.[49] The liberals never hesitated to serve with their orthodox brethren on ordaining councils, and they continued to exchange as long as the Calvinists would exchange with them. William Bentley even assisted a Roman Catholic to obtain a hearing in Salem, but it must be admitted that this was going farther in the direction of toleration than most of the liberals were willing to follow.[50]

The distaste of the Arminians for religious controversy is a recurrent note in the funeral sermons and biographical sketches of ministers of Bentley's generation. Of Abiel Abbot of Beverly it was said: " He was also earnestly solicitous to unite the divided portions of the Christian Body. . . . He made every possible concession for the sake of peace." [51] Of John Allyn it was reported: " I have seldom known one

---

[48] John Tucker, *The Example of Christ, as a Guide to Ministers & People, Considered and Inforced* (Boston, 1751), p. 26.

[49] Aaron Bancroft, *A Sermon Delivered in Worcester, January 31, 1836* (Worcester, 1836), p. 24.

[50] Bentley, *Diary*, I, pp. 162, 165.

[51] William B. Sprague, *Annals of the American Pulpit* (New York, 1857–1869), VIII, p. 320.

who had so strong an aversion to controversy." [52] John Eliot " rarely, if ever, introduced controversy in the pulpit." [53] Such men were rather concerned to enlarge the area of consensus among Christians, than to rend more deeply the body of Christ.

But the liberals were not interested in peace alone; they were also eager for truth. The orthodox believed that they were already possessed of the truth, and were determined to hold it fast in the protecting shelter of their confessions of faith. But the liberals held, with John Robinson, that there was more light yet to break forth from God's holy word. Free inquiry is the way to truth, whereas creeds perpetuate error and produce hypocrites. How far would natural philosophy have progressed, asked Jeremy Belknap, had the founders of the Royal Society drawn up a scheme of philosophy based on Aristotle, or Descartes, or someone else in vogue, and had required assent to it as a qualification for membership? Would not such a test have impeded new discoveries? Similarly, religious truth thrives only in the soil of free inquiry. [54]

Recognizing that free inquiry must lead to differences of opinion, some of the liberals decided that diversity is a positive good. David Barnes declared: " Different opinions produce inquiry, freedom of inquiry excites discussion, and discussion promotes knowledge. Let mankind be perfectly united in opinion, and, paradoxical as it may seem, in a short time they would have no religion at all." [55] Here is a sober statement of a theme proclaimed with intensity by Channing in his sermon on *Spiritual Freedom*, and with ecstasy by the

[52] *Ibid.*, VIII, p. 211.
[53] *Ibid.*, VIII, p. 96.
[54] Belknap to Hazard, April 11, 1784. *Coll. Mass. Hist. Soc.*, Ser. 5, Vol. II, pp. 324–326.
[55] David Barnes, *The Wisdom of God in Appointing Men, Teachers of Men* (Boston, 1801), p. 15.

" apostles of the newness " who looked to Emerson as their leader.

The Arminians had come a long way from the time of the Great Awakening, when Charles Chauncy's chief concern was to prove that the revivalists, not the opposers, were the innovators. Of course they still clung to the Bible as the infallible revelation of God's plan of salvation. But they looked forward to a fuller knowledge of God's will, not backward to a revelation completely understood. Just as they had discovered that virtue is embedded in the process of living, so too they had learned that truth survives in the process of growth. When regarded as a complete and perfect thing, it withers and dies.

CHAPTER ELEVEN

The Threat of Infidelity

1780–1805

I

In 1759, the Reverend Ezra Stiles of Newport declared: " I make no doubt, instead of the Controversies of Orthodoxy & Heresy, we shall soon be called to the defence of the Gospel itself." He was afraid that the demoralizing influences of army life, and the contacts between British regulars and American militiamen, would be too much for the unsophisticated colonials. " I look upon it," he said, " that our Officers are in danger of being corrupted with vicious principles, & many of them I doubt not will in the End of the War come home minute philosophers initiated in the polite Mysteries & vitiated morals of Deism. And this will have an unhappy Effect on a sudden to spread Deism or at least Scepticism thro' these Colonies." [1]

Actually, Stiles was one war too early in his prediction. Occasional references may be found to deists in New England in the sixties and early seventies, but it was not until after the Revolution that infidelity became a serious threat. It was then generally agreed that revealed religion was in grave danger.[2] The Arminians may have produced no

---

[1] Quoted from Stiles Mss in I. Woodbridge Riley, *American Philosophy: the Early Schools* (New York, 1907), pp. 215–216.

[2] See Herbert M. Morais, *Deism in Eighteenth Century America* (New York, 1934), Ch. 4; also G. A. Koch, *Republican Religion* (New York, 1933). But note that Koch, like Riley before him, does not discriminate very carefully between Deism and Supernatural Rationalism.

champion of Christianity quite so vigorous as Timothy Dwight (Yale, 1769), grandson of Edwards and president of Yale. Nor did they agree that revivalism was the only answer to skepticism. But they were as firmly convinced that French philosophy was spreading like a contagion. " Probably there has not been an age, since the apostles," declared Thomas Prentiss in 1785, " when infidelity and irreligion, have been more prevalent than in the present: Nor any period, in which the gospel of Christ, and its sacred institutions, have been treated with more alarming indifference, and contempt. . . ." [3]

So intolerant was the spirit of the age that even the appearance of an interest in Deism could be damaging to one's reputation. William Bentley got his fingers burned twice. In November, 1787, he jotted down a reminder in his diary under the heading: " The danger of Loan of Books, for whose sentiments, you wish not to be accountable." He had lent a copy of Tindal " to Capt. Jo. W. upon the solemn promise of a private examination." The captain left it hidden under a pillow, where it was " found by a woman, lent to an Aunt, read before her husband, & by him reported to Col. Carlton." Luckily, before the colonel was able to get his hands on the book, it was returned and hidden. On another occasion, Bentley lent a copy of Ethan Allen's *Reason the Only Oracle of Man* " under solemn promise of secrecy." It was lent in turn to a Mr. Grafton, who died soon after.

The book was found at his death in his chamber, examined with horror by his female relations. By them conveyed to a Mr. Williams, whose shop is remarkable for news, & there examined — reported to be mine from the initials W. B., viewed as an awful curiosity by hundreds, connected with a report that I encouraged infidelity in Grafton by my prayers with him in his dying hour, & upon the whole

[3] Thomas Prentiss, *A Sermon, Preached at the Ordination of the Reverend Mr. Henry Wight* (Providence, 1785), p. 7.

a terrible opposition to me fixed in the minds of the devout & ignorant multitude.

Bentley's journal entry concludes wryly, "Beware of the third time." [4]

If the eighties were a decade of tension, the nineties were a decade of turmoil. Although the news of the French Revolution was at first welcomed, after 1793 its excesses were attributed to the adoption of an atheistic philosophy, and the New England clergy were fearful lest something of the sort occur at home.[5] Their concern turned into alarm when Tom Paine's *Age of Reason* made its appearance in 1794. The book was undiluted Deism, with something of an anticlerical flavor which Paine had absorbed from his French experience. Arminian and Calvinist agreed in condemning it. Bentley called it "a contemptible publication." [6] Jeremy Belknap referred to it as a "species of vulgar infidelity, founded partly in pedantry, partly in debauchery and partly in ill manners." [7] And Thomas Barnard, Jr., complained because those treatises which represented the truths of revealed religion "as the whimsies of affrighted minds, or the fictions of politicians to keep mankind in awe" were read "with great avidity." [8]

Paine's popularity among the students was a matter of concern to the authorities both of Harvard and of Yale. For a

[4] William Bentley, *The Diary of William Bentley, D.D.* (Salem, 1905–14), I, p. 82. Dr. Thomas Young probably wrote more of the book of which Allen claimed authorship than did Allen himself. See George P. Anderson, "Who Wrote 'Ethan Allen's Bible'?" *New England Quarterly*, X (1937), pp. 685–696. Since almost all the copies were accidentally destroyed by fire, the book was doubtless more talked about than read.

[5] Anson E. Morse, *The Federalist Party in Massachusetts* (Princeton, 1909), Chs. 6, 7.

[6] Bentley, *Diary*, II, p. 107.

[7] Jeremy Belknap, *Dissertations on the Character, Death & Resurrection of Jesus Christ* (Boston, 1795), p. 8.

[8] Thomas Barnard, Jr., *A Sermon, Delivered at Salem, on March 31, 1796.* Fast Day Sermon. (Salem, 1796), p. 17.

time it almost looked as though irreligion would conquer both colleges. Lyman Beecher afterwards recalled that at Yale " most of the students were skeptical " and the college church was almost extinct.[9] Timothy Dwight accepted the presidency of Yale in 1795 because of his conviction that the college had to be restored to sound principles, if orthodoxy were to survive in the Connecticut valley.[10] At Harvard a similar situation prevailed. William Ellery Channing testified that " the tendency of all classes was to skepticism," and Judge Daniel A. White spoke of " the infidel and irreligious spirit, which prevailed at that period among the students at Cambridge." In 1796, the Corporation presented a copy of Watson's *Apology for the Bible* to each student, as an antidote to the *Age of Reason*.[11]

The peak of excitement was reached in 1798, when the Reverend Jedidiah Morse (Yale, 1783) of Charlestown preached a Fast Day Sermon, in which he asserted that a secret conspiracy was afoot to undermine both the political institutions and religious principles of the new republic. Morse had been reading a book by Professor John Robison of Edinburgh, called *Proofs of a Conspiracy against All the Religions and Governments of Europe*. Robison claimed that a secret organization, known as the Order of the Illuminati, founded in Bavaria in 1776 by Adam Weishaupt, was responsible for all the political and social unrest of the times. In particular, working through an alliance with Freemasonry, it had conspired to bring about the French Revolution and to supplant Christianity with the Cult of Reason. Admittedly there had been such an organization, though its ob-

---

[9] Charles Beecher, ed., *Autobiography, Correspondence, etc., of Lyman Beecher, D.D.* (New York, 1864), I, p. 43.

[10] Charles E. Cuningham, *Timothy Dwight, 1752-1817* (New York, 1942), Ch. 9.

[11] William Henry Channing, *Memoir of William Ellery Channing* (Boston, 1848), I, pp. 60, 61.

jectives were far less ambitious and subversive than Robison claimed, and it had been dissolved in 1787.[12] But Morse was convinced that a conspiracy still existed. For him there was no other good explanation for the rising tide of Deism in religion and Jeffersonianism in politics. He was sure that there had been an underground connection between the Illuminati and the Democratic clubs that sprang up in 1793 and 1794.[13]

Most of the liberals, however, were less concerned about the alleged conspiracy, which remained unproven, than about the infidelity itself, which they saw wherever they looked. John T. Kirkland warned the Harvard chapter of Phi Beta Kappa against " the poison of the skeptical and disorganizing philosophy, which is now perverting and corrupting man ";[14] Thomas Thacher referred to " the open insolence and active malignity of infidelity ";[15] and Henry Cumings told his congregation to be on guard against " the ensnaring sophistry of that false unhallowed philosophy, which teaches, as a fundamental doctrine, that all religion is enslaving superstition, inconsistent with true liberty and the rights of man." [16]

These quotations are no more than a sampling of opinion; they might be matched by similar ones from almost any of the leaders of that generation: from John Clarke and Aaron Bancroft; from Alden Bradford, John Lathrop, and William Emerson; from Henry Ware and John Pierce. This was

[12] Vernon Stauffer, *New England and the Bavarian Illuminati* (New York, 1918), Ch. 3.

[13] *Ibid.*, pp. 234–235. See also William B. Sprague, *Life of Jedidiah Morse, D.D.* (New York, 1874).

[14] John T. Kirkland, *An Oration, Delivered, at the Request of the Society of ΦBK* (Boston, 1798), p. 21.

[15] Thomas Thacher, *A Sermon Preached at the Third Parish in Dedham, January 11, 1801* (Dedham, 1801), p. 11.

[16] Henry Cumings, *A Sermon, Preached at Billerica, April 9th, 1801.* Fast Day Sermon. (Amherst, N. H., 1801), p. 22.

one issue on which orthodox and liberals stood together, for to their dying day, they insisted that morality and religion had never been in graver danger than in the 1790's.

II

Emerson once remarked that from 1790 to 1820 "there was not a book, a speech, a conversation, or a thought" in the state of Massachusetts. Certainly not a single new idea was developed in reply to Tom Paine. The arguments of Supernatural Rationalism were restated countless times; the internal evidences, the external evidences, and the miracles were zealously re-examined; the doctrine of Providence was argued once more in countless Thanksgiving sermons; but the pamphlets and sermons that resulted were uncorrupted by the slightest taint of originality.

Two small volumes may be taken as representative of the Arminian counterattack on Paine. The first was Jeremy Belknap's *Dissertations on the Character, Death, and Resurrection of Jesus Christ*. The author himself disclaimed all originality for his book. "It is not pretended," he wrote in the preface, "that any new arguments are advanced in this performance. . . ." He acknowledged indebtedness to the writings of Ditton, West, Lardner, Stackhouse, Doddridge, and Butler, where the reader may find "the same subjects treated with more learning and energy, than in this compendium; which is designed for those who have not leisure or opportunity to look into more voluminous works." [17]

Belknap was chiefly concerned to refute Paine's argument that revelation is valid only for the person who receives it directly; for anyone else it is merely hearsay. Belknap pointed out that we rely all the time on the testimony of others as to things which we have not ourselves observed.

[17] Jeremy Belknap, *Dissertations on Jesus Christ*, p. 3.

The crucial questions are these: Is the testimony credible? Is it contradicted by testimony of equal credibility? Is the point to be proved inherently unreasonable? It is surely rational, he said, " to admit that degree of moral evidence, which is founded on credible testimony." [18]   In this case we rely on the testimony of Jesus Christ and his apostles.

Belknap pointed out that Paine himself admitted Jesus Christ to possess an amiable and pure character. But the sources of our knowledge of Christ's character are also the sources of our knowledge of his divine mission. It is vain, therefore, for Paine to accept the virtuous character of the man and reject the truth of his miracles and resurrection. " They rest on the same evidence and must stand or fall together." A man whom Paine himself described as virtuous and good would not have appealed to his miracles and resurrection " as the proofs of his divine mission, unless they had been realities." [19]   In short, we have as good evidence for the miracles and resurrection as for any event in history; they were facts " seen and known, witnessed and believed, by persons who could not have mistaken the fact; by numbers, by great numbers of them." [20]   On this firm foundation rests the whole structure of Christian faith.

The other pamphlet on which the Arminians chiefly relied was John Clarke's *Answer to the Question, Why are you a Christian?* In sponsoring a London edition, Theophilus Lindsey remarked: " Not that you will meet with any thing that has not been observed before by our best writers, particularly some now living." [21]   Like Belknap, Clarke sought only to put into brief compass some of the arguments that

[18] *Ibid.*, p. 19.
[19] *Ibid.*, pp. 57, 58.
[20] *Ibid.*, pp. 109, 110.
[21] John Clarke, *An Answer to the Question, Why are you a Christian?* (Boston and Cambridge, 1848), p. 7.

had long been familiar. He first reviewed the internal evidences, reaching the conclusion that the system of morals inculcated by Jesus was too excellent to have been the work of human wisdom. He turned next to the external evidences, devoting one chapter to the miraculous spread of the new religion in the early days of the church, another to the fulfillment of prophecy, and another to the miracles.

Judging by the number of times it was reprinted, Clarke's tract was even more popular than Belknap's. There were two Boston editions in 1795 when it first came out; and before a decade had elapsed, there were at least four more in Boston, two in New York state, and five in London. The American Unitarian Association reprinted it in 1832; as late as 1848, an edition was printed especially for the teachers in the Reverend William Newell's Sunday School in Cambridge.

III

The concluding section of Clarke's book has subtle overtones that must not be missed. All that the religion of Christ asks, it declares, is a fair examination by informed people who are familiar with the original texts and with the early history of the church. Those who make such an examination, even if they remain unconvinced themselves, will acknowledge that others may be Christians without yielding to " uncommon weakness, credulity, or fanaticism." [22] The informed people to whom Clarke appealed were Harvard men, slated to be the social, intellectual, and commercial leaders of eastern Massachusetts. " Credulity and fanaticism " were regarded as typical of lower-class, evangelical, religious movements. One may be a Christian in Boston, Clarke seems to be saying, without jeopardizing his social standing.

If Clarke seems a bit insecure and on the defensive, it should be recalled that much was involved in his insecurity

[22] *Ibid.,* p. 54.

besides the spread of Deism. A major shift in values had long been under way, which threatened the prestige of the New England clergy. For a century, the tendencies towards democracy and secularism had been growing stronger. Ever since the Great Awakening, democratic spokesmen had attacked the ministers of the Standing Order for their privileged position and aristocratic tendencies.[23] Ever since the Revolution, the power to influence opinion had been shifting from ministers to lawyers and politicians. By 1789, Jeremy Belknap was protesting that the ministers " are entitled to as much respect as those who prudently conduct the affairs of government and administer public justice." [24] And in 1797, John Eliot warned a newly-ordained minister: " As an order of men, the ministers are not respected in this country as they once were." [25]

The continued prestige of the ministry depended, not only on the survival of Christianity, but also on the preservation of a social structure in which the role of the minister was a significant one. The congregational clergy, therefore, preached Federalism as well as Christianity, believing that it was all the same battle. Thomas Jefferson and Tom Paine stood as convenient symbols of all the forces — political and social as well as religious — which threatened the clergy. Jefferson's rationalism was mild and tolerant, not anti-clerical and anti-Christian like that of Paine, but both men were assailed for infidelity, and both of them were considered to stand for French democracy, Jacobin clubs, and egalitarianism. The net result was that the ministers of the Standing Order were mainstays of the Federalist party.

With few exceptions — William Bentley was one — the

---

[23] Morse, *Federalist Party*, pp. 220–221.
[24] Jeremy Belknap, *A Sermon, Preached at the Installation of the Rev. Jedidiah Morse* (Boston, 1789), p. 8.
[25] John Eliot, *A Sermon, Preached . . . at the Ordination of the Rev. Mr. Joseph M'Kean* (Boston, 1797), p. 33.

Arminian ministers were staunch Federalists. Sometimes their Federalism appears in the form of an anti-egalitarian social philosophy. " Wherever religion spreads an universal influence through society," declared Abiel Abbot of Coventry, " there is nothing out of place; there is no crowding for the highest seats. It teaches each one to think others better than himself, and to wait unambitious, till he is bidden to go up higher." [26] Thaddeus Mason Harris pointed out that " equality of station and possession " is an idle dream; that instead of " making any vain attempt to bring the conditions of mankind to a common standard," we should insist that rich and poor " contribute to each other's accommodation and comfort." [27] And John T. Kirkland defined American equality as " an equality which secures the rich from rapacity, no less than the poor from oppression; the high from envy, no less than the low from contempt; an equality, which proclaims peace alike to the mansions of the affluent, and the humble dwellings of the poor." [28]

But the Arminians did not confine themselves to general statements of a conservative social philosophy; they also made use of special days of fasting or thanksgiving to commend the national administration and support the policies of Washington and Adams. In a Thanksgiving sermon, preached on February 19, 1795, Henry Ware condemned abuse of President Washington and praised him for maintaining neutrality. [29] On a similar occasion in 1796, Henry Cumings enumerated the many blessings which the nation enjoyed, beginning with constitutions of government which

[26] Abiel Abbot (of Coventry), *A Discourse, Delivered at North-Coventry, July 4th, 1799* (Hartford, 1799), p. 8.

[27] Thaddeus M. Harris, *Discourses . . . Vindicating the Design of Free Masonry* (Charlestown, 1801), pp. 76, 77.

[28] Kirkland, *ΦBK Oration*, p. 9.

[29] Henry Ware, *The Continuance of Peace and Increasing Prosperity a Source of Consolation and Just Cause of Gratitude* (Boston, 1795), pp. 16, 17.

maintain a nice balance between despotism and anarchy, continuing with defeat of the machinations of those who would involve us in war with Great Britain, and ending with the services to his country of George Washington.[30] Indeed, particularly in the orations delivered on the occasion of the death of Washington, the ministers may be seen making of him a symbol of national unity to be achieved under the guiding hand of God's providence. This symbol might stand in contrast to the image of Jefferson, the infidel promoter of factional discord.

The new century brought to an end the threat to revealed religion. A new revival movement began to spread, of such importance that it is sometimes called the Second Great Awakening.[31] It won converts especially among those very frontiersmen to whom Jefferson appealed. When a new administration came to power in 1801, therefore, the identification of Jeffersonian democracy with infidelity no longer was as plausible as it had been in 1794. Besides, after the XYZ Affair, even the Republicans lost much of their enthusiasm for France and things French.

In the nineties, Arminians and Calvinists stood together against Paine and Deism. Beneath the surface unity, however, there was a cleavage two generations old. The French Revolution may have postponed for a decade the split between liberal and orthodox. Certainly, once the common danger was past, the two wings of the congregational churches moved quickly toward the period of controversy that was to divide them permanently.

[30] Henry Cumings, *A Sermon Preached at Billerica, December 15, 1796.* Thanksgiving Sermon. (Boston, 1797), pp. 16–24.
[31] Charles R. Keller, *The Second Great Awakening in Connecticut* (New Haven, 1942).

CHAPTER TWELVE

The Eve of Controversy

1804–1805

I

A series of conversions in the church in Northampton at the close of 1734 proved to be the beginning of an era in the ecclesiastical history of New England. An equally parochial event early in 1805 brought that era to a close. The election of Henry Ware as Hollis Professor of Divinity at Harvard precipitated a controversy which altered the New England scene as profoundly as the Great Awakening had seventy years earlier. The Arminian phase of religious liberalism in Massachusetts, then, lasted exactly two generations.

What had the Arminians achieved by the year 1805? Intellectually, they had accomplished a great deal. They had rewritten Christian theology to conform with the basic principles of the Age of Reason; they had found a middle ground between Calvinism and infidelity. They had shaped their system of thought into a fairly self-consistent logical structure, which had finally reached a point of stabilization. Two generations of Arminians amassed the intellectual capital on which the liberals drew in the Unitarian Controversy. Their accomplishment remained relatively unchanged until Emerson and his generation began to challenge its basic presuppositions.

If in this sense the Arminians had accomplished a great deal, in another sense they had achieved very little. Their numbers and influence were growing very slowly; they had had very little success except in eastern Massachusetts. Most of New England remained Calvinist, and orthodoxy was vigorous and expanding.

Boston was the chief stronghold of liberal Christianity. Of the nine congregational churches there in 1804, only the Old South remained orthodox, under the ministry of Dr. Joseph Eckley (Princeton, 1772). William Emerson was at the First Church, as the successor of Charles Chauncy and John Clarke. At the Second Church was John Lathrop, whose Princeton training had been modified by almost forty years of contact with Boston liberalism. The Brattle Street Church was on the point of calling Joseph Stevens Buckminster, the brilliant young preacher whose untimely death in 1812 was to deprive the Unitarians of a leader who might well have ranked with Channing. The New North was under John Eliot, and the New South under John T. Kirkland, later president of Harvard. At the Federal Street Church, where Jeremy Belknap had served from 1787 to 1798, William Ellery Channing was just beginning his ministry, though it was not yet clear where his sympathies really lay. The year 1804 saw the death of Simeon Howard, Mayhew's successor at the West Church, but he was followed by Charles Lowell. Samuel West was at the church in Hollis Street. Although not regarded then as a congregational church, King's Chapel should be listed with the others; James Freeman was approaching the mid-point of his ministry there.

Most of the other important Arminians were to be found within twenty miles of Boston. Closest to the center were Thaddeus Mason Harris in Dorchester, John Pierce in Brookline, Eliphalet Porter in Roxbury, and Joseph Tuckerman in Chelsea. A little further out were Thomas Bar-

Arminian Ministers, 1801-1805.

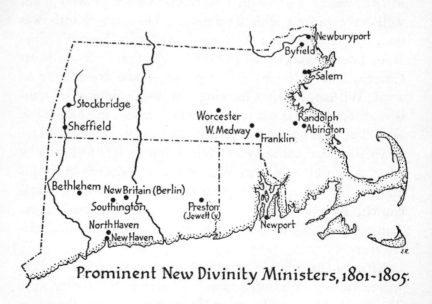

Prominent New Divinity Ministers, 1801-1805.

nard, Jr., William Bentley, and John Prince, occupying three of the five congregational meetinghouses in Salem. West of Boston were Henry Cumings at Billerica and Ezra Ripley at Concord. South of Boston were Thomas Thacher in Dedham and Henry Ware in Hingham. Outside the twenty-mile radius, there were only a few prominent Arminians. William Symmes was in North Andover, Nathaniel Thayer in Lancaster, Aaron Bancroft in Worcester, James Kendall in Plymouth, the other Samuel West in New Bedford, John Allyn in Duxbury, Paul Coffin in Buxton, Maine, and Samuel Deane in Falmouth (Portland), Maine. James Dana was still at the First Church in New Haven, but the Arminianism of which he had been accused in 1758 was hard to discern in his later ministry. Bezaleel Howard still lived in Springfield, but he was not active in the ministry after 1803. Thus two old outposts of Arminianism in Yale territory were no longer important.

Because these Arminians were almost without exception Harvard men, it does not follow that Harvard graduates were predominantly Arminian, or that the theological bent of the college was hostile to moderate Calvinism. President Willard, who served from 1781 until his death in 1804, and David Tappan, Hollis Professor of Divinity from 1792 to 1803, were both Calvinists. To be sure, ever since the days of William Brattle and John Leverett, a tolerant spirit of free inquiry had prevailed. When the Overseers insisted on inquiring into the religious beliefs of the first Hollis Professor in 1722, their actions were viewed with dismay by the Corporation, which was directly charged with the administration of the college. At no time was any specific religious test established, as at Yale.[1] Arminians were always interested

---

[1] Josiah Quincy, *The History of Harvard University* (Cambridge, 1840), II, pp. 70–71.

in the affairs of the college, and Arminian ministers served on the Board of Overseers by virtue of their settlement over several of the nearby churches. But throughout the eighteenth century their influence did not predominate, nor did they try to control the college for narrow or exclusive partisan ends. So long as the spirit of free inquiry prevailed, they were content. And so, while some Harvard graduates became Arminian ministers, a great many more became Calvinists. The Harvard influence might mean anything from middle-of-the-road Calvinism to Arminianism.

Yet the territory was gradually shrinking in which ministers trained at Harvard were acceptable to the people.[2]   In 1740, Harvard-trained ministers occupied pulpits in both Massachusetts and Connecticut as far west as the Connecticut River. By 1775, Harvard had been pushed out of Connecticut, except for the northeast corner, had yielded most of the southern third of old Hampshire County, and had made gains only in the northern third of Hampshire.[3]   The Yale area had expanded to include all of Connecticut, except for a town or two along the eastern boundary; and in Massachusetts it now took in all of Berkshire County, old Hampshire County west of the Connecticut River, and the southern third of Hampshire east of the river. The overlap between the two areas involved the southeastern part of Hampshire County in Massachusetts, and Windham County in Connecticut.

By 1804, Yale territory included all of Berkshire and Hampshire counties, and the southwestern part of Worcester County. Harvard had lost her last foothold in Connecticut;

---

[2] For references, see the source listed on p. 35, note 11.

[3] The division of Hampshire County into the present Franklin, Hampshire, and Hampden Counties did not take place until the nineteenth century. In other parts of the Commonwealth, only minor changes have been made in county boundaries since the eighteenth century.

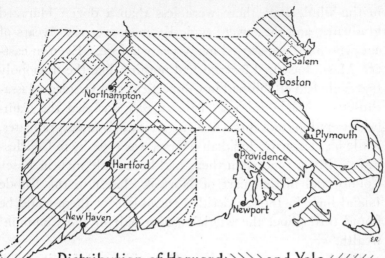

Distribution of Harvard \\\\\ and Yale ////// graduates in S. New England pulpits in 1775

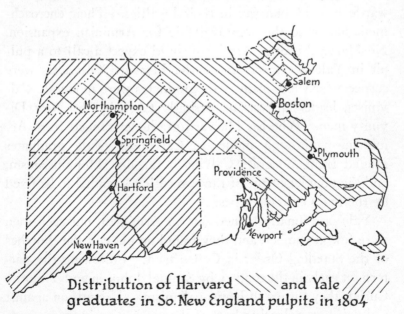

Distribution of Harvard \\\\\ and Yale ////// graduates in So. New England pulpits in 1804

in the whole state there were less than a dozen Harvard graduates, and these were typically men over sixty years of age who had been settled many years before. Even in eastern Massachusetts, Harvard had nothing like the monopoly that Yale had established in Connecticut and western Massachusetts. Abiel Holmes (Yale, 1783) occupied the Cambridge pulpit and preached to Harvard undergraduates, while his classmate, Jedidiah Morse, was close by in Charlestown. For a generation there had been Yale men in Essex County and in that part of Norfolk closest to the Rhode Island line; in 1804, a decided sprinkling of them could be found throughout the whole eastern half of the Commonwealth.

The Yale men were of course Calvinists, and they included some of the most prominent of the New Divinity men, Edwardean or Hopkinsian in their loyalties. Their encroachment narrowed the area available for Arminian expansion. No Harvard-trained Arminian could expect a call to a pulpit in Yale territory. Even the Harvard Calvinists were suspect; for while many Yale graduates were moderate Calvinists, leadership was increasingly taken by the New Divinity men. Whereas Harvard graduates ranged from Arminianism through moderate Calvinism, Yale graduates ranged from moderate Calvinism through Hopkinsianism, and the popular image of the two colleges tended to be fixed by the more extreme types.

Yale occasionally turned out an Arminian, but such men were few in number, and they found no place in the churches of the Standing Order in Connecticut. Following the pattern set early in the century by Samuel Johnson and Timothy Cutler, they turned to Episcopalianism. A revulsion against Calvinism was clearly a part of the motivation in many cases. The Episcopal churches in Connecticut were not numerous, and they were small and struggling, but virtually all were ministered to by Yale graduates. The fact that in Massachusetts, Arminianism developed within the Standing Order, while in Connecticut it developed as Episcopalianism, is reflected to this day in the distribution of Unitarian churches in New England.

II

Even in eastern Massachusetts, where Arminianism was strongest, its popular appeal was limited. Its tone was set by urban merchants, lawyers, and doctors. They nodded assent when Jonathan Mayhew advised young men that sobriety would be rewarded with the esteem of their fellows; they agreed completely with " the elegant Dr. Clarke," who assured them that to prove that " we are not of the world, it is not necessary that we should absolutely refuse its riches, honours, and pleasures." [4]

In the larger towns, the existence of two or more churches made differentiation among the congregations possible. Where there were Baptist, Universalist, or Methodist churches, the social position of their members was inferior to that of the members of the Congregational churches. But even among the latter, in Boston, Salem, and Worcester, there was a tendency to divide along class lines; and the liberal ministers had more than their share of the old families of wealth and prestige in their congregations. This is, of course, only a statement of tendency; social class distinctions were not so sharp as to be all-controlling in New England. But the trend was obvious enough for Jedidiah Morse to assert that his liberal opponents were " a formidable host . . . combining wealth, talents, and influence." [5]

---

[4] John Clarke, *Sermons* (Boston, 1799), p. 154.
[5] Jedidiah Morse, *An Appeal to the Public* (Charlestown, 1814), p. vi.

There are two ways of demonstrating the class character of the Arminians in the larger towns. One is to analyze the lists of members, or proprietors, or pewholders of the liberal churches. Of King's Chapel it has been said that " Dr. Freeman had among his parishioners during his entire ministry a large proportion of the men of high standing and commanding influence in Boston." [6] In Salem, three of the five congregational churches were liberal, and an examination of the records has shown that " the great majority of the men of influence in these three parishes were foreign merchants and ship-masters; and also that these parishes were almost wholly made up of these men, their families, and those who were naturally associated with them in trade, either as assistants or dependants." [7]   Aaron Bancroft himself testified that the Second Parish in Worcester, which was organized for him in 1785, included " a large proportion of the professional and distinguished men of the town, and a fair proportion of the farmers and mechanics." [8]

[6] Henry Wilder Foote, *Annals of King's Chapel* (Boston, 1881, 1896), II, p. 397. Among those associated with King's Chapel were John Amory, a leading merchant; Judge George Richards Minot; Dr. Thomas Bulfinch and his son, Charles Bulfinch, the architect; Governor Christopher Gore; Dr. Aaron Dexter; Judge John Lowell; and Joseph Coolidge, merchant. *Cf.* Foote, *Annals,* II, pp. 338n, 342, 343, 364, 379n, 397.

[7] George Batchelor, *Social Equilibrium* (Boston, 1887), p. 277. Elias Hasket Derby and William Gray, for example, both attended the East Church; Joseph Peabody supported the North. These names were among the most prominent in the town.

[8] Aaron Bancroft, *A Sermon Delivered in Worcester, January 31, 1836* (Worcester, 1836), p. 19. Among the incorporators were Levi Lincoln, afterwards Attorney General of the United States; Timothy Paine, Clerk of Courts, Selectman, member of the General Court; David Bigelow, hotelkeeper, and a leader during the Revolution; Joseph Allen, nephew of Samuel Adams, Clerk of Courts and Member of Congress; Isaiah Thomas, printer, founder of the American Antiquarian Society; Cornelius Stowell and his sons, manufacturers of textiles; and Thaddeus Maccarty, son of the minister of the same name who died in 1784 after serving the First Church for almost forty years. A complete list of the incorporators with biographical notes is given in Samuel S. Green, " Gleanings from the Sources of the History of the Second Parish, Worcester, Massachusetts," *Proceedings of the American Anti-*

A second way to relate the liberals to social class structure is through analysis of the membership lists of upper-class clubs and societies. In Boston, there were more than a dozen literary, scientific, philanthropic, and social organizations formed by men of influence and prestige in the decades immediately following the Revolution. They included the American Academy of Arts and Sciences (1780), the Humane Society (1786), the Massachusetts Historical Society (1791), and the Charitable Fire Society (1794), as well as more informal social groups like the Wednesday Evening Club (1777) and the Anthology Club (1805). In almost every case, Arminian ministers were prime movers in these organizations, supported by members of their own congregations.

The Wednesday Evening Club was begun in 1777 with nine members, but the number was soon increased to sixteen: four clergymen, four lawyers, four physicians, and four merchants. The membership list throughout the decades is a roll of the social élite of Boston. In 1803, there appear to have been fourteen members, at least thirteen of whom belonged to the liberal churches. King's Chapel and the First Church contributed three; Federal Street, Brattle Street, and the New South, two each; and the New North, one. There was no representative of the Old South, which was the one congregational church that was holding fast to orthodoxy, nor of course of the unfashionable religious groups like the Baptists, Methodists, Universalists, or Catholics.[9]

---

quarian Society, New Series, II (1882–83), pp. 304, 310–313. See also biographical sketches in Caleb A. Wall, *Reminiscences of Worcester* (Worcester, 1877).

[9] The membership lists of the Club are given in *The Centennial Celebration of the Wednesday Evening Club* (Boston, 1878), pp. 141–145. Because the early records are defective, these lists do not always indicate clearly when members resigned from the club. The manuscript diary of John Eliot in the Massachusetts Historical Society makes it possible, however, to reconstruct

The American Academy of Arts and Sciences was chartered in 1780. Both orthodox and liberals were elected Fellows of the Academy, but the liberal party dominated the organization. In 1804, six of the seven officers, and at least five of the nine counselors were liberals. Twenty ministers were members; half of them were Arminians. The nonclerical members included ample representation from King's Chapel, First Church, Brattle Street, and Federal Street.[10]

The Massachusetts Historical Society was formally organized in 1791 with ten members; at least seven of them were Arminians, including Jeremy Belknap, who was the prime mover in the enterprise. Its membership was drawn from precisely the same classes, and even the same cliques, as the American Academy. Of the fifteen officers in 1804,

---

the list of active members in 1803. The clergymen were William Emerson (First Church), John T. Kirkland (New South), James Freeman (King's Chapel), and John Eliot (New North). The lawyers were John Quincy Adams (First Church), Judge John Davis (Federal Street), Rufus Amory (King's Chapel), Josiah Quincy (New South), and Judge Thomas Dawes, Jr. (Federal St.). The physicians were Dr. John Warren and Dr. William Spooner of Brattle Street, and Dr. Aaron Dexter of King's Chapel. The merchants were William Smith (First Church) and John Welles (undetermined). Interestingly enough, Judge Dawes came from a family that had attended the Old South for five generations. His father, a mason and contractor, was one of the pillars of the church. The son, who was the first of the family to attend Harvard, moved from the Old South to Federal Street soon after 1800. Similarly Josiah Quincy was baptized at the Old South and attended there until about 1800. He then moved to the New South, under Dr. Kirkland, and afterwards to Federal Street, under Dr. Channing. See Henry A. Hill, *History of the Old South Church* (Boston, 1890), II, pp. 233, 267n.

10 The officers and counselors who may be listed as liberal were: John Adams, Robert Treat Paine (First Church), Reverend Simeon Howard, Reverend John Lathrop, Dr. John Warren, Judge John Davis, John Quincy Adams, Reverend James Freeman, Dr. William Spooner. Other liberals who were members in 1804 included Reverend Thomas Barnard, Charles Bulfinch, Judge Thomas Dawes, Jr., Reverend Samuel Deane, Reverend William Emerson, Hon. Christopher Gore, Reverend John T. Kirkland, Judge John Lowell, Hon. Harrison Gray Otis (Brattle Street), Josiah Quincy, Dr. Isaac Rand (King's Chapel), Reverend Henry Ware, Dr. Aaron Dexter, Hon. Levi Lincoln, Reverend John Prince, Reverend Zedekiah Sanger, Reverend Samuel West. *Memoirs of the American Academy of Arts and Sciences*, I (1785), pp. xx, xxi; II (Part II, 1804), pp. 162–164.

at least eleven were liberals; of fifty-five members, at least twenty-four were liberals.[11]

A final example is the Anthology Society, organized in 1805. Its purpose was ostensibly to assume responsibility for the editing of the *Monthly Anthology;* actually, congenial social intercourse among intimate friends was quite as important. Dinners of widgeon and teal, or woodcock, were recorded in the minutes, together with the assignment of books to the members for review in the pages of the *Anthology.* Four of the original fourteen members were ministers of liberal churches; of the lay members, at least three were from Brattle Street, two from King's Chapel, and one from Federal Street. When, in 1805, Jedidiah Morse declared war on the liberals by publishing his *True Reasons on which the Election of a Hollis Professor of Divinity in Harvard College, was Opposed,* it was the gentlemen of the Anthology Society who replied with a scathing review in their magazine.[12]

[11] The original members included the following liberals: Reverend Jeremy Belknap (Federal St.); James Sullivan (Brattle St.); Dr. Freeman, William Tudor, James Winthrop, George R. Minot, and Thomas Walcutt of King's Chapel; and Reverend John Eliot of the New North. The officers in 1804 included James Sullivan, Reverend John Eliot, Dr. Freeman, James Winthrop, William Tudor, Josiah Quincy, Reverend John T. Kirkland, Judge John Davis, Reverend William Emerson, John Quincy Adams, and Reverend Thaddeus M. Harris. Other liberals who were members in 1804 included Dr. Aaron Dexter, Hon. Alden Bradford, Reverend John Prince, Reverend John Allyn, Reverend William Bentley, Dr. William Spooner, Hon. Josiah Quincy, Hon. Christopher Gore, Hon. Benjamin Lincoln of Hingham, Dr. Isaac Rand, Hon. William Sullivan, Hon. John Adams, and Charles Bulfinch. *Proceedings of the Massachusetts Historical Society,* I, (1879), pp. xiv, xlii, xliii, 164.

[12] The ministers were William Emerson, J. S. Buckminster, Joseph Tuckerman, and Thomas Gray. The remaining members included Samuel Cooper Thacher, later minister of the New South; Peter O. Thacher, and Dr. John Collins Warren of Brattle Street; William Tudor, Jr. and Dr. James Jackson of King's Chapel; and William Smith Shaw of Federal Street. J. S. J. Gardiner, Rector of Trinity, was the first President. The other three members were of the liberal sect, but I have not pinned down their church connections. See M. A. DeW. Howe, ed., *Journal of the Proceedings of the Society which Conducts the Monthly Anthology and Boston Review* (Boston, 1910), pp. 16, 298, 299.

III

The clubs and societies of Boston brought the leading liberals together in frequent and varied social contacts, and undoubtedly contributed to their coherence as a group within the congregational churches. John Clarke and John Lathrop belonged to seven of the ten most important of these organizations.[13] William Emerson, John T. Kirkland, John Eliot, Jeremy Belknap, and Simeon Howard were members of six, and James Freeman of five. Certain laymen — Josiah Quincy, Dr. Aaron Dexter, Judge Thomas Dawes, Jr., George Richards Minot, and John Quincy Adams, for example — were equally gregarious. Ministers in surrounding towns could participate less actively, of course, but they were often tied into the Boston group through membership in one or two of the organizations.

Other links also held the group together. College friendships were important. James Freeman and William Bentley of the class of 1777 corresponded with one another, exchanged pulpits, traded copies of their printed sermons, did favors for one another, and visited back and forth as long as they lived. In the same class were Eliphalet Porter of the church in Roxbury, and Judge Dawes. John Prince and Ezra Ripley were a year ahead of them, together with Dr. Dexter; Aaron Bancroft and George Richards Minot were a year behind. Similarly, William Emerson, Nathaniel Thayer, and John T. Kirkland were all in the class of 1789; Thaddeus Mason Harris and John Quincy Adams were their

---

[13] The ten organizations used for analysis were: Board of Overseers of Harvard College, American Academy of Arts and Sciences, officers of the Massachusetts Humane Society, Massachusetts Congregational Charitable Society, Society for Propagating the Gospel among the Indians and Others, Massachusetts Historical Society, Charitable Fire Society, Society for the Information and Advice of Immigrants, Anthology Club, Wednesday Evening Club. The count given in the body of the text includes memberships held prior to 1805 only.

seniors by only two years, while Josiah Quincy was a year their junior.[14]

The interrelationships among the liberals also involved traditional acts of fellowship among churches and clergy. Party lines were not systematically drawn before 1805 in such matters as pulpit exchanges, ordinations, and meetings of ministerial associations; yet the tendency was already apparent for liberals to favor their own kind. In Salem in 1785 and 1786, for example, William Bentley exchanged half a day with Thomas Barnard on twelve different occasions, while William Hazlitt preached for him three times. None of the neighboring orthodox ministers traded pulpits with him more than once.[15] In Worcester, at about the same time, Aaron Bancroft's ordaining council was composed predominantly of Arminian ministers and laymen from their churches.[16]

Here was a closely-knit clique of liberals in Boston, with ministers and prominent laymen in surrounding towns tied to it in a variety of ways. Yet this group did not cut itself off from friendly intercourse with moderate Calvinists. A visiting Presbyterian discovered to his dismay in 1791 that the Boston Association of Ministers included men of all shades of belief: " Some are Calvinists, some Universalists, some Arminians, some Arians, and one at least is a Socinian." If the purpose is to " shake hands, and talk of politics and science, and laugh, and eat raisins and almonds, and apples and cake, and drink wine and tea, and then go about their business when they please," he offered no objection. " But

[14] *Harvard University Quinquennial Catalogue* (Cambridge, 1930), pp. 196–198, 201–203.

[15] Bentley Mss, Vol. IV, in the American Antiquarian Society, Worcester.

[16] They were: Timothy Harrington of Lancaster, Zabdiel Adams of Lunenburg, Drs. Howard and Lathrop of Boston, Timothy Hilliard of Cambridge, and Thomas Barnard of Salem. See Bancroft, *Sermon Delivered in Worcester*, p. 41.

for the purposes of church government, to me, at least, it appears ludicrous." [17]

A man like Dr. Peter Thacher of Brattle Street, though reputed orthodox, was as much a part of the élite social group, and a member of as many of the societies, as John Eliot or John Clarke. With the ministers of the First Church he was on the most intimate terms, a close relationship being encouraged by the union of the churches in sponsoring a lecture on the Friday before the celebration of communion, ever since 1719. Thacher preached Clarke's funeral sermon; his own was preached in turn by William Emerson. It is significant, however, that before his death in 1802, his Calvinism became so very mild that one of his successors described him as " ranked among the conservative, but liberal clergy of his day." [18] William Emerson defined Thacher's position in his funeral sermon: " He was considered a disciple of the calvinistic school; but he religiously avoided the metaphysical subtleties, with which some adherents to Calvin bewilder themselves and their hearers." [19] The liberals in Thacher's congregation could listen to his mild orthodoxy without concern, or loss of affection for their minister. On his death, however, the three men approached as possible successors were all liberals. [20]

In eastern Massachusetts, the gradation from Arminians to moderate Calvinists was so smooth that there were many ministers who cannot now be placed with certainty. The line between these groups and the Hopkinsians was much plainer.

[17] Joseph H. Jones, ed., *Life of Ashbel Green* (New York 1849), p. 225.
[18] Samuel K. Lothrop, *A History of the Church in Brattle Street, Boston* (Boston, 1851), p. 155.
[19] William Emerson, *A Sermon, on the Decease of the Rev. Peter Thacher, D.D.* (Boston, 1803), p. 13.
[20] They were William Ellery Channing; Abiel Abbot, who went to Beverly instead; and Joseph Stevens Buckminster, who accepted the call. See Lothrop, *Church in Brattle Street*, pp. 159, 160.

The Hopkinsians were widely scattered throughout New England, instead of being concentrated as were the liberals, yet they were at least as closely knit. Jedidiah Morse referred to them as " also a sect ";[21] and William Bentley remarked: " It is the unsocial character of the professors of this sect which makes them odious." [22]

Bentley was uncommonly sensitive to the connection between theology and social structure, and he attributed the exclusiveness of these " Farmer Metaphysicians " [23] to their attempt to win positions of influence and prestige. " There always has been a sect to whom uncharitableness seems particularly to have belonged. Once it was the Anabaptists but they have now risen to some importance & can subsist without it. It is now left to others, who are struggling to rise." [24] Other factors, however, were probably far more important in producing cohesion among the Hopkinsians. They were almost all of them Yale men, rather than Harvard graduates, and a large number of them studied theology under Joseph Bellamy, Stephen West, or Nathanael Emmons. Thus Levi Hart of Preston, Connecticut, and Ammi R. Robbins of Norfolk, were both members of the Yale class of 1760, and both went on to study under Bellamy. Kinship ties were of great importance also. Hart married Bellamy's daughter. Daniel Hopkins of Salem was the younger brother and student of Dr. Samuel Hopkins of Newport, Rhode Island. Samuel Hopkins of Hadley was their cousin; while not a Hopkinsian himself, he was surrounded by five Hopkinsian sons-in-law: Nathanael Emmons of Franklin, Samuel Spring of Newburyport, Samuel Austin of Worcester, William Riddel of

---

[21] William B. Sprague, *Life of Jedidiah Morse, D.D.* (New York, 1874), p. 65.
[22] *The Diary of William Bentley* (Salem, 1905–1914), II, p. 139.
[23] *Ibid.*, I, p. 275.
[24] *Ibid.*, I, p. 161.

Bristol, Maine, and Leonard Worcester of Peacham, Vermont. Worcester was the brother of the Samuel Worcester whose Hopkinsianism got him in trouble in Fitchburg in 1802; but another brother, Noah, drifted into the liberal camp.[25]

Despite the distances involved, the leading Hopkinsians were in constant communication with one another. Hopkins' own circle of intimate personal friends included Dr. Bellamy, Dr. Hart, Dr. Emmons, Dr. Spring, Ephraim Judson, and Dr. Stephen West. Hopkins had served the church in Great Barrington before he removed to Newport; West was his neighbor and Edwards' successor at nearby Stockbridge. With West and Hart in particular, Hopkins carried on an extensive correspondence; Hart preached his funeral sermon and West was his first biographer.[26]

In 1799, the Hopkinsians became institutionalized with the founding of the Massachusetts Missionary Society. Although there were moderate Calvinists who joined it, the society was dominated by the Hopkinsians, just as the Arminians dominated organizations like the Historical Society. In 1804, the president was Nathanael Emmons, the secretary was Samuel Austin, and the trustees were almost all Hopkinsian. In 1803, the society sponsored a new journal, the *Massachusetts Missionary Magazine*, which may be regarded as the Hopkinsian counterpart of the *Monthly Anthology*.[27]

---

[25] William B. Sprague, *Annals of the American Pulpit* (New York, 1857–1869), I, p. 520; II, p. 399.

[26] *Ibid.*, I, pp. 428–435.

[27] The officers and trustees in 1804 were: Nathanael Emmons (Yale, 1767), Franklin; Samuel Austin (Yale, 1783), Worcester; David Sanford (Yale, 1755), West Medway; Daniel Hopkins (Yale, 1758), Salem; Samuel Niles (Princeton, 1769), Abington; Samuel Spring (Princeton, 1771), Newburyport; Jonathan Strong (Dartmouth, 1786), Randolph; Jedidiah Morse (Yale, 1783), Charlestown; Elijah Parish (Dartmouth, 1785), Byfield; Jacob Norton (Harvard, 1786), Weymouth. Deacon John Simpkins of Boston was treasurer. See *Massachusetts Missionary Magazine*, II (1804), p. 7.

Of all that went to make a Hopkinsian, David Sanford of West Medway may serve as the epitome. He was born in New Milford, Connecticut, and was named for David Brainerd, the young missionary whose untimely death had once so deeply affected Jonathan Edwards. He graduated from Yale in 1755, then studied with Dr. Bellamy. He lived for a time at Great Barrington, where Dr. Hopkins and he married sisters. Dr. West of Stockbridge preached his ordination sermon in 1773. He was one of the founders and first trustees of the Missionary Society; he was on the Board of Editors of the *Missionary Magazine*. After a protracted illness, he died in 1810; his funeral sermon was preached by his intimate friend and neighbor, Dr. Emmons of Franklin. On the map, West Medway is some twenty-five miles from Boston; yet the world in which Sanford lived was almost as far removed from the metropolis as it was possible to get.[28]

IV

In 1804, the Reverend Jedidiah Morse, D.D., of Charlestown was the only trustee of the Massachusetts Missionary Society who was definitely not a Hopkinsian. Yet it may be surmised that his presence on the board was no accident. It was rather an essential part of a bold scheme which he had very clearly in mind: a realignment of the religious groups in Massachusetts. Connecticut-born and Yale-trained, Morse was accustomed to fellowship between Old Calvinists and New Divinity men, and to the isolation of Arminians, who were chiefly Episcopalian. In Massachusetts, he was horrified to discover friendly relations between Arminians and moderate Calvinists, while the Hopkinsians were isolated. What Morse intended was to remake Massachusetts in the image of Connecticut. His presence in the Missionary

[28] Sprague, *Annals*, II, pp. 48–53.

Society was enormously significant because it placed him, a moderate Calvinist, in personal touch with all the leading Hopkinsians in Massachusetts. There can be no denying that Morse was a brilliant ecclesiastical strategist. The final outcome was exactly as he intended, and he was the key figure in the whole sequence of events. He was successful because he realized almost instinctively that cooperation would not be brought about by exhortation, but by setting up an institutional framework within which it would develop naturally. He was successful also because he understood that it would be necessary to begin with existing social structures and established networks of communication. He was successful because he was one of the few men in New England who had direct personal contact with the leaders of all three factions, so that the information he got was authentic and the channels through which he might operate were open. He was successful, finally, because the situation demanded a man who would not shrink from controversy.

Morse was born in Woodstock, Connecticut, in 1761. Although this town had once been part of Massachusetts, and a Harvard graduate was installed over the First Church as late as 1763, Yale had pretty well conquered the whole county by the time Morse was ready for college. He went to New Haven, therefore, and not to Cambridge. At Yale, where he was a member of the class of 1783, he encountered Calvinists of various shades of orthodoxy. President Stiles was an Old Calvinist, decidedly critical of the Hopkinsians. The minister of the White Haven Church was Jonathan Edwards, Jr., a New Divinity man, though not an extreme Hopkinsian. He was one of Morse's guides in theological studies following graduation. Among Morse's classmates, his circle of friends included both Abiel Holmes, a moderate

Calvinist who married Stiles' daughter, and Samuel Austin, later a prominent Hopkinsian. It was a council already called to ordain Austin which examined Morse also, and the two were consecrated together on November 9, 1786, in a ceremony in which Holmes participated.[29]

In 1788, Morse accepted a call to the church in Charlestown, where he was installed on April 30, 1789, at the very hour that General Washington was taking the oath as president in New York. Morse was already known as the author of the *American Geography;* indeed he may have owed his call to Charlestown to his authorship of this book, since it was the historian Jeremy Belknap who originally suggested his name. Morse's reputation as a geographer quickly brought him membership in the American Academy and the Historical Society, while his position as minister in Charlestown automatically gave him a seat on the Board of Overseers of Harvard College. As a member of the Boston Association of Ministers, he exchanged frequently with his less orthodox colleagues and met with them fortnightly for discussion and social intercourse.[30]

Morse seemed to have every qualification, intellectual and social, for easy assimilation into the Boston élite. But he had three serious handicaps. He was a Yale man; his standard of orthodoxy was rigid; and to his dying day, he could never resist the temptation to become involved in controversy. By degrees, therefore, hostility developed between him and the liberals. He began his ministry by preaching a series of Thursday Lectures in defence of the divinity of Christ. This was an obvious slap at the liberals, and particularly at James Freeman, the Socinian. In 1790, Freeman sponsored a reprint of a revised edition of Isaac Watts' *Di-*

[29] Sprague, *Morse,* pp. 1–10; James K. Morse, *Jedidiah Morse* (New York, 1939), pp. 14–25.

[30] Sprague, *Morse,* pp. 11–27; Morse, *Jedidiah Morse,* pp. 26–34.

vine Songs, from which those stanzas which were explicitly Trinitarian had been omitted. Morse immediately sent to the *Columbian Centinel* a letter headed " Beware of Counterfeits," which he signed " A Friend to Honesty," in which he implied that the next step would be alteration of the sacred text of the Bible itself.[31]

Evidently Freeman and his intimates felt that this newcomer needed to be put in his place. In 1793, Freeman prepared a sixty-page pamphlet entitled: *Remarks on the American Universal Geography.* He pointed to scores of errors in the book that had made Morse's reputation: inaccurate maps, faulty determinations of latitude and longitude, incorrect measurement of distances, mistakes in simple arithmetic, wrong dates, and reliance on worthless authorities. He also accused the author of gross prejudice: against Universalists; against Massachusetts Congregationalism, which Morse had called degenerate; against the state of Rhode Island, the bulk of whose inhabitants had been dismissed as ignorant; against lawyers; against the inhabitants of Maryland, who had been described as negligent in dress, slothful, and ignorant; in short, against almost everyone and everything except the people and institutions of Connecticut.[32]

Freeman sent a copy of his pamphlet to Morse, explaining that he had no other thought but to help the author make improvements in subsequent editions. " I have," he said, " suppressed many observations, which, though they appeared to be well founded, I was afraid might give you pain. . . . I hope you will believe me when I say that nothing is farther from my thoughts than to injure the sale

---

[31] Sprague, *Morse,* pp. 50–57; Morse, *Jedidiah Morse,* pp. 43–46. The letter " Beware of Counterfeits " appeared in the *Columbian Centinel* for November 17, 1790; other letters appeared in the issues of November 19 and 27, and December 4, 15, and 22, 1790.

[32] J. F. [James Freeman], *Remarks on the American Universal Geography* (Boston, 1793).

of your Geography." [33]   But William Bentley wrote in his Diary: " Mr. Freeman has published his remarks upon Morse's Univ. Geog. which expose that Geographer so fully to the world, as to lay his geographising abilities under suspicion, & perhaps they in future will be in little demand." [34] Morse, certainly, was not deceived; he knew at once that the attack on the geography was the sequel to " his vindication of the *Trinity*, with some other facts of the same nature, particularly the exposure of a *mutilated* edition of Watts's Divine Songs." [35]

For a decade thereafter, relative harmony prevailed, as liberals and orthodox united " to defend the great *outworks* of their common Christianity " against the spread of infidelity. " So long as measures of common concern were pursued . . . ," Morse afterwards recorded, " so long I received their support and their civil and respectful treatment." [36]   But though the bickering ceased for the time being, the basic differences in outlook remained.   The institutional framework in which Morse was placed thrust him in constant contact with the liberals, but he was not genuinely one of them.   His most rewarding friendships were with men more like himself: with Abiel Holmes, his classmate, who was installed over the Cambridge church in 1792; with David Tappan, who became Hollis Professor of Divinity the same year; with Eliphalet Pearson, who was Professor of Languages and a Fellow of Harvard College; and with Dr. Eckley, who was the only Boston congregational minister to join with him in a concert of prayer in 1795.   He was an active supporter of proposals for a General Association of Ministers in Massachusetts, the chief sponsors of which were

---

[33] Sprague, *Morse*, pp. 208, 209.
[34] Bentley, *Diary*, II, p. 64.
[35] Morse, *Appeal to the Public*, p. 2n.
[36] *Ibid.*, p. 2.

moderate Calvinists like President Willard and Professor Tappan.[37]   He also carefully cultivated friendships with Hopkinsians: with Chandler Robbins of Plymouth, who invited him to share in a season of awakening in his church in 1793; with Elijah Parish of Byfield, who collaborated with him on a *Compendious History of New England*, published in 1804; with the Hopkinsians who founded the Missionary Society in 1799 and the *Missionary Magazine* in 1803.[38] These were the contacts which he used so successfully when the period of crisis arrived.

v

In 1803, about a week before Commencement, Professor David Tappan died.   A moderate Calvinist of the Boston variety, he was sincerely mourned by liberals and orthodox alike.

There was immediate speculation as to the name of his successor, but the Corporation was slow to act.   Some people confidently expected an announcement at Commencement the following year, but no word came.[39]   People began to whisper that the college authorities had been disappointed by the failure of the lottery to raise the money needed for the construction of Stoughton Hall, and that the Hollis Professor's salary was being diverted to that purpose.   Others began to complain that the spiritual welfare of the students was being neglected.   A letter to the *Centinel* spoke of the public impatience and dissatisfaction with the situation.   " Clouds and darkness rest over all the proceedings, if indeed any have been had." [40]

    [37] Sprague, *Morse*, pp. 72–91.
    [38] *Ibid.*, p. 23; Morse, *Appeal to the Public, passim.*   The *Compendious History* involved Morse in an extended controversy with Miss Hannah Adams, supported by the liberals, who accused him of plagiarism.   But this controversy belongs to a later period.
    [39] *Columbian Centinel,* Sept. 1, 1804.
    [40] *Ibid.*, Nov. 14, 1804.

But the reason for the delay could not be kept a secret. Both the Hollis professorship and the presidency — now vacant because of the death on September 25, 1804 of Dr. Joseph Willard, a moderate Calvinist — were key positions of influence in the community. The real question was whether the Calvinists could retain control of them, or whether they would be taken over by the liberals. The issue was bluntly put in the *Centinel* on November 24, 1804:

We then ask with a view for seasonable deliberation; — *is there not reason to apprehend that some of the Corporation and Overseers are rather inclined to elect Unitarians or those styled rational Christians, who even deny the proper divinity of the Saviour?* . . . It is believed . . . that the two Clerical Characters most officiously and confidently mentioned abroad for President and Professor are professed Unitarians, and discard the doctrine of CHRIST's proper divinity.

Who the author of this letter was does not appear, but the language and thought of the concluding passage were wholly typical of Jedidiah Morse:

It is a time of great declension both in point of morals and sentiments but the people of *Massachusetts*, except in a few instances, are not so revolutionized and deluded that they will commit their children to the loose and erroneous hands of Unitarians for an education.[41]

Now all the whisperings and accusations and venomous remarks that had been made in intimate circles began to appear in print. A correspondent who signed himself " Mayhew " replied to Morse — if Morse it was — that in a free and Christian country no man may be permitted to charge without proof that a Christian sect is loose and erroneous. " If such are the proofs of your orthodoxy, I most sincerely pray I may never be your disciple. I rejoice, however, that you are alone in your feelings, and that among those in our metropolis who adopt your religious opinions, none engage in or approve of your intolerance." [42]

[41] *Ibid.*, Nov. 24, 1804.   [42] *Ibid.*, Nov. 28, 1804.

Much of the discussion centered on the terms of the gift of Thomas Hollis, who had endowed the chair in 1721 and provided that its holder should be " a man of solid learning in Divinity, of sound or orthodox principles." Hollis was a Calvinist, though no bigot, and obviously had no intention of supporting Arminians or anti-Trinitarians. So the orthodox argued; but the liberals replied " that this munificent man wished to found a Professorship of Divinity, in the large interpretation of the word, and not a Professorship of Calvinism or Arminianism." [43]

After about a month, the editor of the *Centinel* decided to admit no more controversy to his pages, and refused to print a letter signed " Calvinus." He was immediately accused of censorship, and even of attempting to interfere with the publication of the letter in another newspaper: " These, Mr. Russell, are facts, and they but too plainly indicate, that there exist somewhere, dispositions to prevent the public voice being heard and to carry favorite points by means not the most honourable." [44]   But " Constant Reader " ingeniously reopened the argument once more. He congratulated the editor of the *Centinel* on his resolve to print no more controversial letters, and then added — what was the crux of the whole debate — that " whether the candidates for the Presidential and Theological chairs, be Calvinists, Arians, Socinians, or Latitudinarians, is not of so much importance, as whether they are learned, pious, moral men." [45]

Meanwhile, apart from the public clamor, but not unmindful of it, the Corporation was debating its course of action.[46]

    [43] *Ibid.*, Dec. 1, 1804.
    [44] *Ibid.*, Dec. 22, 1804.
    [45] *Ibid.*, Jan. 16, 1805.
    [46] The official record, which is thoroughly uninformative, is in " College Records," Vol. IV, in the Harvard University Archives. The only source for information on the intrigue and manipulation that went on behind the scenes seems to be the " Commonplace Book " of Ephraim Eliot, now in the possession

After the death of Willard, the remaining members were: Ebenezer Storer of the Brattle Street Church, the Treasurer; Dr. John Lathrop, minister of the Second Church; Judge Oliver Wendell, father of Abiel Holmes' second wife; Professor Eliphalet Pearson; Judge John Davis of the Federal Street Church; and Dr. John Eliot, minister of the New North. Storer, Lathrop, Davis, and Eliot were liberals; Pearson and Wendell were orthodox. Various considerations other than theological differences entered into the deliberations, however, and it was two months before the final showdown produced a split along strictly factional lines.

The minutes for the meeting of December 3, 1804, record: "The Corporation conversed at this meeting relative to the choice of a Professor of Divinity; but no question was taken." [47] This meeting was the first at which Dr. Eliot was present, since he had only just been elected to fill the vacancy caused by the death of Dr. Simeon Howard. He was much disgusted by the dilatory fashion in which Professor Pearson presided. Storer pressed for action on the matter of the Hollis professorship. He was a strong supporter of the Reverend Henry Ware of Hingham, a man of gentle spirit and unquestioned integrity. But Pearson was most reluctant to proceed, and would talk only in generalities.

Four days later, another fruitless discussion took place. Pearson made "a most solemn speech," in which he told how much he had prayed and thought about the matter, and about the obligation which rested on the Corporation to elect

---

of Professor Samuel Eliot Morison. Ephraim Eliot was a brother of John Eliot, the newest member of the Corporation, and he copied into his book some extracts from the journal and memoranda of his brother. A few details may be found in the "Pearson Papers" in the Harvard University Archives. See also Sidney Willard, *Memories of Youth and Manhood*, 2 vols. (Boston, 1855), II, pp. 172–177; and John G. Palfrey, "Henry Ware," in William Ware, ed., *American Unitarian Biography* (Boston and Cambridge, 1850), I, pp. 236–238.

[47] "College Records," Vol. IV, under date Dec. 3, 1804.

a Calvinist. " He was ill humoured, he is ever ill mannered," wrote Eliot in his diary. " Upon this occasion he threw the foam of Billingsgate upon me, thinking he had a right to abuse me as I was a new member." [48] Eliot took revenge by referring to him, privately at least, as " Megalonyx."

At the next three meetings, the only accomplishment was the preparation of a statement of the duties attached to the professorship. Pearson continued to urge that its founder had been a Calvinist, while the liberals replied that he would never have insisted " upon a man's believing as he did to be a useful Minister or professor." [49] Finally, on February 1, 1805, Judge Wendell attempted a compromise. The two candidates most frequently mentioned were the Reverend Henry Ware of Hingham, a liberal, and the Reverend Jesse Appleton of Hampton, New Hampshire, a moderate Calvinist. Let Appleton be the professor, Wendell suggested, and then let Ware be elected to the presidency.

This compromise had much to commend it, and was very nearly adopted. Appleton was well liked personally by the liberals. Dr. Lathrop had been seriously considering him, and had solicited information from Dr. Joseph Lathrop of Springfield as to his qualifications and reputation.[50] Eliot afterwards spoke of him in the most affectionate terms; at the time, his chief objections were that Appleton's voice was " dissonant & unpleasant, especially in prayer," and that the professors and tutors who formed the immediate government of the college were against him.[51] Pearson, however, was violently against the compromise because he wanted the presidency for himself, and he suggested Joshua Bates, later

[48] Eliot, " Commonplace Book," Vol. II, R–29, R–30.
[49] *Ibid.*, Vol. II, R–31.
[50] See a memorandum in the " Pearson Papers."
[51] Eliot, " Commonplace Book," Vol. II, R–33.

president of Middlebury, for the professorship. Storer opposed the compromise because he wanted Ware as professor, rather than as president.

Several of the Fellows of the Corporation expressed opposition to the election of a president at this meeting, but they finally assented to a trial ballot. On that basis, Ware got four votes for the presidency, but Appleton received only three for the professorship, so the compromise failed.[52] After four hours of discussion of the matter, the Corporation wearily ended the day by balloting for the professorship. The division came along party lines, four to two: " After much discussion a ballot was taken for a Hollis Professor of Divinity; and it appeared that the Revd. Henry Ware of Hingham was chosen." [53]

The Overseers met on February 14, 1805. They consisted of the ministers of the six adjacent towns, the governor and lieutenant-governor of the Commonwealth, and the members of the governor's council and of the senate. Dr. Morse led the opposition to ratification. The Corporation's failure to examine Ware as to his orthodoxy was criticized, and evidence was presented that he was not orthodox by the standards of Thomas Hollis. It was argued that the college

---

[52] The trial ballot for president showed: Ware, 4; Dr. Kirkland, 1; Dr. Smith, 1. Ware's supporters must have been Wendell, Lathrop, Davis, and Eliot. Storer probably was the one who voted for Dr. Kirkland, and Pearson for " Dr. Smith," perhaps John Smith, professor and librarian at Dartmouth. For professor, the vote was: Mr. Appleton, 3; Mr. Ware, 1; Mr. Pierce, 1; Mr. Bates, 1. The supporters of the compromise, who voted for Appleton on this ballot, must have been Lathrop, Wendell, and Davis. Storer doubtless voted for Ware; Eliot voted for John Pierce, minister in Brookline; and Pearson voted for Bates. On the final ballot, Pearson shifted to Appleton in an effort to stop Ware; but his move was too late. Eliot afterwards regretted that he had not supported the compromise: " My vote for Mr Pierce, prevented the choice of Mr Appleton, for which I am now sorry . . . it was my opinion that Mr [Ware?] should be president, & Mr Pierce professor. But if Mr Appleton had been elected professor, how much easier would things have been managed." Eliot, " Commonplace Book," Vol. II, R–33.

[53] " College Records," Vol. IV, under date Feb. 1, 1805.

would lose the friendship of many supporters, and that it would be better to name a middle-of-the-roader, identified neither with the liberals nor with the Hopkinsians. But when the question was called for, the choice of Henry Ware was confirmed by a vote of thirty-three to twenty-three.[54]

The day after the first meeting at which the Corporation had discussed the problem, Jedidiah Morse had written: " There is a violent struggle to elect an Arminian professor and President for our university, and avowedly to make it the Arminian College. . . . I fear and deprecate a revolution in our university more than a political revolution. I pray God in mercy, to prevent both." [55] Morse lost the battle, and the revolution took place, to be confirmed a year later when Samuel Webber, a liberal, was named president. But Morse gained a point which was almost as valuable to him as control of the college would have been. He had helped to make the election of Henry Ware an act of party warfare, something the liberals were anxious to avoid. After it was all over, the liberals would have liked nothing better than to forget the struggle. But too many bitter words had been spoken, too many pens had been dipped in acid. The Arminian movement had done its work; the Unitarian Controversy had begun.

[54] Jedidiah Morse, *The True Reasons on which the Election of a Hollis Professor of Divinity in Harvard College, was Opposed at the Board of Overseers, Feb. 14, 1805* (Charlestown, 1805).

[55] Morse to Dr. Joseph Lyman, Dec. 4, 1804, quoted in Morse, *Jedidiah Morse*, p. 87.

Biographical Appendix

This biographical appendix is divided into two parts. The first is a list of Arminian ministers, identified as such on the basis of their doctrine as stated in printed sermons and tracts. There were doubtless as many more whose Arminianism cannot now be proved, since they published little; and there were many men in the twilight zone between Arminianism and moderate Calvinism, whose social contacts with the liberal group made them socially, though not theologically, a part of the movement. But the men listed here were the most prominent and representative of the Arminian group.

The second part of the appendix is a much more selective list of New Divinity men, most of them Hopkinsians. It is based on the common reputation of the men, rather than on detailed examination of their writings. Both lists have been arranged in chronological rather than alphabetical order, so as to give some sense of the succession of generations. The basis for this arrangement is the date of graduation from college. The men whose locations are indicated on the maps in Chapter 12 have been designated here by asterisks. The biographical data is based largely on Frederick L. Weis, *The Colonial Clergy and the Colonial Churches of New England* (Lancaster, 1936); William B. Sprague, *Annals of the American Pulpit* (New York, 1857–1869); Clifford K. Shipton, *Sibley's Harvard Graduates*, Vols. 4–8 (Cambridge and Boston, 1933–1951); Franklin B. Dexter, *Biographical Sketches of the Graduates of Yale College*, Vols. 1–6 (New York, 1885–1912).

Arminians

SAMUEL OSBORN, born Ireland, 1685; educated Dublin; ordained Eastham, 1718; settled Eastham, 1718–1719; settled Orleans (Second Parish in Eastham), 1719–1738; dismissed, 1738; died Boston, 1774.

SAMUEL BROWN, born Newbury, Sept. 4, 1687; A.B. Harvard, 1709; ordained Abington, 1714; settled Abington, 1712–1749; died Abington, Sept. 19, 1749.

EBENEZER GAY, born Dedham, Aug. 15, 1696; A.B. Harvard, 1714; ordained Hingham, 1718; settled Hingham, 1717–1787; died Hingham, March 18, 1787. S.T.D. Harvard, 1785. Election Sermon, 1745; Convention Sermon, 1746; Dudleian Lecture, 1759. Close friend of Charles Chauncy; participated in the ordinations of Jonathan Mayhew and his successor, Simeon Howard, at the West Church in Boston.

CHARLES CHAUNCY, born Boston, Jan. 1, 1704/5; A.B. Harvard, 1721; ordained Boston, Oct. 25, 1727; settled Boston (First Church), 1727–1787; died Boston, Feb. 10, 1787. S.T.D. Edinburgh, 1742. Overseer of Harvard College; Fellow of the American Academy. His senior colleague until 1769 was Thomas Foxcroft, a moderate Calvinist, but his intimates were men like Ebenezer Gay, Jonathan Mayhew, and John Eliot.

WILLIAM BALCH, born Beverly, Sept. 30, 1704; A.B. Harvard, 1724; ordained Bradford (Second Church, Groveland), June 7, 1727; settled Bradford, 1727–1792; died Groveland, Jan. 12, 1792. Election Sermon, 1749; Convention Sermon, 1760.

BENJAMIN KENT, born 1708; A.B. Harvard, 1727; ordained Marlborough, Oct. 27, 1733; settled Marlborough, 1733–1735; dismissed, 1735; died Nova Scotia, 1788.

ROBERT BRECK, JR., born Marlborough, July 25, 1713; A.B. Harvard, 1730; ordained Springfield, July 26, 1736; settled Springfield, 1734–1784; died Springfield, April 23, 1784. Convention Sermon, 1771.

THOMAS BARNARD, born Andover, Aug. 17, 1716; A.B. Harvard, 1732; ordained West Newbury, Jan. 31, 1738/9; settled West Newbury (First Church), 1739–1752; settled Salem (First Church), 1755–1776; died Salem, Aug. 15, 1776. Election Sermon, 1763; Dudleian Lecture, 1768. Father of Thomas Barnard, Jr., of Salem.

JOHN ROGERS, born Boxford, Sept. 24, 1712; A.B. Harvard, 1732; ordained Leominster, Sept. 14, 1743; settled Leominster (First Church), 1743–1758; dismissed, 1758; settled Leominster (Second Church), 1762–1787; died Leominster, Oct. 6, 1789.

JOHN BASS, born Braintree, March 26, 1717; A.B. Harvard, 1737; ordained Ashford, Conn., Sept. 7, 1743; settled Ashford, 1743–1751; dismissed, 1751; settled Providence, R.I. (First Congregational Church), 1752–1758; died Providence, 1762.

SAMUEL WEBSTER, born Bradford, Aug. 16, 1718; A.B. Harvard, 1737; ordained Salisbury, Aug. 12, 1741; settled Salisbury, 1741–1796; died Salisbury, July 18, 1796. S.T.D. Harvard, 1792. Election Sermon, 1777; Convention Sermon, 1779.

LEMUEL BRIANT, born Scituate, Feb. 1721/2; A.B. Harvard, 1739; ordained Braintree, Dec. 4, 1745; settled Braintree (First Church, Quincy), 1745–1753; dismissed, 1753; died Hingham, Oct. 1, 1754. Close friend of Jonathan Mayhew.

JOHN BROWN, born Haverhill, March 9, 1723/4; A.B. Harvard, 1741; ordained Cohasset, Sept. 2, 1747; settled Cohasset, 1747–1791; died Cohasset, Aug. 22, 1791.

JOHN TUCKER, born Amesbury, Sept. 19, 1719; A.B. Harvard, 1741; ordained Newbury, Nov. 20, 1745; settled Newbury (First Church), 1745–1792; died Newbury, March 22, 1792. S.T.D. Harvard, 1787. Convention Sermon, 1768; Election Sermon, 1771; Dudleian Lecture, 1778.

*GAD HITCHCOCK, born Springfield, Feb. 12, 1718/9; A.B. Harvard, 1743; ordained Hanson, Oct. 1748; settled Hanson, 1748–1803; died Hanson, Aug. 8, 1803. S.T.D. Harvard, 1787. Election Sermon, 1774; Dudleian Lecture, 1779; Convention Sermon, 1787.

*DANIEL SHUTE, born Malden, July 19, 1722; A.B. Harvard, 1743; ordained South Hingham, Dec. 10, 1746; settled Hingham (Third Parish), 1746–1802; died Hingham, Aug. 30, 1802. S.T.D. Harvard, 1790. Election Sermon, 1768; Convention Sermon, 1783. Incorporator of the Congregational Charitable Society.

JONATHAN MAYHEW, born Chilmark, Oct. 8, 1720; A.B. Harvard, 1744; ordained Boston, June 17, 1747; settled Boston (West Church), 1747–1766; died Boston, July 8, 1766. S.T.D. Aberdeen, 1749. Election Sermon, 1754; Dudleian Lecture, 1765. Overseer of Harvard College. His close friends included Charles Chauncy, Ebenezer Gay, and Lemuel Briant; his widow married Simeon Howard.

*WILLIAM SYMMES, born Charlestown, Nov. 1728; A.B. Harvard, 1750; ordained Andover, Nov. 1, 1758; settled Andover (North Parish), 1757–1807; died Andover, May 3, 1809. S.T.D. Harvard, 1803. Election Sermon, 1785; Dudleian Lecture, 1786.

*DAVID BARNES, born Marlborough, March 24, 1731; A.B. Harvard, 1752; ordained Scituate, Dec. 4, 1754; settled Scituate (Second Church, Norwell), 1754–1811; died Norwell, April 26, 1811. S.T.D. Harvard, 1799. Dudleian Lecture, 1780.

JAMES DANA, born Cambridge, 1735; A.B. Harvard, 1753; ordained Wallingford, Conn., Oct. 11, 1758; settled Wallingford, 1758–1789; settled New Haven, Conn. (First Church), 1789–1805; died New Haven, Aug. 18, 1812. S.T.D. Edinburgh, 1768. Connecticut Election Sermon, 1779. An Arminian at the beginning of his ministry, but later on indistinguishable from moderate Calvinists.

*SAMUEL WEST of New Bedford, born Yarmouth, March 3, 1729/30; A.B. Harvard, 1754; ordained Dartmouth, June 3, 1761; settled Dartmouth (New Bedford), 1761–1803; died Tiverton, R.I., Sept. 24, 1807. S.T.D. Harvard, 1793. Election Sermon, 1776; Dudleian Lecture, 1782. Fellow of the American Academy.

*SIMEON HOWARD, born Bridgewater, April 29, 1733; A.B. Harvard, 1758; ordained Boston, May 6, 1767; settled Boston (West Church), 1767–1804; died Boston, Aug. 13, 1804. S.T.D. Edinburgh, 1785. Election Sermon, 1780; Dudleian Lecture, 1787; Convention Sermon, 1790. Overseer and Fellow of Harvard College; Fellow of the American Academy; member of the Immigrant Aid Society, Humane Society, Congregational Charitable Society, and the Society for Propagating the Gospel among the Indians and Others.

PAUL COFFIN, born Newbury, Jan. 16, 1737/8; A.B. Harvard, 1759; ordained Buxton, Maine, March 16, 1763; settled Buxton, 1761–1818; died Buxton, June 6, 1821. S.T.D. Harvard, 1812. Election Sermon, 1799.

*HENRY CUMINGS, born Hollis, N.H., Sept. 16, 1739; A.B. Harvard, 1760; ordained Billerica, Jan. 26, 1763; settled Billerica, 1763–1823; died Baltimore, Md., Sept. 5, 1823. S.T.D. Harvard, 1800. Election Sermon, 1783; Dudleian Lecture, 1791; Convention Sermon, 1795.

SAMUEL DEANE, born Dedham, July 10, 1733; A.B. Harvard, 1760; ordained Falmouth, Maine, Oct. 17, 1764; settled Falmouth (Portland), 1764–1814; died Portland, Nov. 12, 1814. S.T.D. Brown, 1790. Election Sermon, 1794. Fellow of the American Academy.

*SAMUEL WEST of Boston, born Martha's Vineyard, Nov. 19, 1738; A.B. Harvard, 1761; ordained Needham, April 25, 1764; settled Needham, 1764–1789; settled Boston (Hollis Street), 1789–1808; died Boston, April 10, 1808. S.T.D. Dartmouth, 1798. Election Sermon, 1786. Overseer of Harvard College; member of the Charitable Fire Society, and the Society for Propagating the Gospel among the Indians and Others. Originally a Calvinist.

JEREMY BELKNAP, born Boston, June 4, 1744; A.B. Harvard, 1762; ordained Dover, N.H., Feb. 18, 1767; settled Dover, 1767–1786; settled Boston (Federal Street), 1787–1798; died Boston, June 20, 1798. S.T.D. Harvard, 1792. New Hampshire Election Sermon, 1785; Dudleian Lecture, 1790; Convention Sermon, 1796. Overseer of Harvard College; Fellow of American Academy; founder of Massachusetts Historical Society; member of Charitable Fire Society, the Congregational Charitable Society, and the Society for Propagating the Gospel among the Indians and Others. Married Ruth Eliot, cousin of the Reverend John Eliot. Originally a Calvinist.

*JOHN LATHROP, born Norwich, Conn., May 6, 1739; A.B. Princeton, 1763; ordained Boston, May 18, 1768; settled Boston (Second Church), 1768–1816; died Boston, Jan. 4, 1816. S.T.D. Edinburgh, 1785. Dudleian Lecture, 1793; Convention Sermon, 1800. Overseer and Fellow of Harvard College; Fellow of the American Academy; member of the Massachusetts Congregational Charitable Society, Society for Propagating the Gospel among the Indians and Others, Immigrant Aid Society, Humane Society, and Charitable Fire Society. Calvinist in the early years of his ministry. Preached at ordination of William Bentley.

TIMOTHY HILLIARD, born Kensington, N.H., 1746; A.B. Harvard, 1764; ordained Barnstable, April 10, 1771; settled Barnstable (East Church), 1771–1783; settled Cambridge, 1783–1790; died Cambridge, May 9, 1790. Dudleian Lecture, 1788. Overseer of Harvard College; incorporator of the Society for Propagating the Gospel among the Indians and Others; incorporator of the Congregational Charitable Society.

*THOMAS BARNARD, JR., born Newbury, Feb. 5, 1748; A.B. Harvard, 1766; ordained Salem, Jan. 13, 1773; settled Salem (North Church), 1773–

1814; died Salem, Oct. 1, 1814. S.T.D. Brown, 1794; Edinburgh, 1794. Convention Sermon, 1793; Dudleian Lecture, 1795. Fellow of the American Academy; incorporator of the Congregational Charitable Society; member of the Humane Society and the Society for Propagating the Gospel among the Indians and Others. Neighbor and friend of William Bentley; preached ordination sermons for Aaron Bancroft at Worcester, 1786, and Ichabod Nichols at Portland, 1809.

*JOSEPH THAXTER, born Hingham, April 23, 1744; A.B. Harvard, 1768; ordained Edgartown, 1780; settled Edgartown, 1780–1827; died Edgartown, July 18, 1827. Studied theology under Ebenezer Gay.

*ZEDEKIAH SANGER, born Sherborn, Oct. 4, 1748; A.B. Harvard, 1771; ordained Duxbury, July 3, 1776; settled Duxbury, 1776–1786; settled South Bridgewater, 1788–1820; died Bridgewater, Nov. 17, 1820. S.T.D. Brown, 1807. Convention Sermon, 1805. Fellow of the American Academy.

*JOHN ELIOT, born Boston, May 31, 1754; A.B. Harvard, 1772; ordained Boston, Nov. 3, 1779; settled Boston (New North), 1779–1813; died Boston, Feb. 14, 1813. S.T.D. Edinburgh, 1797. Fellow of Harvard College, replacing Dr. Howard, deceased 1804. Overseer of Harvard College; Fellow of the American Academy; founder of the Massachusetts Historical Society; member of the Wednesday Evening Club, Humane Society, Charitable Fire Society, Society for Propagating the Gospel among the Indians and Others, and the Congregational Charitable Society. Friend of Jeremy Belknap, who married his cousin.

*JOHN REED, born Framingham, Nov. 11, 1751; A.B. Yale, 1772; ordained Bridgewater, Jan. 7, 1780; settled Bridgewater (West Bridgewater), 1780–1831; died West Bridgewater, Feb. 17, 1831. S.T.D. Brown, 1803. Convention Sermon, 1807; Dudleian Lecture, 1812.

*CHARLES STEARNS, born Leominster, July 19, 1753; A.B. Harvard, 1773; ordained Lincoln, Nov. 7, 1781; settled Lincoln, 1781–1826; died Lincoln, July 26, 1826. S.T.D. Harvard, 1810. Convention Sermon, 1815. Fellow of the American Academy.

JOHN CLARKE, born Portsmouth, N.H., April 13, 1755; A.B. Harvard, 1774; ordained Boston, July 8, 1778; settled Boston (First Church), 1778–1798; died Boston, April 1, 1798. S.T.D. Edinburgh, 1795. Overseer of Harvard College; Fellow of the American Academy; member of the Massachusetts Historical Society, the Humane Society, Wednesday Evening Club, Charitable Fire Society, and the Society for Propagating the Gospel among the Indians and Others. Colleague of Charles Chauncy.

*THOMAS THACHER, born Boston, Oct. 24, 1756; A.B. Harvard, 1775; ordained Dedham, June 7, 1780; settled Dedham (Third Church), 1780–1812; died Dedham, Oct. 19, 1812. Fellow of the American Academy.

*JOHN PRINCE, born Boston, July 22, 1751; A.B. Harvard, 1776; ordained Salem, Nov. 10, 1779; settled Salem (First Church), 1779–1836; died Salem, June 7, 1836. LL.D. Brown, 1795. Fellow of the American Academy; member of the Massachusetts Historical Society; Wednesday Evening Club in 1779 prior to settlement in Salem; and the Congregational Charitable Society.

*EZRA RIPLEY, born Woodstock, Conn., May 1, 1751; A.B. Harvard, 1776; ordained Concord, Nov. 7, 1778; settled Concord, 1778–1841; died Concord, Sept. 22, 1841. S.T.D. Harvard, 1816. Step-father of William Emerson.

*WILLIAM BENTLEY, born Boston, June 22, 1759; A.B. Harvard, 1777; ordained Salem, Sept. 1783; settled Salem (East Church), 1783–1819; died Salem, Dec. 29, 1819. S.T.D. Harvard, 1819. Member of the Massachusetts Historical Society. Barnard and Prince of Salem, and Lathrop of Boston participated in his ordination; James Freeman was an intimate friend; active in Masonic affairs; Jeffersonian in politics.

*JAMES FREEMAN, born Charlestown, April 22, 1759; A.B. Harvard, 1777; ordained Boston, Nov. 18, 1787; settled Boston (King's Chapel), 1782–1835; died Newton, Nov. 14, 1835. S.T.D. Harvard, 1811. Fellow of the American Academy; founder of the Massachusetts Historical Society; member of the Wednesday Evening Club, Humane Society, and the Charitable Fire Society. Intimate friend of William Bentley.

*ELIPHALET PORTER, born North Bridgewater, June 11, 1758; A.B. Harvard, 1777; ordained Roxbury, Oct. 2, 1782; settled Roxbury (First Church), 1782–1833; died Roxbury, Dec. 7, 1833. S.T.D. Harvard, 1807. Convention Sermon, 1810. Fellow of Harvard College, 1818–1833. Overseer of Harvard College; Fellow of the American Academy; member of the Massachusetts Congregational Charitable Society, Immigrant Aid Society, and the Society for Propagating the Gospel among the Indians and Others. Preached at ordination of Charles Lowell, 1806.

*AARON BANCROFT, born Reading, Nov. 10, 1755; A.B. Harvard, 1778; ordained Worcester, Feb. 1, 1786; settled Worcester (Second Parish), 1786–1839; died Worcester, Aug. 19, 1839. S.T.D. Harvard, 1810. Election Sermon, 1801; Convention Sermon, 1820. Fellow of the American Academy.

*JOSEPH MOTTEY, born Salem, May 14, 1756; A.B. Dartmouth, 1778; ordained Lynnfield, Sept. 24, 1783; settled Lynnfield, 1780–1821; died Lynnfield, July 9, 1821.

*BEZALEEL HOWARD, born Bridgewater, Nov. 22, 1753; A.B. Harvard, 1781; ordained Springfield, April 27, 1785; settled Springfield, 1784–1809; died Springfield, Jan. 20, 1837. S.T.D. Harvard, 1824. Fellow of the American Academy. Studied under Ebenezer Gay; ordination sermon preached by Timothy Hilliard; his successor in the First Church in Springfield was a Calvinist, and when the church divided in 1819, he joined the new Unitarian church.

*WILLIAM EMERSON, born Concord, May 6, 1769; A.B. Harvard, 1789; ordained Harvard, May 23, 1792; settled Harvard, 1792–1799; settled Boston (First Church), 1799–1811; died Boston, May 12, 1811. Overseer of Harvard College; Fellow of the American Academy; member of the Massachusetts Historical Society, the Wednesday Evening Club, the Anthology Society, the Charitable Fire Society, and the Humane Society. Ezra Ripley was his step-father; Ralph Waldo Emerson was his son; Nathaniel Thayer preached at his installation at Boston.

*JOHN T. KIRKLAND, born Herkimer, N.Y., Aug. 17, 1770; A.B. Harvard, 1789; ordained Boston, Feb. 5, 1794; settled Boston (New South), 1794–1810; President of Harvard, 1810–1828; died Boston, April 26, 1840. S.T.D. Princeton, 1802; LL.D. Brown, 1810. Election Sermon, 1816. Overseer of Harvard College; Fellow of the American Academy; member of the Massachusetts Historical Society, the Wednesday Evening Club, the Immigrant Aid Society, Charitable Fire Society, the Anthology Society, the Society for Propagating the Gospel among the Indians and Others, and the Congregational Charitable Society.

*NATHANIEL THAYER, born Hampton, N.H., July 11, 1769; A.B. Harvard, 1789; ordained Lancaster, Oct. 9, 1793; settled Lancaster, 1793–1840; died Rochester, N.Y., June 23, 1840. S.T.D. Harvard, 1817. Election Sermon, 1823. Preached installation sermon for William Emerson at Boston, 1799.

*JOHN PIERCE, born Dorchester, July 14, 1773; A.B. Harvard, 1793; ordained Brookline, March 15, 1797; settled Brookline, 1797–1849; died Brookline, Aug. 24, 1849. S.T.D. Harvard, 1822. Dudleian Lecture, 1821; Convention Sermon, 1825; Election Sermon, 1849. Overseer of Harvard College; Fellow of the American Academy; member of the Massachusetts Historical Society, and the Society for Propagating the Gospel among the Indians and Others. Thaddeus Mason Harris preached his ordination sermon.

*JAMES KENDALL, born Sterling, Nov. 3, 1769; A.B. Harvard, 1796; ordained Plymouth, Jan. 1, 1800; settled Plymouth, 1800–1859; died Plymouth, March 17, 1859. S.T.D. Harvard, 1825. Member of the Society for Propagating the Gospel among the Indians and Others.

*SAMUEL KENDAL, born Sherborn, July 11, 1753; A.B. Harvard, 1782; ordained Weston, Nov. 5, 1783; settled Weston, 1783–1814; died Weston, Feb. 15, 1814. S.T.D. Yale, 1806. Preached ordination sermons for Thaddeus M. Harris, 1793, and Isaac Allen, 1804.

*JOHN ALLYN, born Barnstable, March 21, 1767; A.B. Harvard, 1785; ordained Duxbury, Dec. 3, 1788; settled Duxbury, 1788–1833; died Duxbury, July 19, 1833. S.T.D. Harvard, 1813. Dudleian Lecture, 1809. Fellow of the American Academy; member of the Massachusetts Historical Society. His theological study was under Dr. West of New Bedford, who preached the ordination sermon; other participants were Gad Hitchcock and David Barnes.

*HENRY WARE, born Sherborn, April 1, 1764; A.B. Harvard, 1785; ordained Hingham, Oct. 24, 1787; settled Hingham (First Church), 1787–1805; Hollis Professor of Divinity, 1805–1840; died Cambridge, June 12, 1845. S.T.D. Harvard, 1806. Convention Sermon, 1818; Election Sermon, 1821. Fellow of the American Academy; member of the Society for Propagating the Gospel among the Indians and Others, and the Congregational Charitable Society. Studied theology under Timothy Hilliard, who preached his ordination sermon; at Hingham was the successor of Ebenezer Gay.

*PETER EATON, born Haverhill, March 25, 1765; A.B. Harvard, 1787; ordained Boxford, Oct. 7, 1789; settled Boxford, 1789–1845; died Boxford, April 14, 1848. S.T.D. Harvard, 1820. Election Sermon, 1819.

*THADDEUS MASON HARRIS, born Cambridge, July 7, 1768; A.B. Harvard, 1787; ordained Dorchester, Oct. 23, 1793; settled Dorchester, 1793–1836; died Boston, April 3, 1842. S.T.D. Harvard, 1813. Overseer of Harvard College; Fellow of the American Academy; member of the Massachusetts Historical Society, the Humane Society, the Congregational Charitable Society, and the Society for Propagating the Gospel among the Indians and Others. Active in Masonic affairs.

*SIMEON DOGGETT, born Middleborough, March 6, 1765; A.B. Brown, 1788; preceptor of Bristol Academy, Taunton, 1796–1813; ordained Mendon, 1813; settled Mendon, 1813–1831; settled Raynham, 1831–1845; died Raynham, March 19, 1852. Theological study under Dr. West of New Bedford.

*WILLIAM ELLERY CHANNING, born Newport, R.I., April 7, 1780; A.B. Harvard, 1798; ordained Boston, June 1, 1803; settled Boston (Federal Street), 1803–1842; died Bennington, Vt., Oct. 2, 1842. S.T.D. Harvard, 1820. Dudleian Lecture, 1821; Election Sermon, 1830. Overseer of Harvard College; Fellow of Harvard College, 1813–1826; Fellow of the American Academy; member of the Society for Propagating the Gospel among the Indians and Others, and the Congregational Charitable Society.

*JOSEPH TUCKERMAN, born Boston, Jan. 18, 1778; A.B. Harvard, 1798; ordained Chelsea, Nov. 4, 1801; settled Chelsea (Revere), 1801–1826; Minister-at-Large, Boston, 1826–1840; died Havana, April 20, 1840. S.T.D. Harvard, 1824. Member of Anthology Society and the Society for Propagating the Gospel among the Indians and Others. Studied theology under Thomas Thacher of Dedham, who preached at his ordination.

*WILLIAM FROTHINGHAM, born Cambridge, March 14, 1777; A.B. Harvard, 1799; ordained Saugus, Sept. 26, 1804; settled Saugus, 1804–1817; settled Belfast, Maine, 1819–1845; died Belfast, June 24, 1852.

*JOSEPH STEVENS BUCKMINSTER, born Portsmouth, N.H., May 26, 1784; A.B. Harvard, 1800; ordained Boston, Jan. 30, 1805; settled Boston (Brattle Street), 1805–1812; died Boston, June 9, 1812. Overseer of Harvard College; Fellow of the American Academy; member of the Massachusetts Historical Society, Anthology Society, Charitable Fire Society, Humane Society, and the Wednesday Evening Club.

New Divinity Men

JOSEPH BELLAMY, born New Cheshire, Conn., Feb. 20, 1718/9; A.B. Yale, 1735; ordained Bethlehem, Conn., April 2, 1740; settled Bethlehem (Woodbury), 1740–1790; died Bethlehem, March 6, 1790. Trained many candidates for the ministry in his home.

*SAMUEL HOPKINS, born Waterbury, Conn., Sept. 17, 1721; A.B. Yale, 1741; ordained Great Barrington, Dec. 28, 1743; settled Great Barrington, 1743–1769; settled Newport, R.I., 1770–1803; died Newport, Dec. 20, 1803. S.T.D. Brown, 1790. A student and intimate friend of Edwards; brother of Daniel Hopkins of Salem; close friend of Joseph Bellamy, Levi Hart, Nathanael Emmons, Samuel Spring, Ephraim Judson, and Stephen West.

*DAVID SANFORD, born New Milford, Conn., Dec. 11, 1737; A.B. Yale, 1755; ordained Medway, April 14, 1773; settled Medway (Second Church at West Medway), 1772–1810; died Medway, April 7, 1810. Studied under Bellamy; married sister of Samuel Hopkins' wife; ordination sermon preached by Stephen West; sermon on his death preached by Nathanael Emmons. Trustee of the Massachusetts Missionary Society and editor of the *Massachusetts Missionary Magazine*.

*STEPHEN WEST, born Tolland, Conn., Nov. 2, 1735; A.B. Yale, 1755; ordained Stockbridge, June 15, 1759; settled Stockbridge, 1758–1818; died Stockbridge, May 13, 1819. S.T.D. Dartmouth, 1792. Edwards' successor at Stockbridge; intimate with Bellamy, Hopkins, and the younger Edwards.

CHANDLER ROBBINS, born Branford, Conn., Aug. 24, 1738; A.B. Yale, 1756; ordained Plymouth, Jan. 30, 1760; settled Plymouth (First Church), 1759–1799; died Plymouth, June 30, 1799. S.T.D. Dartmouth, 1792; Edinburgh, 1793. Studied under Bellamy. New Divinity, but not necessarily Hopkinsian.

*JOHN SMALLEY, born Columbia, Conn., June 4, 1734; A.B. Yale, 1756; ordained New Britain, Conn., April 19, 1758; settled New Britain (First Church, Berlin), 1757–1820; died New Britain, June 1, 1820. S.T.D. Princeton, 1800. Emmons a pupil; commonly classed with the Hopkinsians, though he differed from them on some points.

*DANIEL HOPKINS, born Waterbury, Conn., Oct. 16, 1734; A.B. Yale, 1758; ordained Salem, Nov. 18, 1778; settled Salem (Third Church), 1775–1814; died Salem, Dec. 14, 1814. S.T.D. Dartmouth, 1809. Studied under Samuel Hopkins, his older brother. Helped found Massachusetts Missionary Society; editor of the *Massachusetts Missionary Magazine*.

*BENJAMIN TRUMBULL, born Hebron, Conn., Dec. 19, 1735; A.B. Yale, 1759; ordained North Haven, Conn., Dec. 24, 1760; settled North Haven, 1760–1820; died North Haven, Feb. 2, 1820. S.T.D. Yale, 1796. Edwardean rather than specifically Hopkinsian.

*LEVI HART, born Southington, Conn., April 10, 1738; A.B. Yale, 1760; ordained Preston, Conn., Nov. 4, 1762; settled Preston (Second Church, Griswold), 1762–1808; died Jewett City (Griswold), Oct. 27, 1808. D.D. Princeton, 1800. Member of Corporation, Dartmouth College; member of Corporation, Yale College; studied under Bellamy; married daughter of Bellamy; Bellamy and Hopkins his closest friends.

*EPHRAIM JUDSON, born Woodbury, Conn., Dec. 11, 1737; A.B. Yale, 1763; ordained Norwich, Conn., Oct. 3, 1771; settled Norwich, 1771–1778; settled Taunton, 1780–1790; settled Sheffield, 1791–1813; died Sheffield, Feb. 23, 1813.

JONATHAN EDWARDS, JR., born Northampton, May 26, 1745; A.B. Princeton, 1765; ordained New Haven, Conn., Jan. 5, 1769; settled New Haven (White Haven Church), 1769–1795; settled Colebrook, Conn., 1796–1799; President Union College, 1799–1801; died Schenectady, N.Y., Aug. 1, 1801. D.D. Princeton. Installation sermon preached by Dr. Trumbull;

preached ordination sermon for Timothy Dwight, his nephew. Edwardean; not specifically Hopkinsian.

*NATHANAEL EMMONS, born East Haddam, Conn., April 20, 1745; A.B. Yale, 1767; ordained Franklin, April 21, 1773; settled Franklin, 1769–1840; died Franklin, Sept. 23, 1840. S.T.D. Dartmouth, 1798. Election Sermon, 1798; Convention Sermon, 1804. Studied under John Smalley; second wife was step-daughter of Samuel Hopkins of Hadley; brother-in-law of Samuel Spring, Samuel Austin, William Riddel, and Leonard Worcester, all Hopkinsians; President of the Massachusetts Missionary Society; editor of the *Massachusetts Missionary Magazine.*

*TIMOTHY DWIGHT, born Northampton, May 14, 1752; A.B. Yale, 1769; ordained Greenfield Hill, Conn., Nov. 5, 1783; settled Greenfield Hill (Fairfield), 1783–1795; President and Professor of Divinity at Yale, 1795–1817; died New Haven, Feb. 11, 1817. D.D. Princeton, 1787; LL.D. Harvard, 1810. Grandson of Jonathan Edwards. Edwardean, rather than specifically Hopkinsian.

*SAMUEL NILES, JR., born Braintree, Dec. 3, 1743; A.B. Princeton, 1769; ordained Abington, Sept. 25, 1771; settled Abington, 1770–1814; died Abington, Jan. 16, 1814. Trustee of the Massachusetts Missionary Society; editor of the *Massachusetts Missionary Magazine.*

*SAMUEL SPRING, born Northbridge, Feb. 27, 1746; A.B. Princeton, 1771; ordained Newburyport, Aug. 6, 1777; settled Newburyport, 1777–1819; died Newburyport, March 4, 1819. D.D. Princeton, 1806. Brother-in-law of Nathanael Emmons, William Riddel, Samuel Austin, and Leonard Worcester. Studied under Bellamy, Hopkins, and Stephen West. Trustee of the Massachusetts Missionary Society; editor of the *Massachusetts Missionary Magazine.*

*WILLIAM ROBINSON, born Lebanon, Conn., Aug. 15, 1754; A.B. Yale, 1773; ordained Southington, Conn., June 13, 1780; settled Southington, 1778–1821; died Southington, Aug. 15, 1825.

*SAMUEL AUSTIN, born New Haven, Conn., Oct. 7, 1760; A.B. Yale, 1783; ordained Nov. 9, 1786; settled New Haven (Fair Haven), 1786–1789; settled Worcester, 1790–1815; President of the University of Vermont, 1815–1821; died Glastonbury, Conn., Dec. 4, 1830. D.D. Williams, 1807. Classmate of Abiel Holmes and Jedidiah Morse; brother-in-law of Nathanael Emmons, Samuel Spring, William Riddel, and Leonard Worcester; Samuel Worcester was one of his students, and he preached ordination sermons for both Samuel and Leonard Worcester. Trustee of the Massachusetts Missionary Society, and editor of the *Massachusetts Missionary Magazine.*

*ELIJAH PARISH, born Lebanon, Conn., Nov. 7, 1762; A.B. Dartmouth, 1785; ordained Byfield, Dec. 20, 1787; settled Byfield, 1787–1825; died Byfield, Oct. 15, 1825. D.D. Dartmouth, 1807. Studied under Ephraim Judson; collaborated with Jedidiah Morse on a gazetteer; trustee of the Massachusetts Missionary Society; editor of the *Massachusetts Missionary Magazine.*

*JONATHAN STRONG, born Bolton, Conn., Sept. 4, 1764; A.B. Dartmouth, 1786; ordained Randolph, Jan. 28, 1789; settled Randolph, 1789–1814; died Randolph, Nov. 9, 1814. D.D. Brown, 1814. Studied under Ephraim Judson;

trustee of the Massachusetts Missionary Society; editor of the *Massachusetts Missionary Magazine.*

*AZEL BACKUS, born Norwich (Franklin), Conn., Oct. 13, 1765; A.B. Yale, 1787; ordained Bethlehem, Conn., April 6, 1791; settled Bethlehem, 1791–1812; President, Hamilton College, 1812–1817; died Clinton, N.Y., Dec. 9, 1817. D.D. Princeton, 1810. Successor at Bethlehem of Joseph Bellamy, whose theological views he accepted.

*SAMUEL WORCESTER, born Hollis, N.H., Nov. 1, 1770; A.B. Dartmouth, 1795; ordained Fitchburg, Sept. 27, 1797; settled Fitchburg, 1797–1802; settled Salem, Tabernacle Church, 1803–1821; died June 7, 1821. Studied under Samuel Austin, who preached at his ordination. Brother of Leonard Worcester.

Bibliographical Note

A complete bibliography for this book would have to begin with a list of all the published writings of the ministers of the churches of the Standing Order who can be identified as Arminians. The most important of these writings have been cited in the footnotes; a virtually complete list may be compiled by using Charles Evans' *American Bibliography*, 12 vols. (Chicago, 1903–1934).

The best biographical sketches of the earlier Arminians are to be found in Clifford K. Shipton's *Sibley's Harvard Graduates*, IV–VIII (Cambridge and Boston, 1933–1951). William B. Sprague's *Annals of the American Pulpit*, 9 vols. (New York, 1857–1869) are still invaluable. Recent dissertations, as yet unpublished, are: Charles W. Akers, " The Life of Jonathan Mayhew, 1720–1766 " (Boston University, 1952), which amasses a good deal of information about the Boston of Mayhew's day; and Harold E. Bernhard, " Charles Chauncy, Colonial Liberal, 1705–1787 " (University of Chicago, 1948), which is little more than a summary of Chauncy's publications. Other sources of biographical data are: Joseph Allen, *The Worcester Association and its Antecedents* (Boston, 1868); Alden Bradford, *Memoir of the Life and Writings of Rev. Jonathan Mayhew, D.D.* (Boston, 1838); Jane B. Marcou, *Life of Jeremy Belknap, D.D.* (New York, 1847); and Frederick L. Weis, *The Colonial Clergy and Colonial Churches of New England* (Lancaster, Mass., 1936).

The most useful available manuscript material has been published. It includes the Belknap Papers at the Massachusetts Historical Society, and the diary of William Bentley at the American Antiquarian Society in Worcester. The relevant parts of the Belknap Papers may be found in the *Collections of the Massachusetts Historical Society*, Series 5, Vol. II (1877), and Series 6, Vol. IV (1891). Bentley's diary has been published as *The Diary of William Bentley, D.D.*, 4 vols. (Salem, 1905–1914). Other Bentley manuscripts are also deposited at the American Antiquarian Society. The Massachusetts Historical Society has papers of Benjamin Colman, Andrew Eliot and

John Eliot, and Thomas Hollis, and also scattered letters to and from various Arminian ministers. The bulk of the surviving Mayhew Papers is at Boston University. The Harvard University Archives contain most of the unpublished Dudleian Lectures, as well as official records and papers of the College.

For most of the churches, the available information, for what it is worth, is to be found in historical addresses or in town histories, which must be tracked down individually. The following histories are more inclusive than most: Henry Wilder Foote, *Annals of King's Chapel*, 2 vols. (Boston, 1882, 1896); Arthur B. Ellis, *History of the First Church in Boston, 1630–1880* (Boston, 1881); and John Cuckson, *A Brief History of the First Church in Plymouth* (Boston, 1902). Although the Old South Church remained orthodox, Henry A. Hill's *History of the Old South Church*, 2 vols. (Boston, 1890) contains a great deal of data about all the Boston churches. See also *The Manifesto Church: Records of the Church in Brattle Square, Boston* (Boston, 1902); and " Plymouth Church Records," in *Publications of the Colonial Society of Massachusetts*, XXI, XXII (Boston, 1920, 1923).

For an understanding of seventeenth-century Puritanism, the various writings of Perry Miller are quite indispensable. The items most relevant for the later Arminian development are: *The New England Mind: the Seventeenth Century* (New York, 1939), and " Solomon Stoddard, 1643–1729," in *Harvard Theological Review*, XXXIV (1941), pp. 277–320. Of the books of an older generation, Williston Walker's *History of the Congregational Churches in the United States* (New York, 1894), and *The Creeds and Platforms of Congregationalism* (New York, 1893), are still useful.

Previous treatments of eighteenth-century religious liberalism in New England, which this book supplements, and to some extent supplants, are: George W. Cooke, *Unitarianism in America* (Boston, 1902); Francis A. Christie, " The Beginnings of Arminianism in New England," *Papers of the American Society of Church History*, Series 2, III (1912), pp. 152–172; Joseph Haroutunian, *Piety versus Moralism* (New York, 1932); G. Adolf Koch, *Republican Religion* (New York, 1933); and Herbert M. Morais, *Deism in Eighteenth Century America* (New York, 1934).

Other works dealing with eighteenth-century New England, and especially the development of evangelical orthodoxy, are: Joseph Tracy, *The Great Awakening* (Boston, 1842); John C. Miller, " Religion, Finance, and Democracy in Massachusetts," *New England Quarterly*, VI (1933), pp. 29–58; Perry Miller, *Jonathan*

Edwards (New York, c. 1949); Franklin B. Dexter, ed., *The Literary Diary of Ezra Stiles,* 3 vols. (New York, 1901), and *Extracts from the Itineraries and other Miscellanies of Ezra Stiles, D.D., LL.D.* (New Haven, 1916); Frank Hugh Foster, *A Genetic History of the New England Theology* (Chicago, 1907); Charles E. Cuningham, *Timothy Dwight, 1752–1817* (New York, 1942); William B. Sprague, *Life of Jedidiah Morse, D.D.* (New York, 1874); Vernon L. Stauffer, *New England and the Bavarian Illuminati* (New York, 1918); and Jacob C. Meyer, *Church and State in Massachusetts from 1740 to 1833* (Cleveland, 1930).

The following are some of the more recent books dealing with English latitudinarianism and dissent: Earl Morse Wilbur, *A History of Unitarianism in Transylvania, England and America* (Cambridge, 1952); H. John McLachlan, *Socinianism in Seventeenth-Century England* (London, 1952); Roland N. Stromberg, *Religious Liberalism in Eighteenth-Century England* (London, 1954); G. R. Cragg, *From Puritanism to the Age of Reason* (Cambridge, England, 1950); Basil Willey, *The Eighteenth-Century Background* (London, 1940); and Olive M. Griffiths, *Religion and Learning* (Cambridge, England, 1935).

Index